For Buc Nasty
and the other hard workers at
Double-Knuckle Espresso, Inc.,
the baddest bunch of zombie hunters we know
—*Beautiful and Silky Johnson*

For Heather, who always hid behind
the sofa to watch "Creature Feature"
—S. M.

For Lehne, *je t'adore, je t'aime,* and *le roi et la reine*
—M. L.

No anchorage is safe.
Sleep is not, death is not;
Who seem to die live.

—*Ralph Waldo Emerson*

Nothing is more dangerous than a monster whose story is ignored.

—*Annalee Newitz*

Contents

INTRODUCTION

~

Giving the Living Dead Their Due

Marc Leverette and Shawn McIntosh

And here we are as on a darkling plain
Swept with confused alarms of struggle and flight,
Where ignorant armies clash by night.

—Matthew Arnold, "Dover Beach"

In a 2000 interview with Ulrich Beck, one of our leading social theorists, the language of sociology and horror was combined in what he has come to term "zombie categories," spaces such as family, class, and neighborhood which, because of individualization, are at once both alive and dead.[1]

The (un)dead, it would seem, have come a long way, baby, indeed.[2]

For example, in one of the first mass-market photobooks in popular culture on the monster, Rose London's *Zombie: The Living Dead* (1976), actual "zombies" are given only about twenty pages of coverage, with the rest of the book being devoted to other kinds of walking corpses such as mummies and vampires.[3] This is not to say that the mummy and Dracula aren't a kind of (un)dead—this is a quibble we aren't prepared to defend—but rather that, from our perspective, they are *not zombies*. Culturally, and common-sensically, we prefer to define the zombie like Justice Potter Stewart defined pornography and say that definitions are up for grabs, but we know one when we see one. Or do we?

To speak to the need for a critical study of the living dead, consider the following mention (the sole mention) of the classic, definitive zombie film, George A. Romero's *Night of the Living Dead*, found in London's book in a discussion of the schlock that followed on the heels of Don Siegel's *Invasion of the Body Snatchers*:

> Although none of the later alien-controlled zombie films had Siegel's touch of class, *Invisible Invaders* was interesting in its scene of the corpses walking forwards, animated by intelligences from the Moon. Only blasts of sound could destroy these risen dead. Unfortunately, its relative success led to sequels such as *The Earth Dies Screaming* of 1964 and *The Night of the Living Dead* of 1968, in which radiation from space caused the dead to get up and devour the living. Why this last film has become something of an underground cult remains as much a mystery as the actual alien influence controlling the Living Dead.[4]

Delicately put, this makes no sense whatsoever. Mind you, *Invisible Invaders* isn't at the pinnacle of American cinema; mistaking influence for actually being a sequel is another matter entirely. While Terrence Fischer's *The Earth Dies Screaming* has, sadly, been left to rot in the dustbin of history (perhaps, one day, to rise!), it is difficult to ignore the lasting influence and effect of Romero's $114,000 directorial debut. While the debate still rages regarding what exactly it was about that Venus gas that made it revive the dead, there is little denying that London simply got it wrong—in the comment, in the book, and in general.

As a contranymic creature, meaning that the two definitions of *zombie* are actually their own opposites, the zombie is tough to pin down—which is odd, considering its cultural identity as the slowest of the monsters. From the living made to appear dead (as in Haitian culture, described by ethnobotanist Wade Davis)[5] to the dead rendered living (as in most of the zombie cinema that has appeared since Romero's *Night*), zombies have held a unique place in film and popular culture throughout most of the twentieth and now twenty-first centuries. Rare in that this enduring monster type originated in non-European folk culture rather than the Gothic tradition from which other movie monsters such as vampires, werewolves, and Frankenstein have emerged, zombies nevertheless have in many ways superseded these Gothic monsters in popular entertainment and the public imagination and have increasingly been used in discussions ranging from the philosophy of mind to computer discourse to the business press.

Why have zombies resonated so pervasively in the popular imagination and media, especially films? Why have they proved to be one of the most versatile and popular monster types in the growing videogame industry? What makes zombies such widespread symbols of horror and dread, and how have portrayals of zombies in movies changed and evolved to fit contemporary fears, anxieties, and social issues?

Zombie Culture: Autopsies of the Living Dead has brought together scholars from fields such as cinema studies, popular culture, and videogame studies to examine the role of zombies within a variety of forms and discourses. By looking at how portrayals of the (un)dead have evolved from their folkloric roots and entered popular Western culture, primarily from the cinema of the early 1930s through present-day "twitch media" such as videogames, we hope that this collection will allow you to gain deeper insight into what zombies mean in terms of the public psyche, how they represent societal fears, and how their evolving portrayals continue to reflect underlying beliefs of the Other, contagion, and death.

In the opening chapter, Shawn McIntosh discusses some of the folkloric tradition of zombies from Haiti and their introduction to American popular culture. Through the writings of William Seabrook, in his book *The Magic Island*, along with other contemporary writings, McIntosh provides important cultural, historical, and geographic contexts that help inform the chapters throughout the book, each of which looks at more specific aspects of zombies as they have been portrayed in film and in video games.

Mikel J. Koven then considers the folklore of zombies as depicted across popular horror cinema. His chapter explores issues of narrative, considering Stith Thompson's *Motif Index of Folk Literature* for motifs similar to those found across zombie cinema, to attempt to understand the seemingly primordial fear of the walking dead. Additionally, Koven contextualizes the motifs of vampires, giants, and monsters and how they relate to portrayals of zombies more fully, particularly as they pertain to contemporary horror cinema.

As Linda Badley argues, though, until very recently the modern zombie film was as hilarious as it was horrific, a fact that might be attributed simply to "horrality" and defined as a postmodern blend of parody, body horror, escalating special effects, and the self-reflexive humor of a saturated genre. For Badley, in zombie comedies from directors such as Sam Raimi, Stuart Gordon, Brian Yuzna, Michele Soavi, and Peter Jackson, comedy and body horror are almost completely fused, as social critique in George Romero's *Dead* series yields to the grotesque, the absurd, and what Bruce Campbell has called "splatstick," a comedy of regression—of disgusting food gags, vomit jokes, articulating body parts, and exploding mothers. Employing cultural analysis and theory as they are relevant, especially Bakhtin and Kristeva, Badley attempts to account for why movie zombies in the previous three decades were funny, and she comes to some tentative conclusions about why, in the early morning hours of the twenty-first century, they no longer are.

For his chapter, Brad O'Brien focuses on the zombie with an accent. Although the existence of the Italian zombie film is largely due to the success of George Romero's *Dawn of the Dead* in Italy, Italian filmmakers such as Lucio Fulci, Umberto Lenzi, Marino Girolami, Andrea Bianchi, and Michele Soavi created a subgenre that's distinctly Italian. While critics seem to disagree about when the Italian zombie film began, for O'Brien there's no debating the fact that it emerged as a distinct subgenre in 1979 with Fulci's *Zombie*. As O'Brien argues, gore, a certain sense of ridiculousness (sometimes intentional), and atmospheric settings (mostly on mysterious Caribbean islands) are elements that help define the Italian zombie film.

David Pagano looks at the Italians as well, but for very different reasons, in his chapter on the spaces of apocalypse. For Pagano, at least since Romero's 1968 *Night of the Living Dead*, the cinematic zombie has heralded the end of the world as we know it. Insofar as they usually represent the catastrophic end of the human *habitus*, then, zombie films can be called "apocalyptic." Pagano argues, for example, that one could observe the appearance of other Judeo-Christian apocalyptic images in these films as well: evocations of a degraded society, end-time pestilence, and, of course, the very idea of the risen dead. However, in his chapter, Pagano concentrates on how the zombie film also tends to undermine the apocalyptic point of view by staging and undercutting what he calls the apocalyptic trope of the "safe space." In Romero's films, we find the trope of the imagined safe space with its country home, shopping mall, and military bunker inaugurated and codified. In each case, the narrative stages an ironic inverting of the apocalyptic, and the inside fails to stay secure against the onslaught of the outside. Always in these films, the walls come down, and space and time end up blurring in complex ways. When considered as anti-apocalyptic, the zombie film (and not only Romero's, as Pagano illustrates) can even come to appear as an ethical gesture, as its own kind of revelation.

With Patricia MacCormack's chapter, we explore the representation of zombies and their cinematic effect through Italian zombie films of the 1970s and 1980s. Focusing on the ways in which gory zombie movies, particularly those which privilege spectacles of visceral flesh over narrative, reorganize the human body in a way that challenges the traditional form, function, and expression of flesh in cinema and culture, MacCormack offers a Deleuzoguattarian reading of zombies as "bodies without organs," that is, bodies divested of their organization. As such, MacCormack celebrates the perversion of bodies as directly impacting the perversion of traditional definitions of cinematic pleasure that the zombie film affords. Thus, the pleasure of the internal made external and the specificity of the joy of excess seen in gore is, far from being the threshold of offense, the moment where subjectivity is available beyond the reified positions culture accepts.

Whereas MacCormack expands on psychoanalysis toward a more corporeal cinematic experience, Natasha Patterson shows in her chapter that feminist psychoanalytic film theory has informed much of the gender/genre debates surrounding women and horror film, often reinforcing essentialist assumptions about women. Gender and genre debates circulate around discussions of how and why certain "genres" can be viewed as either masculine or feminine, through examination of the text, as well as the audience. Feminists' employment of psychoanalytic theories in the early criticisms of horror films, argues Patterson, reinforced mainstream assertions that horror was no place for women, giving little recourse for those women who do not experience horror film consumption negatively or masochistically. Thus, her chapter explores Romero's zombie films through the feminist "gender/genre" debates, showing the ways in which his films provide rich textual spaces in which not only to consider the relationship between gender and genre but also to suggest that his narrative solution may actually offer a more "radically democratic" vision of the gender/genre system.

Moving in for a closer look at a singular work within larger genre debates, Martin Rogers argues that Danny Boyle's *28 Days Later* is a zombie film of a whole different order—one significant to our understanding of where the zombie genre is headed in the so-called post-human age. *28 Days Later* modifies the traditional concern of the horror film over physical violation—anxiety depicted by a certain "disgust" with the body and a suspicion of its "fluid" productions—into a concern over medical technology. While technological anxieties are typically the concern of science-fiction film, the two genres' intersection becomes a third, hybrid genre in *28 Days Later* with startling effects. As Rogers argues, our traditional film genres have become unstable because our conception of the body is unstable: it is so thoroughly confused and implicated in the technological that body-horror and science-horror have become the same thing. Human consciousness is no longer solely transmitted through bodies; now a technological state of being, human consciousness has shed the body as a containing space. In this post-human world, it is science fiction (or some hybrid strain of it) that will do the worrying about the body.

Annelise Sklar's chapter moves us away from the cinematic meditation of the zombie to how the aesthetics of the living dead manifest in the psychobilly subculture. Psychobilly, "a mutant mixture of rockabilly, punk music, and subcultures, with a hearty dose of horror-genre kitsch thrown in for good measure," as she describes it in her chapter, appropriates numerous visual aspects of the horror genre, but specifically focuses on zombie imagery—as evidenced by their turning up in "band names, song titles and lyrics, visual artwork, and theatrical costuming."

Moving across media platforms again, Tanya Krzywinska asks how the interactive elements of video games affect the meaning and representation of zombies. Does the interactive format of horror-based video games undermine the critique of consumption that has been read through zombies in other media? Do video game zombies express a disdain for the flesh by the new "wired" generation? What allegorical meanings accrue within the particular context of twitch-based "new" media? In examining the specific interactive qualities of video game media—focusing in particular on the *Resident Evil* cycle, along with *Painkiller* and *Silent Hill*, among others—Krzywinska considers how zombies in horror-based video games measure up to film-based representations and their interpretations.

Video games are also the concern of Ron Scott. As he argues, the game form relies intensely on demonic possession to draw "readers" in, as the popularity of *Everquest*, *Resident Evil*, the *Final Fantasy* series, and many other games attest. Each game relies on the creation of zombies to drive the narrative, but as games they also offer players the opportunity to enter more fully into a Kristevan place "where meaning breaks down." The combination of corporate decision making and creative energy resulted in the reliance of these new media texts on the zombie as an important theme, but the response in the marketplace to this trope speaks to the cultural anxieties awakened and the pleasure found by "readers" as well. The best example of this combination, as Scott argues, may be the *Warcraft* series developed by Blizzard. After players started increasingly to adopt the "evil" race as characters they wished to play, Blizzard created a new "evil" class, the undead, in order to provide a boundary line for good and evil. As Scott examines in his chapter, the undead also became a race of choice for many online players, and a decision that was made at the corporate level—one that also factored in sales and streamlining production in order to control costs—speaks directly to the desire to find the "place where meaning breaks down."

This place is also at the heart of Marc Leverette's chapter, "The Funk of Forty Thousand Years," with which we close the volume. Ultimately offering a philosophy of the (un)dead as a kind of deconstructive trope, Leverette shows how their undecidable ontology is central to their function as conveyors of terror. By reading the zombie through the lenses of deconstruction and undecidability, as well as the ideologies of cannibal narratives and speciesism,

Leverette concludes this study by questioning the past, present, and potential future of this most liminal, or "queer," of creatures.

Finally, we must take this opportunity to heap thanks and praise on Stephen Ryan for his inestimable patience as the process of compiling this volume started to resemble the lumbering of the living dead it spends so much time discussing. Thanks also to Brenda Hadenfeldt for her initial interest. In addition, we must thank our contributors for their bottomless patience and understanding as life kept getting in the way. As such, we wish to extend our sincerest appreciation to those who lent us their insights here: Linda Badley, Mikel Koven, Tanya Krzywinska, Patricia MacCormack, Brad O'Brien, David Pagano, Natasha Patterson, Martin Rogers, Ron Scott, and Annelise Sklar. We must also thank George Romero for his time and for being the bad motherfucker who reinvented the living dead.

Shawn wishes to thank Marc for suggesting and carrying through the idea to make this a book. What was initially one of Shawn's typical mind-farts on a lazy Sunday afternoon—"Why is it that zombies have become so popular even in sci-fi movies like *Resident Evil* and in videogames?"—would have likely remained a paper sitting in a drawer if it wasn't for Marc's enthusiasm for the idea and expanding it. Shawn would also like to thank Naren, who finally learned to stop asking why he was watching some gory, "stupid" horror movie, but who never stopped wondering how that could somehow be called "work."

Marc wishes to thank his family for suffering through his permanent case of omphaloskepsis, while supporting him in pursuing a career that makes him pay close attention to "all the shit he was interested in instead of doing schoolwork." He also wants to thank his wonderful "Auntie," Julie Wolfe, for continually telling him to stop whining and quit covering his eyes as she tried to convince him that being scared was a good thing. Marc also wants to thank Carl Burgchardt and Jason Hockney for so many great conversations about movies and other important life issues, as well as all the assistants and students who are always willing to listen to him natter on about zombies or any other topic on his mind (and if they weren't willing, thanks for being such great liars). And he must thank Lehne, too, for listening to him prattle on about everything and for making this life so terribly wonderful. Finally, thanks to Pooty, whose epic bark always keeps the (un)dead at bay.

Notes

1. Ulrich Beck, "Zombie Categories," in *The Art of Life: On Living, Love and Death*, ed. Jonathan Rutherford (London: Lawrence & Wishart, 2000), 35–51.

2. Readers will notice that here, and throughout Leverette's chapter, a parenthetical conjoining links the dead and undead, implying their status as at once (not) alive and (not) dead.

3. Rose London, *Zombie: The Living Dead* (New York: Bounty Books, 1976).

4. London, *Zombie*, 91, 93.

5. Wade Davis, *Passage of Darkness: The Ethnobiology of the Haitian Zombie* (Chapel Hill: University of North Carolina Press, 1988).

CHAPTER ONE

~

The Evolution of the Zombie: The Monster That Keeps Coming Back

Shawn McIntosh

.

They have appeared in the steamy jungles of Haiti, on the dry plains of Transvaal, in Welsh tin mines, underwater, and in space. They have shuffled onto the silver screen, the Broadway stage, video games, and annually the streets of Manhattan, San Francisco, and Minneapolis. They have shown up in computer lingo and philosophical treatises on the nature of consciousness. Zombies, it seems, are everywhere.

Few monster types have embedded themselves in the popular imagination as thoroughly as zombies have, even though zombies are often upstaged by the flashier monster types such as vampires, Frankenstein's monster, and fantastic science-fiction creatures. However, their plodding, "never say die" quality is one reason among several that they have managed to endure as frightening monsters when other traditional monster types that scared past generations have largely been defanged on the covers of children's cereal boxes or relegated to Saturday afternoon television reruns and self-conscious spoofs. The unique balancing act that zombies represent between control and enslavement, strength and weakness, us and them, and group versus individual identity offers a window into better understanding why we enjoy the horror genre in particular and how we perceive ourselves and certain aspects of popular culture in general.

Zombies are one of the few monsters that originate from a non-Gothic, non-European tradition and that have passed directly from folk culture into popular culture without first being established in literature.[1] Furthermore, some Western researchers have claimed that zombies actually exist, particularly in Haiti, and ethnobiologist Wade Davis has documented at least two cases of people who claim to have been zombies. He provides convincing ethnobiological and physiological evidence that people can in fact be made to seem as if they have arisen from the dead.[2] Despite these controversial claims, there is no doubt that many Haitians believe zombies exist and fear them, although *voudoun* (voodoo) practitioners, who can supposedly create zombies, argue that black magic and creating zombies are done only by evil Voudou sorcerers, known as *bokor*. Voudou was in fact recognized as an official religion by Haiti in April 2003, with the government requiring Voudou priests to register with the authorities. Despite this official recognition, some voudoun say that it will take much more effort to erase the stigma of the popular perceptions of them as practitioners solely of black magic.[3] Haitian government officials have long tried to combat both the popular stereotypes of Haiti as a backward country dominated by beliefs in witchcraft and the Western fascination with zombies that in some ways helps support that stereotype.

Although there is still some debate over the origin of the word *zombie*, most authorities believe the term is a derivation of a word of West African origin, whence many of the slaves who ended up in Haiti were sent. The word likely comes either from a tribe from Gabon called the Mitsogho, who have the term *ndzumbi*—which means the cadaver of the deceased—or from the Kongo *nzambi*, which means "spirit of a dead person." Davis chooses the latter interpretation, as he argues in *Passage of Darkness*:

> Death's essence is the severance from the mortal body of some elusive life-giving principle, and how a culture comes to understand or at least tolerate this inexorable separation to a great extent defines its mystical worldview. In Haiti, the zombie sits on the cusp of death, and the beliefs that mediate the phenomenon are rooted in the very heart of the peasant's being. The existence of zombies is but a confirmation of a fundamental conviction that the dead wield power in the world of the living. . . .
>
> The permeability of the frontier between life and death—indeed, between the material and the immaterial—provides an important backdrop for appreciating the magical beliefs evident in all the popular tales of zombies.[4]

In Haitian folklore, there are two types of zombies: spirit zombies (*zombi jardin*), and the type that has made its way into popular culture, the body raised from the dead (*zombi corps cadavre*). For Haitians, spirit zombies are much more powerful and frightening than physical zombies, because a bokor controls the spirit of a dead person and can inject that spirit into a variety of living creatures to do the bokor's bidding. Davis recounts an episode in which he asked a bokor to bring him a zombie that he could take back to the United States. The bokor later proudly brought a small clay jar, saying that was his zombie. When Davis explained that he expected a walking, physical zombie, the bokor expressed surprise, asking Davis how he expected to bring a zombie through immigration and saying that, at any rate, the spirit zombie he provided him was much more powerful and useful than a *zombi corps cadavre*.

An easy way to classify the two types of zombies is that spirit zombies are souls without bodies and "walking" zombies are bodies without souls. It is the latter type of zombies that Davis explores through ethnography and ethnobiology in *Passage of Darkness*, and, to some extent, in his popularized 1985 account *The Serpent and the Rainbow*, which was made into a movie of the same name, directed by Wes Craven.[5] Davis explains that there are many popular accounts of zombies in Haiti, although he is able to document to his satisfaction only two people who claim to be "recovered zombies." He provides convincing scientific evidence for the poison mixture (made in part from the toxin of the blowfish) that bokors create, putting their victims in a state of near-death, only to revive them later with another mixture. Davis claims that the victims lose many of their higher mental faculties and thus are easily controlled by the bokor through a combination of near-death poisoning, the physiological reaction to the poison, and the traumatic revivification process.

However, it is important to understand the social and cultural milieu surrounding the creation of zombies, as bokors do not randomly choose victims to turn into zombies. Although a full exploration of the social forces at work in Haitian peasant society is beyond the scope of this chapter, a brief summary will show how the zombie in modern Western popular culture has changed from its folkloric traditions. In Haitian society, being turned into a zombie is a form of social sanction, and the bokor usually performs this ritual only at the request of someone who wants the victim to become a zombie.[6] In both cases documented by Davis, the victims were greatly disliked by others in the community and their own family members for their antisocial behavior, and their transformation into zombies was largely seen as "just rewards" for their past actions. For Haitian peasants, the threat of being ostracized from the social community and having one's body controlled by another is one method that serves as a powerful sanction to regulate people's behavior. In other words, Haitian peasants greatly fear being removed from "the many" and becoming "the one." This is the exact opposite of what causes fear among modern audiences in industrialized society, who are afraid of losing their individuality and becoming one among "the many."

There is no clear date as to when zombies first stumbled their way into the limelight of Western popular culture, although William Seabrook's fanciful 1929 travelogue of Haiti and descriptions of Voudou, *The Magic Island*, could certainly be considered a pivotal point in spreading awareness of zombies.[7] However, prior to 1929 there are several intriguing strands of zombie folklore that stretch back all the way to the late eighteenth century with Samuel Coleridge, who wrote in the margin of his friend Robert Southey's *History of Brazil* a brief passage about Zambi, whom he identified as an Angolan god and then further clarified as the devil.[8]

In the latter part of the nineteenth century, Lafcadio Hearn spent two years in Martinique collecting folk tales and ghost stories (much as he ended up doing later in his career in Japan, for which perhaps he is best known). Marina Warner states that some of the tales he collected were of zombies, although he never used that word. In fact, the zombie tales he retold were closer to the spirit zombies, or ghost stories, than tales of revived dead people. There are also reports of zombie-like beings, although again not using the term *zombie*, among nineteenth-century missionary accounts regarding tribal witchcraft in the Transvaal.[9]

But despite differences in nomenclature, the strong fear of possession by another is obviously a common thread through the West Indies and other parts of the world. Warner traces this fear in Martinique and Jamaica (where she also states Voudou exists) directly to the cultural memories of the horrific slave years, and Davis's brief recounting of some of the practices and conditions during the colonial era in Haiti provide further support that the scars of those years run deep in the cultural memory.

However, there is no doubt that the U.S. military occupation of Haiti from 1915 to 1934, with news reports coming from the island related to the occupation, also stoked awareness of Haitian culture and Voudou that helped make Seabrook's 1929 book popular, even as many contemporary experts criticized the book for its fantastic and inaccurate depictions. Subsequent books in the early 1930s further sensationalized Voudou. These included books by former marines who were stationed in Haiti, such as Faustin Wirkus's *The White King of Gonave* (for which Seabrook wrote the introduction) and John Houston Craige's *Black Baghdad* and *Cannibal Cousins*.[10] The titles generally make it clear what type of audience the authors were aiming for.

Zombies entered the stage and screen in 1932, first with Kenneth Webb's stage production *Zombie*, and later that summer with the first zombie film, *White Zombie*, by the Halperin brothers. Webb sued the Halperin brothers over their film, but they were still able to release it. *White Zombie* was one of a spate of horror films, many of which are now classics, that were made following the success of *Dracula*. But unlike *Frankenstein*, *The Mummy*, and *The Invisible Man*, *White Zombie* is admired mostly by a small cadre of avid horror film buffs and researchers of the horror genre. That is not to say that *White Zombie* is without merit, however, as it features a variety of filmic enunciative techniques such as superimpositions, dissolves, split screens, and intercutting that, although widely used by that time in film, could within the context of the story be considered quite experimental.[11] The fact that *White Zombie* was produced by an independent studio may have had something to do with the willingness of the producers and filmmakers to experiment, as well as the fact that it was part of a new generation of sound horror films.

White Zombie touched on themes that have shown up in a number of zombie movies and subgenre horror movies—themes that the zombie as a monster type seems ideal to explore. As Lowry and deCordova explain:

> *White Zombie* offers a formative example of the narrative/filmic figuration of desire in terms of *possession*. Not only is the paradigm of possessor/possessed (which provides a consistent structural bases for the subgenre which *White Zombie* initiated) figured narratively amongst the characters of the film; it is also figured in the enunciative devices employed to situate the viewer on *both* sides of the paradigm at different points.[12]

In other words, the theme of *White Zombie* helps explain a larger issue of the film viewer as *possessor* of the image even as he or she is *possessed by* the image he or she is watching. Other researchers, such as Christian Metz and Raymond Bellour, have also noted the similarities between the dynamic of possessor/possessed and its function in relation to subject and object in voyeurism and fetishism.[13]

Despite whatever groundbreaking enunciative work *White Zombie* accomplished, the plot and acting are considered unremarkable. A young couple is married at a plantation in Haiti, but the plantation owner desires the young wife for himself and so hires a Voudou priest, Murder Legendre (Bela Lugosi), to turn her into a zombie so he can possess her. Legendre's small troop of zombies all follow the traditional Haitian idea of what zombies are: bodies without souls who are controlled by a single master. Madeline, the "white zombie" of the film, breaks out of her state after Legendre is killed, and she is reunited with her husband.

Many of the ten or so zombie films made in the 1930s and 1940s, such as *Ouanga*, *Voodoo Man*, and Val Lewton's production *I Walked with a Zombie*, dealt explicitly with either possession of females for sexual reasons (in the first two films) or touched on white/black racial issues (in the first and last films). *Ouanga* portrayed blacks and natives as ignorant and evil, while Lewton is today widely praised for his sensitive portrayal of natives and the issues surrounding colonialism and race. It was relatively natural to include these themes in the earliest zombie movies, with their Caribbean settings and adherence to the folk culture from which zombies came, but there was also undoubtedly a wellspring of issues upon which to touch regarding the socioeconomic milieu of rich, white plantation owners and downtrodden black peasants and workers.

In the early years, zombies never reached the wild popularity of the flashier types of monsters, such as Dracula, Frankenstein's monster, and the Wolfman. Part of the reason was that zombies in this period were largely portrayed as gaunt, slow-moving, and robotic. They did not have the special effects of the Mummy, Frankenstein, or the Wolfman and lacked the urbane sophistication and air of European culture and history of Dracula. The Halperin brothers' sequel to *White Zombie*, *Revolt of the Zombies*, did not do well at the box office despite its exotic tropical setting of Cambodia and an army of zombies. Yet this flop didn't stop other directors from making more zombie movies in the 1940s, although these movies were largely eclipsed by other types of horror movies.

Revolt of the Zombies did demonstrate how easy it was to transplant zombies to other settings, and as early as the 1940s, zombie movies were starting to put zombies in non-Caribbean settings. Examples include *King of the Zombies* and *Revenge of the Zombies*, in which zombies are used to aid the Nazi cause. It is interesting to note that the theme of Nazis utilizing zombies reappeared not only in the film *Shock Waves* but also in a very popular early video game, *Wolfenstein 3-D*, which was remade as *Return to Castle Wolfenstein* in 2001.

Aside from a few titles, zombies were not widely seen in horror movies during the 1940s. But this also largely saved zombies from the spoofing cycle that befell other classic Universal Pictures monsters such as Dracula, Frankenstein's monster, and the Mummy, all three of which showed up as comedic backdrops to Abbott and Costello in *Bud Abbott Lou Costello Meet Frankenstein*. It is a fine line between horror and laughter—one that modern horror filmmakers increasingly juxtapose—but when the audience starts laughing at the monsters, they stop being afraid of them. Although a zombie does appear in Bob Hope's romantic comedy *The Ghost Breakers*, it is a small, inconsequential part and is not spoofing the zombie as a monster type as such (the film was remade by the same director, George Marshall, in 1953 as the Dean Martin and Jerry Lewis vehicle *Scared Stiff*). *Zombies on Broadway* tried to do what Abbott and Costello later did with other monsters, but largely without success, as the film failed to be either scary or funny.

Two factors removed the classic movie monsters' element of fear for moviegoers in the late 1940s and 1950s: the spoofing cycle in which the monsters appeared in comedies or self-conscious parodies, and the atomic age that created a completely new set of circumstances to be truly frightened about. Compared to the real risk of nuclear annihilation (or to some the equally frightening thought of Communist domination), Frankenstein's monster being chased by torch-bearing villagers and Dracula's Transylvanian accent amid Gothic castles seemed almost quaint.

Zombies did not escape the irradiated and alien-invading 1950s and early 1960s entirely unscathed, as it was a period in which horror films with "zombies" in the title were just as likely feature thinking, planning Martians (*Zombies of the Stratosphere*) or deranged, disfigured ex-lovers going on killing rampages (*The Incredibly Strange Creatures Who Stopped Living and Became Mixed-Up Zombies!!?*) as they were traditional zombies. Leslie Halliwell claims in his book *The Dead That Walk* that he has never met anyone who has actually seen *Strange Creatures* and that it is in fact simply a spoof title rather than an actual film, even though it has a plot summary in Peter Dendle's *The Zombie Movie Encyclopedia* and Dendle claims to have seen all the movies listed. The movie was aired on Comedy Central's *Mystery Science Theater 3000* on April 19, 1997 (with sarcastic running commentary, of course), so it does indeed exist (MST3K Episode 812).[14]

Dendle calls the 1950s and 1960s a "transitional time for the screen zombie," which shows that even after the traditional zombie largely disappeared from the screen, there was still a strong fascination with the word. Dendle, in fact, cites two science-fiction movies—*Plan 9 from Outer Space* and *Invisible Invaders*—as being closer in spirit to the zombie themes of revived dead and possession than some of the movies that had the word *zombie* in their titles. These two movies are good examples of how some of the issues of depersonalization, individuality, and privacy were portrayed during this period.

What the zombie movies of the 1950s and early 1960s did do, however, was further expand the limits of what zombies could be and how they could appear, even to the point of portraying zombies as mutated, irradiated, humanoid fish, as in *The Horror at Party Beach*. One unspoken taboo still remained—showing zombies as rotting cadavers. Up to this point, the human form remained largely inviolate in terms of showing the decay that takes place after death, even as horror fans watched fantastic creatures and humongous, deformed, and disfigured monsters rampage their ways across movie screens.

Although a Mexican director, Rafael Portillo, actually first started showing rotting corpses in 1957 in his *Aztec Mummy* series, it wasn't until the

1966 Hammer release from the United Kingdom of *The Plague of the Zombies* that most English-speaking moviegoers saw decrepit, decomposing walking undead.[15] Up to this point in the movies, zombies were always portrayed simply as gaunt, slow-moving automatons with shabby clothes, as if a trip to the cleaners and a bit of rouge would be the only things needed to freshen one up after a stint underground.

Despite the horrific change of appearance of zombies in *The Plague of the Zombies*, the movie's zombies more or less followed the traditional model in that they were controlled by a master, in this case a tin mine owner, who used them as slave labor. The obvious connection to the plight of Welsh coal miners was noted by critics at the time.[16] Their poor working conditions could easily be compared to those faced by sugar plantation workers in Haiti, as well.

The seminal work that forever transformed how zombies are portrayed is, of course, George Romero's *Night of the Living Dead*. *Night* not only started off a spate of zombie movies and derivative zombie-cannibal movies for the next several years but also ensured that zombies would in many ways replace the classic monster types and science-fiction creatures as one of the most popular, widespread monsters in popular culture, permeating movie practice in various subgenres, as well as the popular lingo of the day in situations ranging from insurance fraud to computer use. It could be said that Romero's original presentation of zombies, although derived from several older zombie traditions and portrayals, including 1950s comic books, breathed new life into zombies. As Dendle states, "Romero liberated the zombie from the shackles of a master, and invested his zombies not with a function (a job or task such as zombies were standardly given by voodoo priests), but rather a drive (eating flesh)."[17]

Romero has said the story of *Night* was derived from Richard Matheson's 1954 novel *I Am Legend*, about the last man alive after everyone else has been changed into vampires. *The Last Man on Earth* and *The Omega Man* are both film versions of *I Am Legend*, but Matheson has said he was not happy with either film and that, although he has "no opinion" about *Night*, it is "awfully close" to *I Am Legend* in tone and spirit, rather than simply derived from it.[18]

Romero essentially conflated the zombie with the ghoul, a cannibalistic monster type that never became very popular. In fact, Romero originally called the zombies "ghouls," but the term "zombies" became the most accepted term for his monsters in *Night*. Over the next several years, more than sixty movies from all over the world would be made that portrayed zombies as cannibals, and the drive continues in modern computer video games, which copied the idea from movies. Romero also popularized the notion that zombies could only be truly killed by a blow or shot to the head or other such head injury that severed the brain core, an idea he further developed in *Day of the Dead* but that had been mentioned in a couple of the older zombie movies of the 1940s.

In *Night*, it is not exactly clear how the dead people were revived or turned into zombies, although shots of newspaper articles mention a meteor passing through the atmosphere or some other source of radiation, perhaps from the government. *Night* has a claustrophobic, apocalyptic feel, as the protagonists are trapped in a farmhouse overnight and face an increasing onslaught of slow-moving zombies driven to break into the house to eat the inhabitants. Only one protagonist survives the night, and that by hiding cowardlike in the cellar, but when he emerges into daylight, he is shot by a truck full of rednecks who mistakenly think he is a zombie. In this sense, order is shown as restored as citizens seem to take back the countryside from the zombie infestation, even though it is too late to help the movie's protagonists.

The apocalyptic theme was taken up enthusiastically by many of the zombie movies that followed *Night* when it started gaining popularity on the midnight-movie circuit after its release. Many of the zombie movies of the 1970s have a plot similar to *Night*'s: a small group of people are trapped in a remote location and have to fight off numbers of slow-moving zombies who want to eat them. Romero himself amplifies the apocalyptic theme in the sequels to *Night*, *Dawn of the Dead*, a social commentary on American mass consumer society as zombies overtake survivors barricaded in a shopping mall, and *Day of the Dead*, when the world is apparently almost completely overrun by zombies and there are only a few survivors left. This theme is reinforced by the latest movie in the series, *Land of the Dead*, in which the remaining humans barricade themselves within a walled city that replicates the divisions of wealth (and safety) of pre-zombie society.

The theme of apocalypse from some ill-defined source or through government shenanigans fits well with a culture that had a generation of people growing up under the threat of nuclear annihilation and that was coming of age and questioning their government's policies, as well as their own identities, in the turbulent 1960s. In zombie movies and video games of later years, reasons for the creation of zombies range from radiation and government experiments to corporate biological experiments gone awry, reflecting a general popular distrust with big government and big business.

The fact that zombies now had a physical and biological drive, and that some aspect of their mentality still existed (thus the need to destroy the brain core to really kill them), nicely conflated the underlying themes that zombies had long represented; the cherished idea of life after death and the connection between our physical bodies and what we consider our souls or spirits, which in secular Western terms translates into "thought" or "mentality." It is an idea that Romero played on in *Dawn*, when one character explains to another that zombies are coming to the mall because they return to places that were important to them when they were alive—essentially saying that consumer culture has become such a core element in the American consciousness that a "drive to the mall" becomes more than a simple descriptive term for a shopping trip.

It is also interesting to note how these movies played on issues of individuality and social cohesiveness. Unlike peasants in traditional Haitian society who fear being taken from the community to become the One (a zombie), the characters in the post-*Night* zombie movies—and, by extension, the audience watching the films and identifying with the characters—fear losing their individuality to become one of the Many. Yet a tension exists within that framework, as the protagonists must also work together to try to overcome the zombie masses and survive. A desire to fight off an uncontrollable transformation likely also plays a role in the popularity of zombies in video games, in which young teens see the approach of puberty and the end of carefree days as students and the looming fate of becoming a corporate drone.

Cultural resonances aside, another element must be considered in the popularity of zombie movies after *Night*, especially in the first spate of zombie movies in what Dendle calls the Golden Age of zombie movies, from 1968 to 1983. That element is production values. Most, if not all, of these movies were produced on extremely low budgets, including *Night*, and it is a fact of movie production that it is much cheaper to shoot indoors with minimal sets, few actors, and no need for expensive special effects. Special-effects technology had become more advanced by the late 1960s and 1970s, but was still largely confined to makeup and lots of fake blood to show the gore that shocked and scared audiences of the time. It was much cheaper to have extras dressed in ragged, everyday clothes with makeup that showed various states of decay than to build elaborate sets or create original, realistic-looking space aliens the size of houses. It was also much cheaper to film in countries like the Philippines, where many of the Italian zombie movies were shot, in which native extras worked for much less than American or European actors and where laws on animal cruelty (and union regulations) were not as stringent as in developed countries.

But even considering the production issues that undoubtedly helped create the spate of zombie and zombie-cannibal movies created during the 1970s and early 1980s, many by Spanish and Italian production companies, the fact is that these movies wouldn't have been made if they did not find audiences willing to be frightened and shocked by the gore, and if there was not some element about their common themes that resonated with the audiences.

Zombies are considered truly to have hit the mainstream in 1983, when they appeared, along with Michael Jackson, in his music video "Thriller." Shortly after this, zombies, like the other popular horror monsters and themes in earlier years, started to get spoofed. A subgenre briefly arose of romantic-comedy zombie movies, with *I Was a Teenage Zombie* and *My Boyfriend's Back*, in which zombies are used as a motif for teen angst about fitting in, being popular, and eventually getting your girl. *Bloodsuckers from Outer Space*, *Hard Rock Zombies*, and *Chopper Chicks in Zombietown* are but three examples of movies that seemed to have the potential to finally put the zombie to rest as a viable and scary monster. Not even the third episode of Romero's zombie series, *Day of the Dead*, in 1985 could seem to maintain the audiences' fear of zombies, who by then had to compete with the super-splatter films of Freddie Krueger and endless *Friday the 13th* sequels.

How could zombies cope with the changed horror environment, in some ways victims of their own success, much like Dracula and Frankenstein's monster many years before them? Zombies had already entered the modern age as victims of evil government experiments or corporate greed and plans for world domination, so where could they go from here? Even if Count Dracula was looking more fruity than fearful in his black cape and decrepit Gothic castle, the vampire legend itself had plenty of room to adapt to the modern age, as Anne Rice's popular vampire novel series shows, as well as the many new milieus in which vampires have appeared in recent years. The workaday, blue-collar zombie, however, with his rotting flesh, tattered clothes, redneck address, and need for human flesh, looked ready for a pink slip.

But zombies were saved from triviality in popular culture and made frightening again, this time by video games. In many ways, in fact, they were and are ideally suited to the video game environment. They are Everyman, or more accurately, Everymonster, and thus can be inserted into any number of scenarios, from Nazi Germany (*Wolfenstein 3-D*) to space stations (*System Shock*) to near-future scenarios on Earth (*Resident Evil*) to the old-fashioned haunted house (*House of the Undead 2*). Because of the interactive nature of video games, they engage players in the content of the game much more than simply passively watching a movie on television.[19] Players must fight and figure their way out of whatever predicament the video game puts them in.

It wasn't the traditional Haitian zombie that made its way into video games, however, but the "new zombie" that had evolved from Romero's

Night. Video game creators borrowed directly from the popular conceptions of zombies of the time when including them in video games, which included their drive for eating flesh (thus reconfirming the fear of what a zombie would do to the player character, rather than of merely being turned into a zombie like in the folklore tradition), the ability to kill them only by blows or shots to the head, the hazy pseudoscientific or evil government origins of what made them zombies in the first place, and the fear of contagion they represented, which was explored in some of the zombie movies from the late 1970s and resonated well in a world just learning about AIDS.

The earliest video games had extremely poor screen resolutions and limited capacity for players, largely because of the lack of computing power on the earliest systems such as the Commodore 64 or Atari game systems. But by the mid-1990s, computer processing power had increased enough to allow for first-person shooter games, which made the perspective not a top-down or distanced view as in earlier games, but that of a character within the scene itself, viewing the situation as that character would.

The first first-person shooter game was *Wolfenstein 3-D*, which had the player take on the role of an Allied soldier held prisoner in a castle in Nazi Germany who had to shoot his way past guards and zombie Nazis to escape. An earlier, non-3-D version of the game and its sequels had been popular since the first release in 1983, so the game makers were not breaking any new ground as far as narrative storytelling went, and the zombies also appeared in an earlier version of the game. Still, the change to a first-person perspective radically changed the video gaming environment, and it was not long before teens were able to shoot directly at the screen with plastic light guns in video arcades. By the late 1990s, light guns were available for home versions of the video games such as *House of the Undead 2.*

Like many new media, video games borrowed from older media forms; in this case, they used many filmic narrative conventions in cutaway set pieces at the beginning to help establish the story line and interspersed throughout the game to continue the narrative. These cinematic flourishes got more accomplished as computers and video graphics cards got more powerful. Game makers quickly learned that players did not buy games to watch animated film shorts, but to actually start playing the games, so these cutaway pieces became shorter as the video game industry evolved.

Zombies are the perfect monster in games for beginning players, who have little patience in reading long instruction manuals and want to start playing quickly. Zombies are slow-moving, allowing players to develop their hand–eye coordination and playing skills of shooting or hitting; are relatively easy to kill, quickly giving players a sense of empowerment within the game environment; and yet continue to frighten with their sudden appearance around corners, their moans, and their relentless, plodding pursuit of the player character. Video game reviewers use terms of fright regarding some games, such as *House of the Undead 2*, that would leave audiences laughing at them if they used the same language in movie reviews.[20] With horror movies, audiences have become jaded, but with video games, they still have the potential to make one jump and be frightened.

The sense of empowering one to kill a monster in a video game should not be overlooked in making zombies a popular monster. It is a feeling that likely carried over from zombie movies, as well. However, in the movies, the audience could of course only watch passively and imagine what they would do in that situation or think how they would run away from the zombies. When playing a video game, the player can do exactly what he or she wants. He or she can stand alone with nothing but a crowbar and a shotgun or choose to run to fight another day.

There are many social and psychological theories on why horror and watching violence are popular, ranging from the aesthetic theory of destruction, in which viewers find a certain beauty in watching something get destroyed, to the pleasure found in violating social norms without fear of reprisal.[21] Many of the theories lack empirical evidence to conclusively show how accurate they might be, although intuitively they do seem to touch on certain aspects of conventional wisdom regarding psychology and enjoyment. Some journalists comment on children's enjoyment of playing violent video games as a way for them to overcome their real-world physical restrictions of small size and lack of strength.[22] It is also noted that—in U.S. society, at least—children are usually constrained and punished when they show aggression, but the video game world gives them a chance to live out their violent fantasies and urges. Although the theory of catharsis has largely been discredited due to lack of empirical evidence, there are echoes of catharsis in the belief that players can experience forbidden behavior in a virtual environment without punishment.

Because zombies evolved in the popular cultural imagination the way they did, they symbolize a monster that can be killed guilt-free. If zombies were still perceived in their folkloric conception—as people who were controlled by someone else to do that person's bidding—then ethical questions could arise on the morality of killing beings who were essentially victims of another's evil plans. However, since the modern conception of zombies has removed the evil master and replaced him with simply a physical or biological drive or craving to kill or eat humans, it becomes essentially a no-brainer—zombies are evil, and we are good.

It should be noted, however, that zombies have not overrun the video game world. They are perhaps the most popular traditional monster type within video gaming, but it is important to keep in mind that other video game types are regularly best-sellers, including sports games, action-adventure, and spy thriller games. In the past two years, a racing/adventure game, *Grand Theft Auto*, and its sequels have been huge sellers.

Two video games featuring zombies were popular in the years they were released: the previously mentioned *Wolfenstein 3-D*, with a PC-game release in 2001 called *Return to Castle Wolfenstein*; and *Resident Evil* and its sequels. The plot of *Resident Evil* has the player character as an amnesic person in a mansion nearby a top secret underground research facility called Raccoon City who accompanies a commando team into the city after the supercomputer controlling the city seems to have malfunctioned. As events unfold and the player gets farther into Raccoon City, it becomes apparent that a secret government program to create a biological agent has gone awry and turned all the citizens and researchers of Raccoon City into flesh-eating zombies. Even in 1996, this unoriginal zombie narrative still generated enough consumer interest to make the game extremely popular, and its sequel, *Resident Evil 2* (1998) for the Sony PlayStation, was the sixth top-selling video game of the year and the only one that year to feature zombies, or any kind of traditional monster. Its popularity resonated enough that the game was turned into more than one movie, putting it in the same league as other popular video games that became the basis for movies, such as the 1983 game *Mario Bros.*, which was made into the 1993 movie *Super Mario Bros.*; the video game *Lara Croft: Tomb Raider II*, made into the movie *Lara Croft: Tomb Raider*; and the light-gun arcade game *House of the Dead*, released in 2003 as a movie of the same name.

Although it has been argued that movies created from popular video games are inevitably a disappointment to fans because the element of interactive play has been removed from the movie, both *Lara Croft* and *Resident Evil* had movie sequels, *Lara Croft Tomb Raider: The Cradle of Life* and *Resident Evil: Apocalypse*, released in 2003 and 2004, respectively. This fact would seem to indicate that, despite some disappointing reviews of both of the original movies, they were popular (or profitable) enough to justify producing sequels, both with their original big-name Hollywood stars.

An interesting turn has taken place in video games regarding players choosing to play as zombies, despite several disadvantages to winning. This option became available in the *Warcraft* and *Diablo* series of games, as Ron Scott discusses further in chapter 11.

In 2005, Wideload Games released its inaugural game, *Stubbs the Zombie: Rebel without a Pulse*, to generally positive gaming reviews.[23] As the title suggests, the player takes the role of a zombie and kills humans, turning them into zombies to then kill others and create more zombies. The player can lob their internal organs at humans and even detach their head and use it as a bowling ball to disable opponents. Made with a healthy sense of parody, it nevertheless highlights how zombies have made yet one more transformation—into the lives of gamers willing to play as a zombie.

The willingness to be "zombified" does not stop at the Xbox console, however. Periodically in the past several years, there have been events held in cities such as New York and San Francisco in which gatherings of people dressed as zombies have walked the streets. Websites offer helpful tips on creating realistic-looking wounds and blood effects, and pictures of the events are posted on sites like Flickr. In the United Kingdom, a group called Terror4Fun for the past few years has hosted ZombieFests, which include zombie-movie nights, workshops on creating good special effects, and live-action role-playing (LARP), in which dozens of participants play various roles over the course of a day (overseen by referees of sorts who direct the story line) and that end up with a sole "survivor."[24]

In Minneapolis on September 9, 2006, a zombie pub crawl was held, attracting 350 participants dressed as zombies in various states of blood and gore, shuffling from one bar to another. The pub crawl website sums up the spirit of the event: "Why the zombie pub crawl? Because it's pretty much the greatest idea for a pub crawl ever conceived. Walking down the street in a horde of zombies and drinking? It's a dream come true."[25] The Minneapolis police did not share the fun spirit at a "zombie dance party" held in July 2006 in Minneapolis, arresting six people dressed as zombies for carrying devices that looked like WMDs—which turned out to be backpacks with homemade stereos in them so the zombies could dance.[26]

The evolution of zombies from the folkloric tradition into their current form in Western popular horror entertainment and the burgeoning D.I.Y. entertainment culture makes it unlikely they will fade into obscurity in the popular imagination. Zombies, or at least the concept of zombies, have also permeated other aspects of our daily lives, ranging from "zombie insurance," in which people claim insurance policies for people who have not yet died, to home PCs being turned into zombies by a hacker who then controls the computer to do his or her own bidding. Zombies have also showed up in online communication environments such as MUDs (multi-user dimensions), in which users create avatars of themselves and communicate with others in real-time chats. Some technologically savvy and malicious users in these MUDs can take control of someone else's avatar and have them do obnoxious or perverse acts. People who have been victims of this type of zombification report feeling personally violated, even sometimes using the term "raped" as they watch helplessly as their characters sexually assault or curse at other characters in the chat rooms. This is an interesting twist in how a new technology reverts back to traditional concepts—in this case, the traditional concept of a zombie as someone taken over by a master.

But in terms of popular culture and entertainment, zombies are versatile enough to be the fall guys for a range of paranoid theories on secret government programs or evil corporate plans. Likewise, in the dress-up and reenactments that people are taking part in at various locales and at times other than Halloween, zombies represent an abandonment of society even as they envelop the individual in a security blanket of community—a community in which not much is asked and where the rules of behavior are clear. There is something terrifying about being turned into a zombie, but something strangely comforting in *choosing* to be one, almost like Cholo (John Leguizamo) in *Land of the Dead*, after he is bitten by a zombie, when he tells his friend to not kill him just yet because he was "always curious about what it would be like"—as if it is a lifestyle choice. In that, perhaps the special power zombies hold over our imaginations is that they show us not only that we can fight powerful societal forces on our own but also that, when dealing with mysterious forces greater than ourselves, there will be a comforting sense of community even in (un)death.

Notes

1. Peter Dendle, *The Zombie Movie Encyclopedia* (Jefferson, NC: McFarland, 2001).

2. Wade Davis, *Passage of Darkness: The Ethnobiology of the Haitian Zombie* (Chapel Hill: University of North Carolina Press, 1988).

3. Michael Norton, "Haiti Officially Sanctions Voodoo," April 10, 2003, http://www.ananova.com/news/story/sm_769262.html.

4. Davis, *Passage*, 57–58.

5. Wade Davis, *The Serpent and the Rainbow* (London: Time Warner, 1987).

6. Milo Rigaud, *Secrets of Voodoo* (San Francisco: City Lights, 1969); Davis, *Passage*.

7. W. B. Seabrook, *The Magic Island* (New York: Harcourt Brace, 1929).

8. Marina Warner, *Fantastic Metamorphoses, Other Worlds: Ways of Telling the Self* (Oxford: Oxford University Press, 2002).

9. Peter Delius, "Witches and Missionaries in Nineteenth Century Transvaal," *Journal of Southern African Studies* 27, no. 3 (2001): 429–43.

10. Faustin Wirkus and Taney Dudley, *The White King of Gonave* (Garden City, NY: Doubleday, 1931); John Houston Craige, *Black Baghdad* (New York: Minton,

Balch & Company, 1933); John Houston Craige, *Cannibal Cousins* (New York: Minton, Balch & Company, 1934).

11. Edward Lowry and Richard deCordova, "Enunciation and the Production of Horror in *White Zombie*," in *Planks of Reason: Essays on the Horror Film*, ed. Barry Keith Grant (Metuchen, NJ: Scarecrow Press, 1984), 346–89.

12. Lowry and deCordova, "Enunciation," 350, emphasis in the original.

13. Christian Metz, *The Imaginary Signifier: Psychoanalysis and the Cinema*, trans. Celia Britton et al. (Bloomington: Indiana University Press, 1983); Raymond Bellour, "Alternation, Segmentation, Hypnosis: An Interview with Raymond Bellour," interview by Janet Bergstrom, *Camera Obscura*, nos. 3/4 (1979): 58–78, 97.

14. Leslie Halliwell, *The Dead That Walk: Dracula, Frankenstein, the Mummy and Other Favorite Movie Monsters* (London: Continuum, 1988).

15. See Dendle, *Zombie Movie Encyclopedia*, 5.

16. Gary A. Smith, *Uneasy Dreams: The Golden Age of British Horror Films, 1956–1976* (Jefferson, NC: McFarland, 2000).

17. Dendle, *Zombie Movie Encyclopedia*, 6.

18. Paul M. Riordan, "He Is Legend: Richard Matheson," *Sci-Fi Station*, Sci-Fi Masters Series, http://www.scifistation.com/matheson/matheson_index.html.

19. Steven Poole, *Trigger Happy: Videogames and the Entertainment Revolution* (New York: Arcade, 2000).

20. Scary Larry, "Dreamcast's *House of the Dead 2* Is Long on Gore," *CNN.com*, October 29, 1999, http://www.cnn.com/tech/computing/9910/29/house.of.dead2.idg.

21. Dolf Zillman and Peter Vorderer, *Media Entertainment: The Psychology of Its Appeal* (Mahwah, NJ: Erlbaum, 2000).

22. G. Jones, "Playing It Out," *Game Developer*, January 1, 2003, p. 64.

23. Chris Kohler, "Mmmmmmmm, Brains," *Wired Online*, October 28, 2005, http://www.wired.com/news/games/0,2101,69349,00.html.

24. Terror4Fun, http://terror4fun.com/zombie_homepage.html.

25. http://www.zombiepubcrawl.com/indexREAL.php.

26. Associated Press, "'Zombies' Booked for Carrying Fake WMDs," July 25, 2006, http://www.twincities.com/mld/twincities/news/state/minnesota/15117272.htm.

CHAPTER TWO

~

The Folklore of the Zombie Film
Mikel J. Koven

With its focus on "peasant superstition," ancient monsters, and antiquarian belief traditions, one would normally expect the modern zombie movie to be full of "folklore." However, closer examination of both the lore itself and several zombie-oriented films reveals a much different phenomenon, one which not only sheds light upon the folklore themes and motifs within zombie films but also challenges and problematizes many of the methodologies drawn upon in studying the intersections of folklore and popular film.

The methodologies employed here are twofold, reflecting different aspects of folklore study: on the one hand is a "literary" approach, looking to the folklore collections, with their largely European–North American bias, to ascertain the degree to which zombie cinema has drawn upon traditional folklore motifs and narrative types. The other approach is more ethnographic, exploring the anthropological literature in an attempt to ascertain the zombie film's verisimilitude with the living Haitian belief traditions. Neither approach is wholly successful, and they require a degree of interpretation—not to try to make the paradigms fit the films, but instead to see the dialogue the folklore has with these perennially popular horror films. This chapter began as an attempt to explore the folklore motifs within the zombie film; however, like most anthropological explorations into the realm of the zombie, the conclusions were slightly different from what was expected.

The study of the intersection between folklore and popular film is not nearly as clear-cut as would be expected if one were merely looking to see visual adaptations of traditional "lore."[1] Leslie Jones, in referring to *The X-Files*'s use of folklore, referred to most popular representations of traditional narrative as being "notionally folkloric," that is, popular film and television writers tend to grab any snippet of lore, without due attention to cultural context or meaning, resulting in invented cultural narratives that are more "Frankenstein-like" monsters, cobbled together from any handy source, than a representation of the narrative traditions from which these stories emerged.[2] However, such cobbling does not necessarily negate these films' use of folklore; Julia George, in 1982, surveyed eleven horror films that she happened to catch on television and, in a close textual study of four, identified very specific folktale motifs within them. None of these films made direct reference to specific folktale or legend narratives—that is, they were not explicitly *adaptations* of popular lore—but in telling their *filmic* narratives, they drew upon folklore as texture.[3]

Between a Type and a Motif

Within folkloristics, the academic study of folklore, studies of traditional narratives distinguish between the tale *type* and *motif*. Stith Thompson defined the former as

> a traditional tale that has an independent existence. It may be told as a complete narrative and does not depend for its meaning on any other tale. It may indeed happen to be told with another tale, but the fact that it may appear alone attests its independence. It may consist of only one motif or of many. Most animal tales and jokes and anecdotes are types of one motif. The ordinary *Märchen* (tales like Cinderella or Snow White) are types consisting of many of them.[4]

Beginning early in the twentieth century, Finnish folklorist Antii Aarne began codifying these tale types into an index, and the project was completed and revised by Thompson.[5] The resulting index, *The Types of the Folktale*, listed all known independent tale types and arranged them according to a specific cataloguing procedure (akin to the Dewey Decimal System within library science), gave a brief synopsis of the tale, and noted the specific literary references to these tales from the known folktale collections and archives. One example, which will be relevant below, is AT 363,[6] "The Vampire"; its synopsis is given as follows: "The bridegroom eats corpses in three churches (E251.3.1, G20).[7] He appears to his bride in the form of her father,

her mother, etc. (D40, D610) and when she tells about his habit he devours her."[8] Aarne and Thompson then list various collections in which this story can be found; in this case, the vampire narrative AT 363 can be found in Finnish, Swedish, Estonian, Livonian, Lithuanian, Norwegian, Danish, Irish, Catalan, Italian, Czech, Serbo-Croatian, Polish, Russian, and Turkish folktale collections.[9]

As can be gleaned from just this single example, with the exceptions of the Catalan and Italian instances, this particular narrative is found across most of northern Europe and down through eastern Europe into the Balkans, a distinct map forms on which one can speculate how this particular tale type has spread. The vampire narrative is a fairly simple one, and though not explicitly about zombies, or at least the zombies of horror cinema, this story does have echoes that can be found in zombie movies, namely, a recognizably human (if not familiar) figure that devours the living.

A related and more complex folktale type is AT 307, "The Princess in the Shroud," which is defined broadly as: "Each morning the watchers are found dead. A youth overcomes the enchantment; the dead girl comes out of the shroud. He wins her hand. (Not always a princess.)"[10] Here the folktale is identified as including three distinct movements:

I. *The Parents' Hasty Wish.* (a) Barren parents wish for a child even if she is a devil. (b) A daughter is born who is diabolical.
II. *Vampire.* After her death she leaves the grave in the church at night like a vampire and kills the soldiers who keep watch.
III. *Disenchantment.* At last she is disenchanted by a youth, on the advice of an old man, when for three nights in prayer, once kneeling before the altar, once prone before the altar, and once lying in her grave, he endures her punishments. The other watchers are resuscitated. Happy marriage.[11]

It is this inclusion of an alternative (to AT 363) vampire narrative that is of particular interest in trying to identify traditional narrative types within the zombie film, for AT 307 and AT 363 are the only tale type references to resurrected monsters that are even vaguely similar to the kinds of cinematic monsters we are concerned with here.

More fruitful, but still not entirely successful, is an exploration of folktale *motifs*, rather than within full tale types. Thompson defines the folktale motif as

the smallest element in a tale having a power to persist in tradition. In order to have this power it must have something unusual and striking about it. Most motifs fall into three classes. First are the actors in a tale—gods, or unusual animals, or marvelous creatures like witches, ogres, or fairies, or even conventionalized human characters like the favorite youngest child or the cruel stepmother. Second comes certain items in the background of the action—magical objects, unusual customs, strange beliefs, and the like. In the third place there are single incidents.[12]

Published between 1955 and 1958 in six volumes, Thompson's *Motif-Index of Folk-Literature: A Classification of Narrative Elements in Folktales, Ballads, Myths, Fables, Mediaeval Romances, Exempla, Fabliaux, Jest-Books, and Local Legends* classifies and catalogues the known folk narrative motifs. Volume 6 itself is an index to the *Index*; however, when searching for similar motif references between zombie movies and the oral narrative tradition, one needs to be highly flexible. There are no specific references to "zombie," "voodoo," or any of the stereotypical references we would expect from horror films. Instead, one needs to think more laterally and look to motifs pertaining to "Cannibal(s)(ism)," "Corpse," "Body," "Ghost," and "The Dead." Needless to say, most of the references under these indexical headings would not be relevant to a study such as this: "Cutting toenails of c[annibal] woman G519.1.2,"[13] for example, is not something I have come across in any horror film. However, one can also find, in this case under "Corpse," "ghosts (eat c[orpse]) E256,"[14] which is much closer to the kinds of motifs horror fans would be familiar with from zombie movies. These, albeit random, examples are further instances of what Thompson referred to as the second category of motifs, those which depict some kind of background action or "unusual custom."

The Dead

Within the various volumes of Thompson's *Motif-Index*, two specific categories of folktale motifs hold possibilities for identifying traditional motifs within the modern zombie film: category E, "The Dead,"[15] and category G, "Ogres."[16] To take each in turn, "The Dead" features a number of significant motifs that should be largely familiar to fans of the zombie movie, although little in the first section of category E, "Resuscitation" (E0–E199), is seemingly relevant to this study. This section focuses more on those motifs wherein a character, like Snow White, is thought to be dead, but is resuscitated and lives "happily ever after," or those more religious in tone, featuring the resurrection of the dead Lazarus-style by Christ or various saints and other holy people.

We do, however, find within this section motif E121.6.1,[17] "Resuscitation by demon's entering corpse," which, depending on the context of its use, could either be a motif pertaining to background action or a single incident. The notes that accompany this citation in Thompson refer to this motif as emerging from Irish mythology, and with only two subsections attached, this does not seem to be a widely circulated or well-known motif within the oral tradition. However, within the horror film, while demons may prefer to possess the living, they can also possess and thereby reanimate the dead. This belief tradition can also be found among certain native groups in Indonesia.[18] That this belief tradition is cited by Thompson as being of Irish rather than Indonesian origin calls attention to one of the central methodological flaws in Thompson's *Index*; the *Index* is clearly Eurocentrically biased, and this perhaps explains the absence of more "traditional" zombie lore within the folktale corpus, as there is little representation outside of Europe and European North America.

The rest of category E focuses on those motifs pertaining to ghosts and revenants, and despite the more ethereal nature of these monsters, in comparison to the more corporeal and visceral zombie of the movies (which I discuss more below), certain motifs are relevant here. The 200s of category E are concerned specifically with the "malevolent return from the dead,"[19] a motif that tends to parallel the zombie film; Romero's living dead, for example, are nothing if not malevolent.

Within this section are the "Return of family members" and motifs wherein "ghosts return to right wrongs,"[20] motifs that appear less relevant to exploring the folkloristic motifs within zombie films. But E250–E259.2 are concerned with "bloodthirsty revenants," and here we begin to see the motifs horror fans are more likely to be familiar with.[21] It is within this section that the vampire lives, for example, as E251—and cross-referenced with AT tale types 301 and 363, as I noted above, a motif that describes a central character or agency within the folktale.[22] More specifically, E251.3.1 tells us that "vampires eat corpses," a tradition from India; relatedly, "ghosts eat corpses," too (E256), a tradition which comes from Africa.[23] These motifs further demonstrate how a single motif initially might describe a character or agency within the narrative (ghost or vampire), but then can extend to descriptions of actions themselves (the eating of the corpses). Motif E259 becomes a miscellaneous reference for other random motifs pertaining to these "bloodthirsty revenants," including (from India again) E259.1, "Corpse bites off woman's nose"[24]—an image that, if it hasn't yet occurred in a zombie film, should.

Elsewhere within category E is motif E267, "Dead tears living to pieces," which Thompson identifies as British, occurring within the ballad tradition noted by Lowry Wimberly.[25] Significantly, what should be the most relevant motif in Thompson's *Index* is one of the tougher to follow up. E422 is identified as "The Living Corpse" and is defined by Thompson as: "Revenant is not a specter but has the attributes of a living person. He wanders around till his 'second death', complete disintegration in the grave."[26] This motif not only describes the character/agency (the "living corpse") but also develops the character slightly by motivating the figure's existence (waiting until the monster's "second death"). This creature is more in keeping with the cinematic zombie.

The problem is that the cinematic zombies are not revenants, specters, or ghosts; they are not ethereal embodiments of evil souls (or souls turned evil) who feast on the blood of the living. Although parenthetical to this study of the zombie, filing the vampire within this category recognizes the ethereal nature of that monster, by aligning it with other "spirit" forms like ghosts. And yet, as I have demonstrated, many of the motifs of the zombie film echo more traditional motifs within "ghost lore," including the lore of the vampire. Elsewhere, Thompson sees E422's "living corpse" (a zombie by any other name, at least within the cinematic tradition) as being an extension of the ghost motif. Thompson notes that

> the ghost is little more than a living dead man in full flesh and blood pacing up and down the earth awaiting the second death when his body shall eventually disintegrate in the grave. Frightful creatures these are, often appearing as vampires living on the wholesome blood of mortals.[27]

Later, Thompson notes that "these revenants of flesh and blood are most often malicious, and their return is usually to punish rather than to reward" the living.[28]

What differentiates Thompson's revenant tradition from that of the cinematic zombie is the specificity of the return of the living dead; within the oral tradition, the dead come back for a specific purpose (whether malicious or benevolent), rather than the seemingly random return of the cinematic zombie, at least in the post-Romero films. That being said, it could be argued that the modern cinematic zombie film has a more sociological purpose behind it: that the dead have come back to life as some kind of unspoken punishment of the living, some punishment for the sins of modernity. "When there is no more room in Hell, the dead shall wander the Earth" indeed.

This "living corpse" tradition of the reanimated dead body has a stronger link to the British and northern European ballad tradition, although Wimberly, like Thompson after him, contextualizes this within the ghost tradition. Wimberly notes that "the ballad revenant is a living corpse . . . for not only does our ghost share in the attributes of the dead and reflect its condition, but appears in certain instances to be identical with it."[29] Wimberly quotes from a Danish ballad the following stanza which could equally have come from any zombie film: "Out from their chest she stretch'd her bones, / And rent her way through earth and stones."[30] Here, the ghostly revenant of the ballad text is the reanimated body of the dead mother, literally coming through the earth of her gravesite. This "materiality" of the revenant, as Wimberly refers to it, even goes so far as to reflect the "incident of the dead man's returning without his arms, which, he says, have rotted off, [and] may be explained by saying that the ghost simply reflects the condition of the dead body."[31] Clearly the ballad ghost is differentiated from the spectral light or sheet-wearing variety. And as Wimberly again notes, "such an expression 'living' or 'vitalized corpse' is much to be preferred."[32]

Within Norse mythology, of course, is the story of the Viking warriors who kill each other in the day, but are revitalized at night to return and kill each other all over again the next day.[33] But beyond that, as Jacqueline Simpson notes, within the Icelandic legend traditions, revenants also can take more corporeal forms. The Icelandic *sending*, literally referring to the act of giving a gift or present, within the context of stories about sorcery "always refers to a malignant ghost raised by conjuring a corpse from its grave (or at least by using a bone or other material object), and sent to destroy an enemy."[34] Despite Simpson's identification of these Icelandic legends using Thompson's motif E422, our living corpse motif, these stories consist more of spectral revenants being sent (via witchcraft) than the reanimation of dead bodies.[35]

In an earlier book, Simpson does give, in great detail, the process by which an Icelandic sorcerer can raise a *sending*, and in this case, rather than a spectral presence, the sending is the reanimated corpse.[36] As the *sending* emerges from the grave, Simpson warns, the wizard must be extremely careful to ensure that the revenant stays under the sorcerer's control. But it is worth including a visual image Simpson gives in her description of the raising of a *sending*, which again zombie filmmakers should take note of:

When the dead first emerge from their graves, their mouths and nostrils are all bubbling with a frothy mixture of mucus and mud known as "corpse-froth"; this the wizard licks off with his tongue. Then he must draw blood from under the little toe of his right foot, and moisten the ghost's tongue with it.[37]

Returning momentarily to the problematic nature of popular filmmakers ransacking folklore (poorly) and not doing proper folkloristic research into the narrative traditions, this means that concepts like "corpse-froth" do not get included in zombie films. When filmmakers actually do proper folklore research into the themes of their films, it not only ensures accuracy and verisimilitude with narrative traditions but also often reveals some really wonderfully repulsive images that are much better than most horror script and story writers can conjure up themselves. The folk have been grossing each other out for centuries.

Parenthetically, and not within category E itself but perhaps vaguely relevant to the zombie film, motif F129.4.4 is "Voyage to the Isle of the Dead," in which, Thompson notes, "visitors who sleep there die."[38] Thompson further notes that, again, this motif is Irish in origin and is closely linked with more Classical voyages to the underworld. But, perhaps with not too much of a stretch of the imagination, one could apply this motif to Lucio Fulci's *Zombi 2*, wherein the zombies are created on such an "Isle of the Dead" and every one of the human visitors stranded on the island (i.e., who end up sleeping there) dies.

Ogres

Thompson's category G concerns ogres, and within this category, the first four hundred motif numbers are concerned with the many different kinds of ogres.[39] And it is in category G that we find closer analogies with the cinematic zombie.

Under the broad category of "Ogre" in Thompson's *Index* are specific references to cannibalism. Thompson distinguishes between those cases of "regular cannibalism" (G10–G49)—including G20, "Ghouls," who are defined as "persons who eat corpses"—and "occasionally cannibalism" wherein often the cannibalism is either from extreme conditions (e.g., facing starvation) or accidental.[40]

Sometimes the ogres themselves are cannibalistic (motif G312), as in the story of Hansel and Gretel.[41] However, one specific form of cannibalistic ogre Thompson notes with its own motif number, G312.1, is worth mentioning in slightly more detail: the piśāca, described as: "Drinks blood and eats human flesh. Eats corpses and makes living waste away."[42] The piśāca appears to share many commonalities with the cinematic zombie, yet Thompson notes that it is a monster from Hindu mythology, and I would suggest it highly unlikely that similarities are intentional.

Within folktales, ogres often take the narrative form of witches, trolls, or otherwise corporeal beings, including the devil. Despite referring to the "*huldre*-folk" Ol' Lanky Tor meets on his journeys as "trolls," rather than "ogres," Reidar Christiansen refers to the story "Trolls Resent a Disturbance" as containing motif G312, the "cannibal ogre" motif, and says that it has been collected frequently in Sweden as well as southern Norway.[43] Thompson notes:

> Three or four different concepts seem to be thoroughly confused when the term "devil" is used by the teller of tales . . . [and] frequently means nothing more than the vague word "ogre". Thus when they speak of the "stupid devil" they may equally well say "the stupid ogre" or "the stupid giant."[44]

In the same work, Thompson notes that storytelling folk often do not make distinctions between their supernatural creatures.[45] Ghosts are the same as the living corpses, who are the same as vampires, and ogres are the same as witches, giants, devils, and trolls. So, to return to the traditional *Märchen*, the witch in "Hansel and Gretel," the giant in "Jack and the Beanstalk," and the wolf in "Little Red Riding Hood" can all be seen as using G312, the "cannibal ogre" motif; witches, giants, and wolves can all be variants of this same kind of ogre figure. What differentiates category E from category G has more to do with their ethereal or corporeal nature. If the supernatural entity is of flesh and blood, then any of these terms will suffice.

Therefore, when it comes to attempting to apply Thompson's *Index* to the zombie film, we need to be equally flexible. Even though the cinematic zombie is, according to its nature, perhaps best classified as E422, a living corpse, which is a more ethereal supernatural being, according to its behavior it is perhaps better classified as a combination of G20, the ghoul, and G312, the cannibal ogre. And yet, neither category E nor G is sufficiently descriptive of what we mean when we refer to zombies, either from the literature or horror movies. Despite the occasional reference in Thompson to such-and-such a motif being from Africa or India, the *Index* is less helpful when one is attempting to research non-European motifs like the zombie. To get to these materials, one needs to avail oneself of a different kind of folklore research.

The Ethnographic Zombie

> Here in the shadow of the Empire State Building, death and the graveyard are final. It is such a positive end that we use it as a measure of nothingness and eternity. We have the quick and the dead. But in Haiti there is the quick, the dead, and then there are Zombies.[46]

There are two main anthropological, ethnographic, and folkloristic studies of Haitian Voudou and the zombie: originally published in 1938, Zora Neale Hurston's *Tell My Horse* is the pioneering African American anthropologist's personal account of her travels in the Caribbean (mostly Jamaica and Haiti) in the mid-1930s and her search for understanding the Voudou culture, including the zombie. Fifty years later, ethnobotanist Wade Davis followed Hurston's footsteps to Haiti, explicitly to find the scientific solution to the secret of the zombie, and his 1987 book, *The Serpent and the Rainbow* was an instant best-seller, with Hollywood quickly buying the rights to Davis's story.[47] The following year saw the release of the film of the same name, directed by Wes Craven.

Despite both the Hurston and Davis books, most casual perceptions of "voodoo" is as a "dangerous" religion, akin to Satanism, and the reality of the zombie as a modern monster has largely been fueled by horror cinema and popular culture. Karen McCarthy Brown refers to a distinct Euro–North American bias against the Haitian people in general and their "unofficial" national religion, Voudou.

> It has been incorrectly depicted as magic and sorcery that involves uncontrolled orgiastic behavior and even cannibalism. These distortions are undoubtedly attributable to racism and to the fear that the Haitian slave revolution sparked in predominantly white nations. Haiti achieved independence in 1804, thus becoming a black republic in the Western Hemisphere at a time when the colonial economy was still heavily dependent on slave labor.[48]

The Euro–North American vilification of Voudou may very well be unconsciously (or even consciously) motivated by racist skepticism of a religion that is largely determined and controlled by nonwhites, and the resultant moral panics about such a culture's (fictional) excesses can be explained. And yet, both Hurston and Davis, in addition to other anthropological literatures, do verify the existence of the Haitian zombie.

McCarthy Brown notes that within Voudou, practices exist that are locally referred to as "work of the left hand," magical beliefs and traditions that can be manipulated for (literally) "sinister" purposes.[49] Included within these "left-handed works" is the creation of zombies, which McCarthy Brown defines as "either the disembodied soul of a dead person whose powers are used for magical purposes, or a soulless body that has been raised from the grave to do drone labor in the fields."[50] Within Hurston's book, we meet Felicia Felix-Mentor, and in Davis's book we hear the story of Narcisse, both of whom, it was claimed, were actual zombies. While within the Voudou belief tradition lies the conceit that both Felicia and Narcisse had died and been raised from the grave as slaves, most believed, like Haitian psychiatrist Dr. Lamarque Douyon, that a more pharmaceutical explanation lay behind the zombie mystery.

> Though convinced zombies were real, [Dr. Douyon] had been unable to find a scientific explanation for the phenomenon. He did not believe zombies were people raised from the dead, but that did not make them any less interesting. He speculated that victims were only made to *look* dead, probably by means of a drug that dramatically slowed metabolism. The victim was buried, dug up within a few hours, and somehow reawakened.[51]

Hurston, thirty years earlier, spoke with then director-general of the Service d'Hygiene, Dr. Rulx Léon, and both held the same belief that zombification was likely pharmaceutical in origin.[52] It was this pharmaceutical solution that Davis sought in the early 1980s and documented in his book *The Serpent and the Rainbow*. Ironically, when Craven came to film Davis's book in 1988, he resorted to exactly the kinds of sensationalistic stereotypes of voodoo and the scary zombies for which McCarthy Brown aptly criticizes popular culture.[53]

An alternative perspective on the zombie emerges from this scientific literature: the zombie ceases to be the mindless monster battering down the shopping mall doors and emerges as more of a tragic figure, whose memory has been chemically erased and who has been sent to live a life of slavery. In Haiti, the fear of zombies does not come from meeting one on a darkened street, but from being turned into one.[54]

And yet, despite the sensationalistic title, the Val Lewton–produced and Jacques Tourneur–directed *I Walked with a Zombie* actually goes out of its way to keep as close to the ethnography as possible within Hollywood. Although based on the nonfiction magazine story by Inez Wallace (as well as lifting a bit, uncredited, from Charlotte Brontë's *Jane Eyre*), Curt Siodmak's screenplay appears to make extensive use of Hurston's travelogue in order not only to create verisimilitude with the Voudou practices but also to weave together, under Lewton and Tourneur's direction, a strong anticolonial discourse about the white presence and exploitation of Haiti.

The Zombie of the Cinema

If we understand the movie monster as a metaphor for some form of social anxiety, the zombie becomes particularly apt. Certainly there seems to be a distinct disjunction in the displacement of the zombie from the Caribbean to the U.S. screen. The early zombie films, most notably Victor Halperin's *White Zombie*, seem distinctly at odds with the ethnographic materials currently available. They do not avail themselves of Euro–North American zombie-like motifs from folk narrative, as demonstrated previously, nor do they seem to be rooted within the Haitian traditions of Voudou, even at its most sensationalistic level. *White Zombie* works more as a melodrama, wherein a "witch doctor," Murder Legendre (Bela Lugosi), is enlisted to enchant a young woman away from her fiancé, but instead the "voodoo priest" falls in love with her himself and turns her into a zombie so she will stay with him forever. In the background are Legendre's zombie slaves toiling away in his mines. Despite the vaguely Caribbean setting of the film and the use of the term *zombie*, not a single character of African descent is visible. While this might not be too surprising for a film made in the early 1930s, Legendre's zombies are made, not through the sensationalistic voodoo rites one would expect, but more through a form of mesmerism. And yet, as David J. Skal notes, *White Zombie* "was in many ways a nightmare vision of a breadline."[55] Skal continues:

> Zombies were especially handy in the present [Depression-era] economy, for, as San Francisco reviewer Katherine Hill quipped, "They don't mind about overtime." And as if to reinforce the notion of zombies-in-the-here-and-now, she noted that the theatre management had positioned costumed members of the living dead throughout the lobby like so many potted palms.[56]

If contemporary film critics in 1932 saw the metaphoric aspect of the zombie figure as reflecting those hardest hit by the Depression, eleven years later in 1943, Steve Sekley's *Revenge of the Zombies* makes this connection even clearer. In this New Orleans–set thriller, Dr. Max Heinrich von Altermann (John Carradine) is a Fifth Columnist raising an army of zombies for the Nazi cause. Here is the ultimate fighting force, obeying orders without question or sense of morality, and once killed, they can be resurrected, as in the stories of the Norse Vikings, to fight another day. In both of these films, despite the clearly expressed fear of the Other as monster, are some echoes of the Haitian fear of losing one's free will, of *becoming* a zombie rather than meeting the monster itself.

Conclusion

The film version of *The Serpent and the Rainbow* is a true anomaly: the anthropological and ethnographic source material is readily available for comparison with the film, and while resisting the immediate rejection of Craven's film as merely a poor adaptation, the trap is clearly set, since the film not only keeps Davis's title but also purports itself to be a "true story" about "real" zombies and tries to cash in on Davis's anthropological credentials. These issues of verisimilitude are beyond the scope of this current chapter, however.

The ethnographic literature on Voudou and the figure of the zombie has not really found much of a home on the cinema screen, despite the brave attempt in *I Walked with a Zombie*. The real fear of zombification—of not *meeting* a zombie, but *becoming* one—is a much too subjective fear to be able to depict filmically. Instead, the study of folklore and film needs to focus on *how* the ethnographic and anthropological materials are being used within a specific film. Are the cultural metaphors emically found within (in this case) Haiti adaptable to Depression-era America in *White Zombie* or to wartime B movies like *Revenge of the Zombies?* This is but one question the folklore-film nexus can explore on this subject.

Would that the search for evidence of folklore within popular culture were as easy as looking up a reference in Thompson's *Index* for "zombie" and finding a series of explicit examples of the living corpse from traditional folklore. This is not to say that similar stories did not occur in the oral tradition, but these references never manifest themselves quite so readily. The *Motif-Index* is, at best, a vague map of traditional storytelling, and the marginal notes that "Here be monsters" are what we need to explore more fully. In attempting to identify traditional tale types and motifs that have parallel references to, in this case, zombie films, the differences between our chosen films and the comparative source materials open up certain questions which, while never being directly answered, at least can be appreciated as landmarks for further research.

So, while the hordes of living corpses attacking remote farmhouses are not readily found within Euro–North American folk narratives, the similarities in behavior of the modern cinematic zombie to folk monsters like the *sending* or various ballad revenants is worth noting. But we can take this even further: recognizing these folk revenants and ogre-like monsters as retributionary figures sent to avenge some kind of particularized wrong within the narrative world of the song or tale, what happens when we apply this notion to those cinematic clambering mobs of the living impaired? Are they, too— implicitly, to be sure—sent to right unspoken social wrongs? Despite no clear-cut correlation between the (European) folk traditions and the modern zombie film, placing these two phenomena side by side does create a discursive juxtaposition. Thus, the real study of folklore and popular film lies not in uncovering direct and explicit representational issues, but in the exploration of new discourses about either in light of the other.

Notes

1. See, for example, Mikel J. Koven, "Folklore Studies and Popular Film and Television: A Necessary Critical Survey," *Journal of American Folklore* 116, no. 2 (2003): 176–95.

2. Leslie Jones, "'Last Week We Had an Omen': The Mythological *X-Files*," in *Deny All Knowledge: Reading the X-Files*, ed. David Lavery, Angela Hague, and Marla Cartwright (London: Faber & Faber, 1996), 79.

3. Julia George, "The Horror Film: An Investigation of Traditional Narrative Elements," *Folklore Forum* 15 (1982): 159–79.

4. Stith Thompson, *The Folktale* (Berkeley: University of California Press, 1977), 415.

5. This is a crude gloss on the early development of European folklore theory; a much more thorough discussion can be found in Thompson, *Folktale*. See also Antti Aarne, *The Types of the Folktale: A Classification and Bibliography*, 2nd rev. ed., trans. and enlarged by Stith Thompson (Helsinki: Suomalainen Tiedeakatemia/Akademia Scientiarum Fennica, 1981).

6. "AT 363" is this type's Aarne-Thompson index number, named after the authors of *The Types of the Folktale*.

7. These alphanumeric references refer to the motifs frequently found within these tale types, which I shall discuss below.

8. Aarne, *Types of the Folktale*, 126.

9. Aarne, *Types of the Folktale*, 126–27.

10. Aarne, *Types of the Folktale*, 99.

11. Aarne, *Types of the Folktale*, 99–100, italics in the original.

12. Thompson, *Folktale*, 415–16.

13. Stith Thompson, *Motif-Index of Folk-Literature: A Classification of Narrative Elements in Folktales, Ballads, Myths, Fables, Mediaeval Romances, Exempla, Fabliaux, Jest-Books, and Local Legends* (Bloomington: Indiana University Press, 1955–58), 6:114.

14. Thompson, *Motif-Index*, 6:165.

15. Thompson, *Motif-Index*, 2:402–517.

16. Thompson, *Motif-Index*, 3:274–366.

17. To break down Thompson's code somewhat, "E121.6.1" equates to category E, motif 121, subsection 6, sub-subsection 1 (Thompson, *Motif-Index*, 2:415).

18. See, for example, Peter A. Metcalf, "Death Be Not Strange," in *Magic, Witchcraft and Religion: An Anthropological Study of the Supernatural*, 2nd ed., ed. Arthur C. Lehmann and James E. Myers (Mountain View, CA: Mayfield, 1989), 332–35.

19. Thompson, *Motif-Index*, 2:419–29.

20. Thompson, *Motif-Index*, 2:419–21; 2:412–24.

21. Thompson, *Motif-Index*, 2:424–25.

22. Thompson, *Motif-Index*, 2:424.

23. Thompson, *Motif-Index*, 2:425. Thompson does not tell us from which part of Africa this motif comes.

24. Thompson, *Motif-Index*, 2:425.

25. Thompson, *Motif-Index*, 2:427. See also Lowry C. Wimberly, *Folklore in the English and Scottish Ballads* (New York: Frederick Unger, 1928).

26. Thompson, *Motif-Index*, 2:445.

27. Thompson, *Folktale*, 254.

28. Thompson, *Folktale*, 254.

29. Wimberly, *Folklore*, 234.

30. Wimberly, *Folklore*, 234.

31. Wimberly, *Folklore*, 235–36.

32. Wimberly, *Folklore*, 238. But *Night of the (Re)Vitalized Dead* just does not have the same ring to it.

33. Thompson, *Folktale*, 255.

34. Jacqueline Simpson, *Legends of Icelandic Magicians* (Cambridge, England: D. S. Brewer and Rowman & Littlefield for the Folklore Society, 1975), 93.

35. Simpson, *Legends*, 115.

36. Jacqueline Simpson, *Icelandic Folktales and Legends* (London: B. T. Batsford, 1972), 149–52.

37. Simpson, *Icelandic Folktales*, 150.

38. Thompson, *Motif-Index*, 3:21. Category F is "Marvels" and features many different kinds of voyages to the Otherworld.

39. Thompson, *Motif-Index*, 3:276–353.

40. Thompson, *Motif-Index*, 3:276–82.

41. Thompson, *Motif-Index*, 3:347.

42. Thompson, *Motif-Index*, 3:348.

43. Reidar Th. Christiansen, *Folktales of Norway*, trans. Pat Shaw Iversen (London: Routledge & Kegan Paul, 1964), 81–82.

44. Thompson, *Folktale*, 42.

45. Thompson, *Folktale*, 42.

46. Zora Neale Hurston, *Tell My Horse: Voodoo and Life in Haiti and Jamaica* (London: Harper & Row, 1938), 179.

47. Wade Davis, *The Serpent and the Rainbow* (London: Time Warner, 1987).

48. Karen McCarthy Brown, "Voodoo," in Lehmann and Myers, *Magic, Witchcraft and Religion*, 321.

49. McCarthy Brown, "Voodoo," 325.

50. McCarthy Brown, "Voodoo," 325.

51. Gino Del Guercio, "The Secrets of Haiti's Living Dead," in Lehmann and Myers, *Magic, Witchcraft and Religion*, 328.

52. Hurston, *Tell My Horse*, 196.

53. Even more ironically, according to the gossip on the *Internet Movie Database*, Davis sold the rights to his book to Universal only on the condition that Peter Weir would direct the film with Mel Gibson starring. Perhaps this explains why the Davis character's name is changed to Dennis Allan (played by Bill Pullman) and so much deviation to Davis's book occurs in the film.

54. Del Guercio, "Secrets," 331.

55. David J. Skal, *The Monster Show: A Cultural History of Horror* (New York: Norton, 1993), 169.

56. Skal, *Monster Show*, 169.

〜

CHAPTER THREE

Zombie Splatter Comedy from *Dawn* to *Shaun*: Cannibal Carnivalesque

Linda Badley

In the modern horror pantheon (*Resident Evil* and *28 Days Later* notwithstanding), zombies tend to be stooges—they specialize in stumbling incoherence, sick jokes, and the splatter film equivalent of taking pies in the face. Certainly from *Dawn of the Dead*[1] through Peter Jackson's *Braindead* (also known as *Dead Alive*)—and occasionally thereafter, as in the recent British sleeper hit, Edgar Wright's *Shaun of the Dead*—zombie cinema has been as hilarious as it has been horrifying. Horror and comedy are hardly strangers to one another, but beyond the parody, "comic relief," and black humor typical of B films, there is something fundamentally funny about zombies. Even in otherwise bleak splatter epics such as *Day of the Dead*, they are ridiculous, disgusting, pathetic, and absurd—at the same time *and for the same reasons* that they are horrifying. As the sheriff in the news bulletin sequences in *Night of the Living Dead* says when asked if zombies are "slow moving": "Yeah. They're dead. They're all messed up."

To put the issue another way, classifying monster icons by primary affect, we might say that ghosts are uncanny, vampires erotic, werewolves bestial and violent, and zombies grotesque. Monsters are grotesque by definition, of course, in the broad sense of being distortions or transgressions of the norm—werewolves, *The Thing*, and the *Hellraiser* films easily come to mind. However, I am following Philip Thomson, Wolfgang Kayser, and Mikhail Bakhtin, for whom the grotesque involves an ambiguous response, a mixture of revulsion and/or fear in the presence of the ludicrous.[2] Zombies (since *Night of the Living Dead*) are grotesque in all of these senses, but *especially* in provoking, often simultaneously and in nearly equal doses, the gut-level responses of disgust, horror, and laughter. True, the humor has ranged from the inadvertently ridiculous (*Plan 9 from Outer Space*) to the pointedly satirical (*Dawn of the Dead*) to "black," existential comedy (*Dellamorte Dellamore*, also known as *Cemetery Man*) to the anarchic splatter comedy of the early films of Sam Raimi and Peter Jackson.

This admittedly sweeping survey also shows how zombie comedy shifted over time: from social allegory in the late 1970s to "splatstick" (splatter slapstick) by the late 1980s and early 1990s, and from concern with the body politic to an obsession with the body itself—the body politicized as a site of anxiety, transgression, adolescent revolt, and liberating laughter. With this shift in mind, I will try to account for why, how, and when movie zombies in the previous three decades were funny and arrive at tentative conclusions about why, in the early twenty-first century—and with *Shaun of the Dead* the notable exception—they rarely are. I begin by analyzing the humor of *Dawn of the Dead*, the film that set the standard for the splatter film and for zombie comedy, from a range of perspectives—from philosophical to psychological to cultural-historical.

Dawn of the Dead: Six Perspectives

The Absurd

Zombie films are based on inherently laughable yet, in our world, absurdly possible premises. The fragmentary and unreliable news reports in *Night of the Living Dead* speculate that a detonated Venus probe carrying radiation brought the dead to life. A decade later, in *Dawn of the Dead*, the zombies are accounted for as a manifestation of "the excesses in our culture," as the trailer puts it. Their cause is often irrelevant or unknowable, the point being that "They're us." The absurdity of such premises calls attention to the absurdity of zombies themselves, who are materializations of the biggest joke of all: the fact that many fans of zombie films love reiterating, "We're all gonna die." At some fundamental level, and like all horror only more so, zombie humor is tragicomic, based in a sense of the absurd. But there is more to it than existential laughter.

The Freudian Joke

In Bill Condon's *Gods and Monsters*, an aging James Whale, plagued by flashbacks from the World War I trenches, escapes by reminiscing with his gardener about making the Universal Pictures Frankenstein films. Through an obviously Freudian process, he comes to understand that the films were "comedies about death." He returns persistently to the memory of a comrade named Barnett who was shot and left dangling on the barbed wire demarcating no-man's land, where he gradually decomposed into a "sick" joke:

> "Good morning, Barnett," we'd say each day. "How's ole Barnett looking this morning?" "Seems a little peaky. Looks a little plumper." . . . Oh, but we were a witty lot. Laughing at our dead. Telling ourselves it was our death too. But with each man who died, I thought, "Better you than me, poor sod."

The film—which is expressly "about" horror cinema and its raisons d'être—advances Freud's theory that jokes provide a socially accepted means of expressing otherwise unacceptable responses toward taboo subjects (such as decomposition). The "Barnett on the wire" joke deflects the horror of the situation even as it expresses terror, repulsion, aggression, guilt, and anxiety, allowing detachment from the death Barnett has come to represent. *Gods and Monsters*, and the coping mechanism it illustrates, might thus be said to explain why *Dawn of the Dead* repeatedly turned the "living dead" into slapstick routines, as in a scene in which a zombie inadvertently steps up on a box and the top of his head is whizzed off by a helicopter blade. The effect provoked laughter and applause in the film's first audiences.

Bergsonian Mechanicalism

Modeled on Dr. Caligari's Caesar and Paul Wegener's golem, the Frankenstein monster was a direct ancestor of the modern movie zombie. Referred to as "it," unable to speak, reduced to moans, grunts, and growls, he had a halting, lurching walk and a somnambulant, mechanical movement that suggested disability and the "repetition compulsion" of the death drive. In *Bride of Frankenstein* and much later in *Young Frankenstein*, the same characteristics that made the living dead our uncanny doubles turned them, detached from their original context, into great, sad clowns.

Further detached, more obvious versions of the same "sick" joke, zombies are the more easily played for laughs. Bub, an homage to Karloff's monster and the real hero of Romero's *Day of the Dead*, becomes the clownish double of his military keepers—relearning how to shave (taking skin and all), grunt to Beethoven's "Ode to Joy" on a Sony Walkman, salute, and (mis)fire a gun. Thus a central joke in zombie cinema is explained by Henri Bergson's theory that laughter is a response to "mechanical" behavior easily converted into slapstick.[3] Oblivious to pain, reduced to basic drives, and represented as a mass, the living dead are prone to pratfalls and exploding heads. In *Dawn*, hordes of zombies return to the center of their former lives, Monroeville Mall, and famously go on shopping, choreographed to the Muzak on the P.A. system (or to the Goblins' "The Gonk," described by one fan as "a kind of kooky clockwork big band number that makes you laugh every time you hear it").[4]

"Mechanicalism" is the obvious device for *Dawn*'s satire on the emerging postmodern consumer culture that was epitomized in "malling." "My zombies have tasted the good things in life and just can't figure out why that's not happening anymore," Romero told Adam Simon.[5] Reanimated by the forces of consumerism advertising seeks to channel, they lend themselves to broad visual puns: they're "born to shop," "live to eat," and walk around with their guts literally falling out. Disemboweling a man—as they scramble for organs and carry off ropes of intestines—they resemble a mob at a sale table. Wearing the clothes in which they expired, they suggest a diverse spectrum of classes, races, tastes, and religious practices that the primary visual image converts into caricatures, making (with deadly irony) the point that as consumers we're fundamentally all alike.[6] Because zombies are "us," we laugh *at* them uneasily, registering that we are laughing at ourselves, our friends, and neighbors.

These explanations only partly explain a central issue *Dawn* represented in 1978: the unprecedented level of violence in a film that also critiques a capitalist culture of violence—and the way the violence *itself* was perceived as funny, as in the helicopter scalping scene or the film's third act, where "The Gonk" offsets the violence of the final biker-versus-zombie bloodbath. Although Romero is often quoted on how the idea was to "numb you to the violence," a strategy he hoped would "open the mind" to the satire and the ideas in the film, things worked another way as well: the satire allowed the film to pass unscathed through several European censors. Undercutting the intensity of film violence and releasing audiences (represented in the film by surrogate audiences of rednecks and bikers) from normal "moral" responses to death, humor became a strategy for filmmakers who wished to push the limits.[7] Thus *Dawn* ushered in the 1980s splatter movies, low-budget films whose aim, according to John McCarty, was not to scare so much as "mortify" audiences with gore.[8]

"Horrality": A Historical Perspective

Departing from the relatively grim demeanor of the early slasher film, splatter comedy infused horror/sci-fi hybrids like *The Thing* and *The Fly* as well as zombie films such as *Evil Dead* and *Re-Animator*. Thus in 1983, Philip Brophy offered the term *horrality* (merging the terms *horror*, *textuality*, *morality*, and *hilarity*) to account for the onslaught, in the late 1970s and early 1980s, of movies that combined "perverse and/or tasteless"—and often self-referential—humor with graphic, fantastically over-the-top body horror effects.[9] Reveling in their excess, they were grounded in the body as the center of vulnerability in an increasingly material and visual culture.[10]

Horrality helps explain *Dawn of the Dead*'s reliance on what makeup effects director Tom Savini refers to as "gags."[11] Romero authorized Savini, a former Vietnam War photographer who found taking pictures and fabricating wounds to be a coping mechanism, to come up with as many ways of killing people as he could. "That became my job," Savini exclaims on the DVD commentary, adding that it was "like Halloween for months!" His "job" was topped off by his improvised role as the machete-wielding leader of the biker gang, a literalization of his extradiagetic role of "gag" coordinator and stuntman. Savini plays his character's pleasure in gore mayhem (for example, in cleaving a zombie's head) with a sadistic glee that refers to his role as splatter-effects auteur and trickster. Led by Savini, the bikers turn the zombies into the pretext for a literal pie-and-seltzer fight that ends in a rapturous orgy of routing, looting, and carnage.

Bakhtinian Carnival

The controversy *Dawn* presented in 1978 is usefully approached from the broader sociocultural perspective of Bakhtin's concept of Carnival as a dialogic space, a temporary liberation from and comic inversion of high culture's ritual fasts and feasts, and a space in which culturally constructed boundaries, especially those distinguishing death from life, become permeable. In the early Renaissance, Bakhtin noted, death was represented as "natural," jolly, and even joyful, as Carnival diffused fear with a festive, nonspecific laughter that went beyond satire.[12] In bringing back the "half-dead forms" of the outcast pagan gods, it was, as Barbara Creed has theorized, the ancestor of modern Halloween rituals or horror films.[13]

Especially applicable to zombies is Bakhtin's concept of a "grotesque realism" that celebrates the "open" and lower body, taking pleasure in its gross functions as processes that connect the individual with the whole. Bakhtin singles out certain Kerch terra-cotta figurines of three pregnant hags representing "a death that gives birth," fusing "a senile, decaying and deformed flesh with the flesh of new life, conceived but as yet unformed."[14] What clinches the image is that the hags are laughing. And so, the grotesque body is laughing, anarchic, joyously ambivalent, transgressing the modern canon that closes off and abjects: all is open, protruding, secreting, decomposing, eating, and being eaten.

Bakhtin's concept became popular in the 1970s and early 1980s, precisely when the "gross-out" began to be embraced by the middle-class youth culture in everything from animal comedy to splatter film and the pleasure of the horror text was, as Brophy put it, "getting the shit scared out of you."[15] Thus, for many viewers, the carnivalesque elements in *Dawn of the Dead* overrode Romero's subtext. The film created a precedent in which zombie movies end in a version of the "feast of fools," an orgy of obscene violence that is perversely procreative, as zombies cannibalistically beget more zombies, the underclass destroys the overlords, the lower body misrules, and we all become zombies. While the film's tone is ambivalent, ranging from nihilism to hilarity, the spectatorial response is "low" pleasure and "inappropriate" laughter.

Seen from this perspective, as biker boss, stuntman, and makeup-effects overlord, Savini found his destiny as a trickster icon, a Lord of Misrule for the horror genre. In *Dawn*, he presided over a space in which pagan rites (of dismemberment and cannibalism, represented as a form of sharing) are restored, death and life are continuous, body parts and fluids that normally remain hidden invade public space, and the underclass prevails. Casting was carnivalesque as well, including scores of unpaid nonactors who masqueraded as zombies, who identified with indie horror film as an underclass, or who wanted to play bikers because they *were* bikers.

Sconce's Politics of (Bad) Taste

Beginning with Romero, zombie movies challenged fundamental concepts of autonomy and rationalism, representing the revolution of the body from the head. Thus *Dawn* was carnivalesque also in its role in the revolution in taste that occurred between the 1960s and the 1980s, and which Jeffrey Sconce has deemed a "politics."[16] Zombie cinema drew from the darkly humorous, graphically violent E.C. Comics that Romero and other horror auteurs had consumed from childhood (and that preceded *Mad* magazine and R. Crumb in carnivalizing middlebrow "adult" values).[17] Enjoying "mindless" zombie movies meant identifying with a youth culture that was positioned against hegemonic "good" taste and expressed the accumulated disillusionment, rage, and war trauma of a generation.

The association between zombies and lowbrow culture was sealed when *Dawn of the Dead* became the bible for splatterpunk, a literary movement that inverted and cannibalized cyberpunk (science fiction's current bid for literary respectability), and also helped to birth the bimonthly fanzine *Fangoria* in 1979. Aimed at "gorehounds," *Fangoria* upended the venerable *Famous Monsters of Filmland* by devoting its coverage primarily to splatter effects and featuring a *Hustler*-style cover foldout of the monster of the moment—for instance, the creature from Cronenberg's *The Fly* in final molt. Celebrating the making of horror effects, and starring effects technicians Savini, Rick Baker, and their like, *Fangoria* portrayed the *production* of the grotesque as a carnival.[18]

1980s Zombie Comedy: "Thriller,"
Return of the Living Dead, and *Re-Animator*

Dawn of the Dead, as Romero says, marked the birth of "a different decade [from the 1960s and early 1970s], a different time. The beginning of prosperity. The major crises seemed . . . over, and everybody was just dancing. Disco. Just listening to the BeeGees, man." Zombie movies reflected the cultural attitude of the moment: you couldn't change the world, but you could dance. By the mid-1980s, zombie cinema had very nearly lost its political-satirical edge. What it offered now was an "open" carnival space in which certain issues of class, gender, and identity might be expressed.[19]

One marker for this shift was the extended John Landis–Michael Jackson video "Thriller," which brought a benignly carnivalesque image of zombies into the mainstream. In the video, Jackson's character ("Michael") suddenly finds himself surrounded by zombies, with no way of escaping except by joining and then leading them in a moonwalking dance. Jackson assimilates their revolutionary Otherness into his performance; they in turn (and however paradoxically) lend him the transformative power associated with 1980s special makeup effects. Other indicators of this shift were two cult classics, Dan O'Bannon's *Return of the Living Dead* and Stuart Gordon's *Re-Animator*.

Poised between political satire (on the military-industrial complex and medical science) and a diffused hilarity that ranged from black humor to spoof (on *Night of the Living Dead*) to conscious B-movie cheesiness, *Return of the Living Dead* revised Romero's premises to make zombies virtually indestructible and formidably funny. Contaminated by the corpse-animating 245 Tri-Oxin gas, the product of a misguided biological weapons experiment, they (that is, their parts) keep twitching and grasping long after they have been destroyed, providing endlessly divisible, permutated gore—and thus, in terms of the film's main metaphor, endless "party time." When a helpful mortician cremates one zombie, the oven's smoke seeds the clouds overhead, raining the chemical down on the cemetery, where a spectrum of teenage stereotypes, from punks to Goths to preppies, are having a party and scream queen Linnea Quigley is inspired to take off her clothes and dance. As the dead jump up out of their graves to the Cramps' "Partytime," the teenagers join them. The dominant mood is suggested by the DVD cover, which depicts a group of pink-and-green-haired, Mohawked, leather- and stud-collar-clad skeletons and features Quigley's substantial (and paradoxically undecomposed) cleavage to complete the image of the fertile hag.

Gordon's *Re-Animator*, based on H. P. Lovecraft's 1922 stories about mad vivisectionist Herbert West, began in all seriousness, focusing its critique on the medicalization of the body for at least forty-five minutes before turning its medical school and morgue settings into anarchic carnival space. While the satire is pointedly "black," the film's cult status has more to do with the mosh pit atmosphere of the last third, the sheer exuberance of its display of bad taste, brought on by a breakdown of the symbolic order. The film makes hash of a hierarchical structure of "loaded" binary oppositions (professors and students, doctors and patients, fathers and daughters, heads and bodies, parts and wholes, sex and death) as all of the characters are turned into raging zombies and/or "mad" scientists.

The catalyst is the boyishly puritanical West (Jeffrey Combs), a Miskatonic Medical School student obsessed with bringing the dead to a grotesque, screaming, frothing version of life by injecting them with an iridescent chartreuse serum. He is joined in his compulsion by the young intern and romantic lead, Cain (Bruce Abbott), and the madder scientist, Professor Hill (David Gale), who, seeking to prove that the soul is located in the brain, plagiarizes West's work. Decapitated by West, Hill's head is invigorated by its liberation (suggesting at first that his hypothesis is true). Sending signals to the trunk, it commandeers a series of lobotomies through which he turns the morgue's cadavers into slaves. When West crushes Hill's head, overdoses the trunk with serum, and Hill's zombies run amok (producing a Dionysian orgy of twitching limbs and rampant organs), the lower body is avenged.

In Rabelais's day, the styles of medical and military manuals leaked into literary texts, resulting in a *Gargantua*, which Katerina Clark and Michael Holquist describe as "a happy Frankenstein's laboratory," with Rabelais as the "madcap scientist stitching together body parts and functions that subsequent generations would call monstrous."[20] *Re-Animator* is similarly inspired in that its grotesqueness is accentuated by the clinical precision with which the concluding chaos is depicted: a dozen reanimated cadavers, each completely naked and distinguished by wound or cause of death—burn victim, slit wrist, malpractice, gunshot wound, and so forth—join a revolution of uncontrollable, "undead" life over the technologies of power.

Re-Animator's best-known moment is an obscene visual pun that is also an elaborate Rabelaisian inversion of hierarchies, as the mad Dr. Hill's libidinous decapitated head performs cunnilingus on the unconscious (and completely naked) dean's daughter, Megan (Barbara Crampton). The film ends as Cain tries to revive Megan, fails, and (of course) injects her with reagent, the screen goes black, and a scream is heard. It is indicative of the "real" message of the film that at this point, in a screening attended by Gordon, the audience shouted, "Use the juice! Use the juice!" They wanted this particular circus to go on. The satire on medical technology was finally a vehicle for the more generalized carnivalesque celebration: of the body in pieces or "without organs," unregulated and grotesque.

"Splatstick": *Evil Dead*

The shift away from social satire is suggested in B-movie star Bruce Campbell's term for his work in the *Evil Dead* trilogy—*splatstick*, which merged the lowest of the low "body" genres, splatter film and physical comedy, to produce the ultimate gross-out.[21] In the mid-1980s, the zombie craze attracted a younger generation of innovative, self-taught indie filmmakers inspired by Romero's production model and fascinated with splatter technology, resulting in a regressive, extremely physical, relatively unironic version of horror carnivalesque.

Sam Raimi's *Evil Dead* had no subtexts other than an understanding of genre formulas and effects, its own effort to produce "the ultimate experience in grueling horror," Raimi's prior filmmaking experience (limited to homemade Three Stooges–style shorts), and the experience of male adolescence. Outside of Ash, the slightly dim, wimpy protagonist, exaggeratedly distraught at having to dismember all his friends, the film lacked characterization or context outside of its postmodern amalgamation of horror-film clichés. Combining Romero's mythos with *The Exorcist*'s possession motif, Raimi turned his "zombies" into cackling, writhing hags that hurtled insults like evil clowns and spewed rainbow-colored fluids. In contrast to Romero's slow-moving hordes, Raimi's cheesy-looking "deadites," facilitated by Raimi's kinetic style and inventive camera work, seemed to be on speed and provoked bevies of nervous laughter. Audiences began talking to the film, telling Ash how stupid he was.[22] In short, the absence of A-film characteristics and the crude ferocity of the effects added up to an audience-participation film and a spook tunnel ride.

Among the first to reduce the horror film to a series of comic-book gags, each more creatively fantastic than the previous, the *Evil Dead* films had a long-term impact. *Evil Dead 2*, which announced itself as the splatstick comedy the first film had been unintentionally, was a sequence of gags developed out of the motifs of the body out of control and the monstrous feminine. In sequences derived from the violent physical humor of early cartoons, the feckless protagonist Ash's (Campbell) body is dismembered, doubled, hybridized, or "possessed"—as in a sequence in which his hand bludgeons him with kitchen implements until he severs it with a chainsaw. Squealing and gibbering to itself (like the Stooges' Curly), it scuttled into a mouse hole, gave Ash the finger, strangled him, and so forth. Replacing the hand with the chainsaw, Ash transformed himself into a carnivalization of the jut-jawed action hero epitomized by Sylvester Stallone and Arnold Schwarzenegger—but whose worst enemy was his own body. Eternally stuck in what Jacques Lacan called the "mirror stage," Ash was destined to be splattered—engulfed in the flesh and flux of comic life.

The latter is personified in nature (POV shots that barrel through the woods, eventually whipping into a whirlwind whose center is a huge, grasping tree) and his girlfriend (whose headless body springs from the grave, performs a lascivious dance, juggling its head while giggling hysterically, before the head, sporting a mouthful of alarmingly pointed teeth, bounces provocatively into Ash's lap). The Übermonster is the professor's wife, buried in the cellar and portrayed (via bodysuit and head puppet) as a campily senile, laughing hag with cheesy flesh and "pregnant" with bowels that spill from her belly. In a final flourish, she becomes a huge Phallic Mother joke, as her neck extends ostrich-like and her head, dangling from above, cackles, "I'll swallow your soul." Mingling male and female anatomies, decaying flesh with maternity, she is the obscene center of the carnivalesque upheaval in which the film *seems* to conclude (before shifting into another time zone).

Kiwi Carnival: *Braindead*

However different from Romero's progressive, political, and relatively "adult" satire, Raimi's carnivals of regression implied a politics of taste: a choice of gross-out physical humor and self-referentiality over an earlier generation's black humor and social content. But top prize in the regressive category is usually given to the early Peter Jackson, whose *Braindead* was a scatological inversion of the hero's journey, proceeding through the inner spaces of the home and the maternal body.[23] As in the *Evil Dead* films, the body was associated with the maternal—it is the protagonist's overbearing, possessive mother straight out of *Psycho* who starts the zombie plague. Merging silent film slapstick with Monty Python routines, it was also, however, a sweet romantic comedy set in 1950s Wellington, New Zealand, with quaint red streetcars and corner groceries told through splatter gags and some three hundred gallons of fake blood.[24]

In Jackson, as in Raimi, Romero's ensemble of embattled, bickering anti-heroes is replaced by a single protagonist, the Keatonesque underdog Lionel Cosgrove (Timothy Balme) who manages to survive in a world in threatening flux—in this case, the flux of the grotesque body—using dismembered parts as tools, negotiating a bloody floor by stepping on heads and organs and swinging from the ceiling by a length of intestine. In an inversion of the conventional zombie siege (in which the goal is to keep zombies *out* of the house), Lionel struggles to domesticate them—starting with his rapacious Mum, Vera (Elizabeth Moody)—by administering animal tranquilizer.

The zoo is a dominant metaphor in *Braindead*, as the film sustains the carnival practice of representing the animal aspects of human materiality—defecating, copulating, eating, decay—and the Feast of Fools, the gluttonous, drunken inversion of the sacred feasts that, Mikita Brottman reminds us, was replete with implied cannibalism, obscene posturings, licentious behavior, filth throwing, and farting.[25] Disgusting food gags contribute greatly to *Braindead*'s carnivalesque tone and theme. In one scene, an appalled Lionel draws the leftovers of a German shepherd from Mum's mouth as his girlfriend Paquita (Diana Peñalver) exclaims, "Your mother ate my dog!" One family dinner scene—in which Lionel attempts to feed his tranquilized surrogate zombie family (Nurse McTavish [Brenda Kendall], Father McGruder [Stuart Devenie], Mum, and Void [Jed Brophy]) porridge, as they sit twitching, nodding, and moaning around the dining room table—is told entirely through linked gore and food gags.[26]

The film's high (read "low") point is an elaborate allegory of toilet training that focuses on Lionel's battle with Void's zombified innards—Void being a 1950s-style "juvenile delinquent" who thinks from his gut and, when bisected and disemboweled, becomes a running scatological visual pun. Thanks to Void, in true Rabelaisian style, the boundary distinguishing the abject from one's true and proper self, inside from outside, is transgressed, lower and upper body priorities are reversed, and (most importantly) "good" taste is affronted as normally unnamed, unseen organs recognize and even "speak" for themselves (in a parody of the mirror phase set in the bathroom). In the final Keatonesque sequence of fantastic physical comedy, Void's guts pursue Lionel through the several stories of the house. At the conclusion of the final "battle" sequence in which Lionel pulverizes a houseful of partying zombies, he looks down at his feet to see Void's indomitable innards on their coils pleading for their "lives." Lionel demonstrates his manhood by applying the lawnmower, the ironic symbol of the domesticated male's territorial control.

On another level, Void's zombified guts are an umbilical cord that Lionel just cannot shake. Like *Evil Dead 2*, *Braindead* represents women as especially rapacious. Mum is a condensation of dominating/toilet training/dead mother jokes and also perhaps horror comedy's ultimate example of the unruly feminine and the pregnant hag. But, as Barry Grant and Barbara Creed have shown, the film may be read as a postcolonial critique in which the proper suburban mother represents the queen and New Zealand's continued (umbilical, economic) ties to the Mother Country.[27] The film thus satirizes the colonialist and bourgeois orthodoxy that proclaims the "sanctity of motherhood" (the theme of Father McGruder's funeral service for Mum).

On yet another level, however, and as the film finally argues, the "forces of death" that (according to the cards) "surround" Lionel (e.g., Mum and the zombie plague she has birthed) are necessary to his coming of age. At the film's climax, swollen to a couple of stories tall, with horselike jaws, pendulous breasts, belly, and ass, devouring Mum is "purged"—but not before Lionel is swallowed and reborn mock-heroically in a pile of afterbirth. The mother is profoundly ambiguous; while she may represent colonialist cultural oppression, it is her mix of orality, aggression, and transgression that destroys the Motherhouse (Mum's colonialist values) and that is the source of the film's final explosion of the bodily canon and the various orders that support it.[28] Carnival's hell is transformed into a Bakhtinian cornucopia as "the monster, death, becomes pregnant" and protrusions and size are symptoms of procreative power.[29]

Although reminiscent of Larry Cohen (*It's Alive*), David Lynch (*Eraserhead*), and David Cronenberg (*Shivers, The Brood, The Fly*), Jackson's fantastic body horror is assimilated into a film with an entirely different tone. In his early films, exuberant spectacle and comic gore gags override the revulsion and fear characteristic of Romantic or Gothic grotesque, as the body— eating, defecating, cannibalized and cannibalizing, dying and reproducing— is associated with comic resilience and vitality. Thus while notoriously adolescent, seemingly misogynistic, and reactionary, *Braindead* also exemplifies Bakhtinian grotesque realism, in which the bodily canon is inverted, the lower body and the feminine are "on top," and death is voraciously procreative.[30] It may be zombie cinema's purest example of a carnival in which political satire is disseminated throughout a text whose tone and purpose are ultimately festive and anarchic. Yet while it provoked wildly carnivalesque responses at various festivals, including Cannes 1993, the film became a cult phenomenon on VHS and DVD rather than a U.S. box-office hit.

By the early 1990s, with the advent of digital video graphics, the mainstreaming of horror, and a backlash against the explicit gore of the previous decade, the zombie splatter comedy cycle was over for the time being. In topping previous efforts, critics said, Jackson had insured its demise. Yet more accurately, it had already begun to mutate and infiltrate genres such as science fiction (*Terminator 2, Species*, etc.) and the films of Quentin Tarantino, while the horror genre itself had already shifted toward self-reflexiveness and suggestion (*Scream, The Blair Witch Project*, etc.). Similarly, Bakhtinian critique, while infiltrating various methodologies, had lost its fascination.

Carnival Domesticated: *Shaun of the Dead*

One product of the shift from the political engagement of the late 1960s and early 1970s was that zombie comedy had changed from Romero's darkly humorous social satire to the increasingly grotesque (but finally targetless) body humor in the 1980s films of Brian Yuzna, Stuart Gordon, Sam Raimi, and Peter Jackson—films that functioned as adolescent fantasies of regression and simultaneously as rites of transgression. The emergence and decline of zombie splatter comedy was like that of most cycles or subgenres, the product of a cultural shift (from progressive to conservative) and several interrelated factors: the rise of a youth culture that came to dominate the box office (but that subsequently aged and changed), technological developments in special-effects makeup, the complicated relations between the horror genre and the MPAA rating system, postmodernism, and the self-cannibalistic and cyclical nature of the horror genre.

Two seeming exceptions to this trend have been Rob Zombie's *House of 1000 Corpses*, which (although not a zombie film) returned to the outrageous Feast of Fools mode of the 1980s in a spirit of parody (primarily of *The Texas Chain Saw Massacre*), and the British zombie comedy *Shaun of the Dead*, directed by Edgar Wright and coscripted by Wright and star Simon Pegg. Originating as an early episode of their popular British sitcom series *Spaced* (in which the protagonists found themselves in the middle of *Resident Evil*), *Shaun of the Dead* advertised itself as an homage to the subgenre Romero had invented but also as something new—a "rom-zom-com," a romantic comedy with zombies.

The real point of 1980s splatstick was the cannibal carnival, with the zombies providing, along with the horror, most of the laughs. The coming-of-age story of an ill-equipped late-bloomer protagonist such as Ash or Lionel, however, was often the vehicle of this grotesque humor. *Shaun of the Dead* features a similar story and protagonist, a balding, thirtyish underachiever (Pegg) who has settled into a comfortable rut in his North London suburb—he plods to his job as an appliance salesman, shares a flat with his loutish best buddy Ed (Nick Frost), and spends his evenings at his favorite pub (the Winchester)—all to the chagrin of his long-suffering girlfriend Liz (Kate Ashfield)—and is slowly recovering from a hangover for much of the film. Much as in *Evil Dead* and *Braindead*, the zombie plague, which coincides with Liz's breakup with him, rouses him to action. What is new is the prohibition of splatstick, director Edgar Wright explains, citing two rules of thumb: "No screaming" and "No zombie pratfalls"—in fact "no funny zombies" at all.[31]

While the film has its share of gore, the humor is character oriented, notably verbal (packed with legendary one-liners), and situational—according to Wright, the zombies simply provide the circumstances that the protagonists, cluelessly and belatedly, find themselves in: "You could go to the script and replace the word 'zombies' with 'traffic jam' or 'power outage' and it would still make sense."[32] At the same time, and in homage to Romero's satire on consumerism (as per the title), *Shaun of the Dead*'s zombies function as the "slacker" generational metaphor for the way people go about their lives. Identically choreographed steadicam sequences make the point by following Shaun's morning routine—from crawling out of bed, shuffling down the street (stumbling on the same curb at crossing), turning into the corner convenience store, and riding a bus full of passengers in bleary-eyed stupor—all the while oblivious to the shuffling zombies he passes or jostles (many of them former neighbors) along the way.[33]

Even though it prohibits the grotesque in the form of splatstick, *Shaun of the Dead* shows reverence toward the spirit of the older cannibal carnivalesque. Making special reference to the mayhem that Savini's gleefully violent biker character relished and that *Dawn of the Dead* was celebrated for, the film embodies (and thus safely contains) the carnivalesque spirit in a single character, that of Shaun's Falstaffian roommate Ed, a crotch-scratching, practical joking, hard-drinking PlayStation addict who shares Shaun's fixation on the Winchester. If, as in the 1980s comedies, the zombie plague allows Shaun a chance to become an unlikely hero in an equally unlikely apocalyptic setting, the pub, it also enables Ed to fulfill his fantasies of speeding in a luxury car, swilling beer, and mindless killing—until he (appropriately) is turned into a zombie himself.

In the epilogue, Shaun is living with Liz in bourgeois respectability, and the remarkably unchanged Ed (secured by dog collar and chain) lives a happily contained undead existence on a couch in the shed out back, where Shaun retreats to play video games. Where Jackson's Lionel failed to housebreak his zombies, Shaun succeeds in containing Ed, but at a price. Like the film itself, which confines the zombie splatter genre within a romantic/slacker comedy, Ed is carnival domesticated for the twenty-first century.

Conclusion: Fast Zombies?

Updating zombie comedy generally and Romero's satire on consumerism specifically for the post-*Simpsons*, post–*South Park*, post-9/11 generation, *Shaun of the Dead* played off culturally attuned viewers' expectations and offered a metaphor for the mindlessness of routinized capitalist culture. Beyond the slacker jokes, however, the zombie plague of *Shaun* (referred to by news commentators as "Z-day") also possibly comments on our post-holocaust retreat into ennui and indifference. Notably, *Shaun*'s zombies are slow. As Wright argues, true zombies are a "bizarre tidal, lava-like encroachment" that resembles the slow inevitability of apathy and of death itself.[34] Accordingly, fast zombies would be a contradiction in terms or another species.

At this writing, of course, as apocalyptic horrors of biological warfare, contagion, and terrorism have become all too real and war once again appears to be perpetual, zombies have returned with a vengeance and in a range of mutated forms. They speak for the cultural moment—expressing paranoia, alienation, and a sense of ever-present threat. In mainstream films such as *Resident Evil*, *28 Days Later*, and the remake of *Dawn of the Dead*—and in contrast to *Shaun*—zombies are virulent, fast, and deadly serious. In the *Lord of the Rings* trilogy, in which zombie-like species are aligned with the forces of good and evil and are treated with the gravity due J. R. R. Tolkien's World War II epic, even Jackson relinquished the more raucous forms of the carnivalesque. The regressive/transgressive spirit of zombie splatter comedy, it seems, has been rendered obsolete by affectionate parody, contained in domesticated forms (as in *Shaun*), or returned underground where it survives in the no-budget, backyard film production mode that inspired *Night of the Living Dead*—in the D.I.Y. movement, the carnivalesque productions of the Troma team, and sundry Internet and cult phenomena. Still, we may take consolation in the hope that, as Bakhtin was fond of stressing, the carnival principle is "indestructible," that even while "narrowed and weakened"—its original forms fragmented, regulated, and commodified—it continues as an occasionally disruptive undercurrent, now and then surfacing "to fertilize various areas of life and culture."[35]

Notes

1. It is symptomatic that the first *modern* zombie film, *Night of the Living Dead*, as much a product of cinema as it was of literature or folklore, began as a parody with Johnny's Boris Karloff imitation, "I'm coming to get you Barbara"—followed by the first zombie's equally Karloffian monster walk. While George Romero's trick was to

modulate from seemingly harmless parody to cinema vérité and abject horror, black humor and social satire inflected the film throughout.

2. Philip Thomson, *The Grotesque* (London: Methuen, 1972), 3, 7–9, 12–19; Wolfgang Kayser, *The Grotesque in Art and Literature*, trans. Ulrich Weisstein (New York: McGraw-Hill, 1966), 186–89 et passim; Mikhail Bakhtin, *Rabelais and His World*, trans. Hélène Iswolsky (Bloomington: Indiana University Press, 1984).

3. Henri Bergson, *Laughter: An Essay on the Meaning of the Comic*, trans. C. Breretson (New York: Macmillan, 1926). The word *slapstick* originally referred to two pieces of wood used by clowns to make a slapping sound when they appeared to be hitting one another and refers more broadly to physical (often aggressive or violent) humor. It is achieved by rendering scenes that normally would be painful or worse cartoonlike, mechanical, or fantastic.

4. "Dawn of the Dead: The Unreleased Incidental Music," http://www.trunkrecords .com/turntable/dawn.shtml.

5. Quoted in the documentary *The American Nightmare*.

6. The Hari Krishna zombie, who limps in balletic circles, his tambourine dangling uselessly, comments on the decidedly unmystical Western sources of the zombie plague. Steve, the would-be romantic lead for most of the film, charges out to fight a group of marauding bikers for possession of the mall (insisting: "It's ours. We took it. It's ours.") and creates an anticlimactic battle won ultimately by the zombies, who finish off the surviving bikers. Bitten in the struggle, Steve leads them back to his comrades' hideout, like the commander of a stumbling, rotting army or a duded-up cowboy with an irrelevant gun dangling numbly from two fingers, his lurch a skewed rendition of the gunslinger's walk. See Tony Williams, *The Cinema of George Romero: Knight of the Living Dead* (London: Wallflower, 2003), 96.

7. The satire could, of course, carry a social or "moral" perspective, if necessary. The extent to which the satire saved *Dawn* from censorship is shown in the controversy over the European versions overseen by coproducer Dario Argento, who cut the humor (and thus the subtext) from the script in order to turn the film into a "flat-out" horror movie (along the lines of the Italian zombie genre developed by Lucio Fulci). As Romero explains on the DVD commentary track, when various European censors mutilated these versions, Romero sent them copies of the original, which they apparently found inoffensive enough to exhibit without cuts. See Donato Totaro's discussion of Peter Jackson's use of humor to undercut the effect of extreme violence in "Your Mother Ate My Dog! Peter Jackson and Gore-Gag Comedy," *Offscreen* 5, no. 4 (September 2001), http://www.horschamp.qc.ca/new_offscreen/ goregag.html. More generally, for a useful discussion of comedy and violence in film, see Geoff King's *Film Comedy* (London: Wallflower, 2002).

8. John McCarty, *Splatter Movies* (New York: Fanta Co Enterprises, 1981).

9. Philip Brophy, "Horrality—The Textuality of Contemporary Horror Films," in *The Horror Reader*, ed. Ken Gelder (London: Routledge, 2000), 277, 284.

10. See Linda Badley, *Film, Horror, and the Body Fantastic* (Westport, CT: Greenwood Press, 1995).

11. Tom Savini, "Fast Foreword," in *Still Dead: Book of the Dead 2* (New York: Bantam, 1992), xiii–xvi.

12. Carnival was licensed and was thus an escape valve and a form of social control. However, Bakhtin insists that it was more than that: it sustained the vital life of the people and continues as an undercurrent whose subversive power can be tapped; Mikhail Bakhtin, *Problems of Dostoevsky's Poetics*, ed. and trans. Carlyl Emerson (Minneapolis: University of Minnesota Press, 1984), 107. See also Peter Stallybrass and Allon White, *The Politics and Poetics of Transgression* (Ithaca, NY: Cornell University Press, 1986), who argue that "for long periods carnival may be a stable and cyclic ritual with no noticeable politically transformative effects and that, given the presence of sharpened political antagonism, it may often act a catalyst and site of actual and symbolic struggle" (14).

13. Bakhtin, *Rabelais*, 24; Barbara Creed, *The Monstrous-Feminine: Film, Feminism, Psychoanalysis* (New York: Routledge, 1993).

14. Bakhtin, *Rabelais*, 25–26.

15. Brophy, "Horrality," 279.

16. Jeffrey Sconce, "Trashing the Academy: Taste, Excess, and the Emerging Politics of Cinematic Style," *Screen* 36, no. 4 (1995): 371–93. Drawing on Pierre Bourdieu and Lester Bangs, Sconce argues that an appreciation of paracinema—which ranges from the "punk" art cinema of Andy Warhol and Paul Morrissey to "trash" or deliberately lowbrow cinema from John Waters to Troma—implies an opposition to middlebrow or hegemonic "good" taste. Romero undoubtedly shared this role with Tobe Hooper, David Cronenberg, John Carpenter, and Wes Craven, who made subversive, deliberately offensive films with similar subtexts in the 1970s, as Adam Simon's documentary *The American Nightmare* makes clear. Romero, however, was first, and *Dawn* had a clear political message.

17. See Williams, *Cinema of George Romero*, 17–32, 84–87, 114–27, on the influence of E.C. Comics on Romero's films, and see David J. Skal, *The Monster Show: A Cultural History of Horror* (New York: Norton, 1993), 263–85, on the impact of 1950s comic book culture on the horror films of the late 1960s and thereafter.

18. The same youth culture that relished zombie splatterfests and *Fangoria* would delight in *National Lampoon's Animal House*, *The Revenge of the Nerds*, and *Porky's*. These gross-out comedies, as William Paul argues in *Laughing Screaming: Modern Hollywood Horror and Comedy* (New York: Columbia University Press, 1994), shared with horror a Bakhtinian mood and social function.

19. In such "open" spaces provided by postmodern horror film, the processes of subject formation were possibly changed by the experience of the grotesque, as Barbara Creed suggested in "Horror and the Carnivalesque: The Body Monstrous," in *Fields of Vision: Essays in Film Studies, Visual Anthropology, and Photography*, eds. Leslie Devereaux and Roger Hillman (Berkeley: University of California Press, 1995), 153–57.

20. Katerina Clark and Michael Holquist, *Mikhail Bakhtin* (Cambridge, MA: Belknap Press of Harvard University Press, 1984), 297.

21. Ian Pryor credits Peter Jackson with the coinage, but the general consensus is for Campbell, who, after all, came first; Ian Pryor, *Peter Jackson: From Prince of Splatter to Lord of the Rings: An Unauthorized Biography* (New York: St. Martin's, 2003), 102.

22. Bill Warren, *The Evil Dead Companion* (New York: St. Martin's, 2000), 95.

23. In Jackson's debut film *Bad Taste*, about invading human-eating aliens who seek to establish an intergalactic fast-food franchise, Jackson played an alien who vomits for several minutes into a huge bowl that is passed around like a communion cup. His next effort, *Meet the Feebles*, returned *The Muppet Show* to its origins in the fabliau as anthropomorphized animals acted out the physiological facts that level the species.

24. In Monty Python's Sam Peckinpah parody "Salad Days," elegant picnickers impale themselves with tennis racquets, hands are severed by a piano lid, limbs inexplicably fall off, volcanic quantities of blood gush forth; in *The Meaning of Life*, Mr. Creosote, a fantastically obese patron, eats until he vomits and vomits until he explodes; and in *Monty Python and the Holy Grail*, the Black Knight is reduced to a blood-spewing, limbless torso, yet continues to challenge his opponents.

25. Mikita Brottman, *Funny Peculiar: Gershon Legman and the Psychopathology of Humor* (London: Analytic Press, 2004), 92. Jackson's version of the zombie plague begins at the zoo, where Mum is bitten by a Sumatran "rat monkey," an unholy hybrid the zoo keeper explains as follows: "All these great big rats [that] came off the slave ships and raped the little tree monkeys." As Mum screeches, the camera cuts to reaction shots of birds in nearby cages. The motif is extended in the romance between Lionel and Paquita, whose unrepressed "animal magnetism" draws out Lionel's repressed sexuality, provoking Mum's jealousy. But it emerges most plainly in the scenes in which Lionel attempts to domesticate his zombie charges, starting with Mum.

26. As McTavish's porridge seeps from her severed neck, Void shoves a spoon into his mouth and out through the back of his head, Mum snatches the porridge off the spoon, McGruder and McTavish eye each other lasciviously and proceed to kiss until Lionel pulls them apart, their lips stretching until McGruder's rip off, leaving him with an even more lascivious rictus grin, a carnivalesque image of "gay death." McTavish and McGruder, having abandoned their socially sanctioned roles, fall to the floor and copulate enthusiastically. Outside the door, as Lionel tries to conceal his disgraceful zombie "family" from Uncle Les (who wants to usurp the family fortune), rutting animal sounds are heard within, and Uncle Les accuses Lionel of having found his dead father's porn flicks: "Is that the one with the donkey and the chambermaid?"

27. See, for example, Barry Keith Grant, *A Cultural Assault: The New Zealand Films of Peter Jackson* (London: Kakapo Books, 1999); and Barbara Creed, "Bad Taste and Antipodal Inversion: Peter Jackson's Colonial Suburbs," *Postcolonial Studies* 3, no. 1 (2000): 61–68.

28. The scene has the grotesque physicality, humor, and miraculous atmosphere of the birth of Gargantua, the labor pains brought on by his mother's consumption of a

vast amount of tripe (the digestive organs of a cow, which contain a certain percentage of dung). See Bakhtin, *Rabelais*, 162–64.

29. Bakhtin, *Rabelais*, 91.

30. Jackson has been accused of using comedy in order to get away with more extreme splatter than otherwise. In an interview with Ian Pryor, Jackson defends splatstick as "totally different" from violence. "You can punch somebody in the face in a drama, and it's an incredibly violent act. Then you can rip somebody's head off in a zombie film, and it's a comedy. . . . Any discussions about violence in a movie should be totally within the context of what the film is, what genre it is, and what it's trying to achieve" (quoted in Pryor, *Peter Jackson*, 102–3). Jackson cites Monty Python and silent comedians Buster Keaton, Charlie Chaplin, and the Keystone Cops as evidence that violence is and always has been "part of comedy" and that the more fantastically "gross" horror effects are, the more comical the film becomes. "That is really the key point: the only harmful violence is believable violence, realistic violence and there's nothing in this film that's realistic at all. It's fantasy" (quoted in Pryor, *Peter Jackson*, 103).

31. Peter Canavese, "Interviews: Simon Pegg and Edgar Wright—*Shaun of the Dead*," *Groucho Reviews*, November 8, 2004, http://www.grouchoreviews.com/index .php?module=subjects&func=viewpage&pageid=26.

32. Todd Gilchrest, "Romero High-Fives *Shaun*," *Filmstew.com*, September 24, 2004, http://www.filmstew.com/showarticle.aspx?contentid=9746.

33. A comic turning point (and another nod to Romero) is the scene in which the usually clueless group of would-be survivors make their way through a sea of zombies by pretending to be zombies. Understanding "being zombie" as a matter of performance means a step in the right direction of becoming "human."

34. Jeff Otto, "*Shaun* and the *Dead* Director," *FilmForce*, September 23, 2004, http://movies.ign.com/articles/550/550221p2.html.

35. Bakhtin, *Rabelais*, 33–34.

~

CHAPTER FOUR

Vita, Amore, e Morte—and Lots of Gore: The Italian Zombie Film

Brad O'Brien

"If . . . zombies could talk, they would probably speak Italian, because that's where most of the really grisly zombie pics come from," writes Allan Bryce in his introduction to *Zombie*, a collection of essays on zombie cinema.[1] Thanks to Italian filmmakers like Lucio Fulci, Umberto Lenzi, Marino Girolami, Andrea Bianchi, and Michele Soavi, not only do zombies bite open throats, feast on human flesh, and skewer eyeballs but they also wrestle sharks, fly airplanes, shoot guns, dress up as monks, fight cannibals, ride motorcycles, and spy on women in the shower. However, because these directors often used elaborate set pieces to deliver the gore and the nonsense, or as Donato Totaro puts it, because they focused on "entertainment as pure spectacle,"[2] their films sometimes display unique visual styles that make them cinematically intriguing instead of simply nauseating and laughable.

For Alan Jones, "the reason why ultra-religious Italy took over the undead issue and made it more infamous, gory and gruesome than its American counterpart—in the late seventies/early eighties—is crystal clear to see."[3] He explains in "Morti Viventi," his comprehensive history of the Italian zombie film:

> Italian zombies are unique in cinema culture because the very idea of death unable to contain the dead is a very strong Catholic notion. . . . To Catholics, the body is the waste product of the departed soul. The flesh case literally lies

around for some diseased evil to infest it and make it rise again in a corrupt version of Christ's resurrection. Italians adore such reverse affirmation of their faith and that's why continental film-makers embraced the zombie genre to become the foremost practitioners of the staple art.[4]

This explanation helps account for the presence of a zombie in the first Italian horror film of the sound era. In his recent essay "The Italian Zombie Film: From Derivation to Reinvention," Totaro points out: "Although one rightly thinks of the late 1970s and early 1980s as the prime period for the classic Italian zombie film, the *idea* of the walking or reanimated dead has been a mainstay of Italian horror cinema since its first modern incarnation, Riccardo Freda's *I vampiri*."[5] *The Vampires* (*I vampiri*), on which Mario Bava worked as an uncredited codirector, has nothing to do with traditional vampires and instead revolves around the aging Parisian Duchesse du Grand, who attempts to preserve her youth with the blood of young women. She's assisted by her mad-scientist cousin, Dr. Julien du Grand, and his cohorts, who rely on a junkie named Joseph Seignoret to kidnap the suppliers of the duchess's new blood. But when Seignoret threatens to confess his crimes to the police, Dr. du Grand murders him, reanimates his corpse, and thus transforms him into the first Italian zombie.

Although zombified, Seignoret eventually leads the police to du Grand's castle and the horrors it conceals. However, he plays just a minor role in the film. He's on screen for less than ten minutes, and his zombie status is left ambiguous. A police inspector claims that Seignoret was simply revived from a state resembling death and is thus not a walking corpse. But according to Tim Lucas, Freda and Bava had planned to take the idea of the zombie much further. In his liner notes to the Image Entertainment DVD of *The Vampires*, Lucas explains that Seignoret "was originally conceived as a criminal who was put to death on the guillotine and later reassembled and reanimated."[6]

Freda and Bava obviously had corrupt resurrections on their minds while filming *The Vampires*. However, it contains none of the key elements that distinguish Italian living-dead films from those made in other countries. Fulci would introduce these elements in 1979 with *Zombie*, the first true Italian zombie film. The conditions leading to this film's release reveal limitations in Jones's explanation of why Italians took their zombie films to such extremes.

As Stephen Thrower notes in *Beyond Terror: The Films of Lucio Fulci*, *Zombie* "had all the hallmarks of a quickie rip-off."[7] Producer Fabrizio De Angelis conceived of *Zombie* as a quick way to cash in on the success of George Romero's *Dawn of the Dead*, which opened in Italy in 1978 and grossed a million dollars in a month and a half. De Angelis even marketed Fulci's film as a sequel to Romero's. In Italy, *Dawn of the Dead* was released as *Zombi*, so De Angelis released Fulci's film as *Zombi 2*. Italy's first zombie film thus owes its existence to the Italian release of an American zombie film.

If Italian filmmakers embraced the idea of the living dead simply because it offered reverse affirmations of their faith, they wouldn't have waited for the success of *Dawn of the Dead* to begin making their own zombie films. The origin of the grisly Italian zombie film thus requires a more complex explanation that accounts for several different economic and sociocultural factors. I'll discuss these factors later in this chapter, but first, I want to identify the key elements of the Italian zombie film and to show how a few filmmakers tinkered with these elements before the release of *Dawn of the Dead* or *Zombie*.

When discussing the trademarks that Fulci introduced, Totaro notes that *Zombie* "has less in common with Romero's classic than one would assume," but then goes on to suggest that Fulci's film is highly derivative:

> [*Zombie*] established and/or perfected much of the Italian zombie lexicon, some of which was taken from Romero, some not. Included among these filmic elements, thematic-narrative conventions and visual iconography are the following: a pulsating soundtrack that establishes dread and drives the film's rhythm; extreme levels of viscerality (through both violence and grotesque imagery); the mixture of zombies in a Third World setting . . . ; an unresolved or open-ended conclusion; and a philosophical bleakness.[8]

With the exceptions of the "pulsating soundtrack" and the "zombies in a Third World setting," each of these elements also features prominently in *Dawn of the Dead*. Totaro's "Italian zombie lexicon" thus fails to specify the distinguishing characteristics of the Italian zombie film.

As Thrower points out, in *Zombie*'s opening scene, "Fulci declares a very different identity to Romero's *Dawn of the Dead*."[9] Instead of simply borrowing key components from *Dawn*, Fulci also invented new ones. Although Totaro lists two of them, the Third World setting and the pulsating sound track, these aren't common to all Italian zombie films.

Two innovations were the use of rotten, worm-eaten zombies and the inclusion of sadistic gore. Totaro mentions each of these, including them under the heading "extreme levels of viscerality," but he doesn't elaborate on how they distinguish Fulci's film from Romero's. *Zombie*'s set pieces also set it apart from *Dawn*, which Totaro acknowledges. He discusses them in great detail, noting that they "typif[y] an aspect of the transformation that perhaps best differentiates the Italian horror film from its American counterpart, which is more character-based, plot-driven and attentive to verisimilitude."[10] Fulci's other innovation, which Totaro ignores, is the way he revels in the ridiculous. A history of Italian zombie cinema that overlooks the element of silliness in them fails to understand one of the significant differences between Italian zombie films and those made in other countries, and one of the reasons why they have such a large cult following.[11]

In 1961, with *Hercules in the Haunted World* (*Ercole al centro della terra*), Bava gave us a taste of what was to come. The living dead whom Hercules fights have rotten skeletal hands, pasty white faces, black eyes, and bald white heads, which make it difficult for us to see these beings as anything other than creatures that just crawled out of their graves. Although these zombies look silly when they fly down on very visible cables to attack Hercules, and their clothes look more like tattered sheets and tinsel than decaying garments, the shots in which they poke their hands out of the ground and out of their tombs make up a very nice set piece that adds eeriness to the silliness and gives us a taste of the ways in which later Italian horror filmmakers would abandon narrative coherency in favor of spectacle.[12]

Kim Newman argues that, "excluding some blue-faced reanimated warriors in the wilder peplum movies," the first Italian zombies appeared in Ubaldo Ragona's *The Last Man on Earth* (*L'ultimo uomo della terra*).[13] A more accurate claim is that Ragona's film is based on Richard Matheson's 1954 novel *I Am Legend*, which has also been cited by Romero as the creative influence behind *Night of the Living Dead*. *The Last Man on Earth* portrays Robert Morgan's struggle to survive alone in a world populated almost entirely with creatures that are something of a cross between a vampire and a zombie. Like vampires, they fear garlic and mirrors, they must sleep during the day to avoid the sunlight, and a stake through the heart is the best way to kill them, but they are zombie-like in that very little intelligence guides their actions as hordes of them stumble around Morgan's house and beat on the doors and windows with two-by-fours. Although the undead in *The Last Man on Earth* aren't the living dead of later Italian zombie films, nor of later living-dead films in general, these vampire-zombies do have a common trait shared by almost all zombies: individually, they're not much of a threat, but in numbers, they're horrifying.[14] *The Last Man on Earth* also anticipates the ridiculousness that later Italian zombie films would revel in with its vampire-zombie dog that Morgan stakes and then buries.

Bava's *Baron Blood* (*Gli orrori del castello di Norimberga*), released in 1972, is another Gothic horror film featuring zombies. Although Jones and Totaro overlook it, *Baron Blood* is important in the evolution of Italian zombie cinema because of the makeup effects Silvani Petri used to create the reanimated corpse of the film's title character. When the sixteenth-century baron rises from his grave, blood oozes from gaping wounds that disfigure his hands and face. While these wounds represent the effects of the fire that took his life, his tattered, gray skin resembles that of the worm-eaten zombies Fulci would unleash seven years later. Gary Morris describes the zombified baron as "a kind of hamburger-faced mock-Phantom of the Opera."[15] He is the first Technicolor Italian zombie and the first to be an image of visceral horror.

While the films I've discussed so far aren't "zombie films," they illustrate that Italian filmmakers were interested in the living dead years before the release in Italy of *Dawn of the Dead*. But why didn't they make their own zombie films before 1979?

Horror and science-fiction director Luigi Cozzi provides one answer: "In Italy, when you bring a script to a producer, the first question he asks is not 'what is your film like?' but 'what *film* is your film like?' That's the way it is, we can only make *Zombie 2*, never *Zombie 1*."[16] In other words, Italian studios are reluctant to fund genre films unless they are imitations of other genre films whose success they can exploit.

Paul Hoffman notes that "Italy's cinema is governed by the law of *filone*—an Italian word meaning 'streamlet'."[17] A successful genre film will inspire dozens of imitations until audiences get bored with the genre. Then, as Hoffman puts it, "the *filone* dries up."[18] For example, a peplum (sword-and-sandal action movie) filone spanned from the late 1950s to the mid-1960s. Mira Liehm points out that between 1957 and 1964, Italian studios released 170 mythological films, but by 1965, audiences had lost interest.[19] In 1964, the success of Sergio Leone's *A Fistful of Dollars* (*Per un pugno di dollari*) inspired the spaghetti western filone. Liehm states that by 1972, when this filone ended, Italian filmmakers had released three hundred westerns.[20] But no zombie films had been popular enough to capture the attention of Italian producers.

In the mid-1950s, this was also true of horror films in general. Fortunately, Riccardo Freda encountered two producers who liked to gamble. Lucas notes that before making *The Vampires*,

Freda met with . . . Ermano Donati and Luigi Carpentieri and told them he was interested in directing a horror film. They were intrigued, but also nervous about producing a film in an unproven genre. Knowing how quickly Bava worked at lighting and cinematography and knowing that Donati and Carpentieri shared his own weakness for gambling, Freda made them a bet: that he could complete the entire picture in only twelve days.[21]

They agreed to produce the film; however, after ten days of shooting, Freda was only halfway finished. When he asked for an extension, Donati and Carpentieri refused, reminding Freda of their bet. He "threw a fit and stormed off the picture," but Bava took over as director and finished the film on schedule.

Although *The Vampires* was produced quickly and cheaply, it didn't make much money. However, as Gary Johnson points out, in the late 1950s, "The immediate success of the [British] productions of *The Curse of Frankenstein* and *Dracula* (American title: *Horror of Dracula*) signaled to filmmakers around the world the power of the old iconic monsters of Universal's reign."[22] As a result, throughout the 1960s, Italian studios were willing to produce Gothic horror films. In the 1970s, most of the horror films released were *gialli*, particularly violent thrillers with plots that are convoluted often to the point of being nonsensical. This subgenre takes its name from a series of Italian mystery novels published with yellow (*giallo*) covers. Producers funded these films because of the popularity of the novels. In "Italian Horror in the Seventies," Robert Firsching notes that "with the huge success of Dario Argento's *The Bird with the Crystal Plumage* (1969), the popularity of the genre exploded. . . . Over one hundred oddly titled horror-thrillers followed, dominating the 1970s as the Gothic had the '60s and the zombie film would the '80s."[23]

But until 1978, a zombie film hadn't performed well enough in Italy for Italian studios to consider producing their own living dead films. Jones explains: "Despite George Romero's landmark *Night of the Living Dead* causing shock waves around the world, the Italian film industry was slow to catch on to the living dead trend."[24]

However, in 1974, Italian producer Edmondo Amati did help finance the Spanish zombie film *Let Sleeping Corpses Lie* (*Non si deve profanare il sonno dei morti*). Written and directed by Spaniards, this film featured a mostly Spanish crew, with one notable exception: the Italian makeup and effects artist Giannetto De Rossi, who would later design the rotten walking corpses for the first true Italian zombie film. While blood oozes from the open wounds of some of the living dead De Rossi created for *Let Sleeping Corpses Lie*, for the most part they simply have the appearance of disoriented living humans with cadaverous, bloodshot eyes. De Rossi's gore effects give viewers a better glimpse of the visceral horrors that would later appear in *Zombie*. In one scene, the living dead tear off a nurse's breast.

When it was released in Italy in late 1974, *Let Sleeping Corpses Lie* didn't inspire any Italian imitations, but a few years later, Dario Argento, an Italian horror director who cared nothing about participating in the latest filone, decided to coproduce *Dawn of the Dead*. Argento's early films were commercially and critically successful all over the world, and in the late 1970s, he began producing films for other directors. In his book *Giallo Argento*, Luigi Cozzi notes that "Argento started financing movies which reflected his own vision of fantastic cinema: he left complete artistic freedom to the directors but often took part in the creative process, cowriting the scripts and paying visits to the sets."[25] The first of these movies was *Dawn of the Dead*, which he coproduced with Richard Rubenstein. Argento also edited the European cut of the film and replaced parts of the sound track with a score composed by the Goblins, the Italian progressive-rock band that had written the sound tracks for his last two films, *Deep Red* (*Profondo rosso*) and *Suspiria* and has continued working with him throughout his career.[26]

Dawn of the Dead's success suggests that it appealed to Italian audiences in ways other zombie films hadn't. In *The Monster Show*, his cultural history of American horror, David Skal argues that audiences respond best to horror films that reflect current cultural anxieties.[27] He links the popularity of films featuring deformed, monstrous babies in the late 1960s and early 1970s with fears about giving birth that resulted from the discovery that thalidomide, a drug widely prescribed to treat morning sickness, caused severe birth defects. He also makes associations between the spread of AIDS and the renewed interest in vampire films in the 1980s. Perhaps Italians responded so well to *Dawn of the Dead* because Romero's vision of a collapsed civilization tapped into their very real fears about their own country.

In *A Concise History of Italy*, Christopher Duggan gives the following description of the social and political climate of Italy in the 1970s:

> The spread of urbanization, higher living standards, greater access to education, and fresh opportunities for leisure helped to raise expectations and made the shortcomings of the state seem worse than ever. In 1970, according to a European survey 72 percent of Italians were 'highly' or 'completely' dissatisfied with the way their democracy operated. In 1976 the figure was more than 80 percent, compared with around 46 per cent dissatisfaction in Britain and under 20 percent in Germany, and an average for the European Community as a whole of 45 percent. Terrorism in the North, and in the South a growth in organised crime, were among the causes and effects of this lack of confidence in the institutions.[28]

Paul Ginsborg explains that in the early 1970s, neo-fascists committed acts of terrorism as part of their "strategy of tension." They hoped "a series of bomb explosions and other outrages would sow panic and uncertainty, and create the preconditions for an authoritarian regime."[29] Evidence that members of the Italian secret service had close ties with the terrorists made their strategy even more alarming. Their plot failed, but in the last half of the decade, left-wing extremists, known as the "Red Brigades," created even more tension. This group consisted of workers who felt exploited by their employers and had grown impatient with negotiations. By the end of the decade, they followed a "strategy of annihilation," which involved "indiscriminate action, aimed at members of the professions and 'servants of the state.' The aim was to terrorize whole sections of the ruling elites and their supporters, so that the state itself would be unable to function properly."[30] These actions, which "shocked and demoralized" Italians, finally ended in the early 1980s. If they hadn't, Ginsborg claims, "there seems little doubt that the Republic would not have survived in its present form."[31]

This was the social and political context in which *Dawn of the Dead* opened in Italy. Perhaps Italians saw something of themselves in Romero's characters attempting to live normal lives in their chaotic surroundings. Jones's claim that zombie films offer Italians a reverse affirmation of their faith might also account for part of the film's success. Whatever the case, it started a new filone.

Fabrizio De Angelis, the producer of *Zombie*, hired Fulci simply to make an imitation of *Dawn of the Dead*. However, Fulci and his crew wanted to create a much more ambitious film. As Thrower notes, they "took full advantage of the opportunity De Angelis offered them, turning a projected rip-off into a nerve-wracking horror classic in its own right."[32] They made a conscious effort to distinguish their film from Romero's, and this helps explain why Italian zombie films are so extreme. In an interview published in the book *Spaghetti Nightmares*, De Rossi tells us:

[De Angelis] wanted to do a remake of Romero's *Dawn of the Dead* and asked me to copy Tom Savini's zombie make-up, which I hadn't particularly liked, because the extreme pallor of the zombies' faces on film gave them a bluish tinge. And so, realizing that our film was going to be a low-cost imitation, I decided to at least try and give the special effects a touch of originality.[33]

Fulci displays this originality in the film's opening scene. When a police officer enters the cabin of a derelict sailboat, he's attacked by a large zombie that grabs his legs and pins him to the floor. The officer tries to escape by clawing the zombie's arm, but when his fingers dig into the zombie's rotten skin, he ends up with a handful of gooey, worm-filled flesh. With this sequence, not even ten minutes into *Zombie*, Fulci and De Rossi reveal that the zombies in their film will be very different from those in *Dawn of the Dead*.

Gaping wounds disfigure the blue faces of Romero's living dead, which are quickly recognizable as not quite human; however, as Thrower explains, these "ghouls are, almost without fail, nothing more than pasty-faced versions of their old living selves."[34] But Fulci's living dead—with worms hanging from their eye sockets; brown, decaying maggot-infested flesh dangling from their bones; blood oozing from open wounds; and teeth that seem as if they are about to rot away—look like nothing other than flesh-eating zombies.

In the same sequence, Fulci introduces another trademark of the Italian zombie film: sadistic gore. After pinning the police officer to the ground, the zombie bites into his neck, making a large gory hole. The camera lingers on this hole long enough for us to see three streams of blood spurt from it. While Romero creates scenes of similar unease in *Dawn of the Dead*, the nastiness of Fulci's gore and the sadistic ways in which he presents it set it apart from the gore in *Dawn*, which Thrower describes as "remarkably clean."[35]

The gore becomes particularly sadistic when Fulci presents it as part of an elaborate set piece. One of the most memorable set pieces of any Italian horror film appears about halfway through *Zombie* when a rotten corpse kills Paola, the wife of a doctor attempting to discover why the dead won't stay in their graves. After she realizes a zombie is in her house, Paola attempts to hide in her bedroom. We then watch as the zombie pokes its hand through the door, grabs Paola's hair and pulls her face toward a large splinter. From the first shot of her wide-open right eye, we know the set piece will end with the splinter puncturing it, but Fulci postpones this moment for several minutes. As Totaro points out in his discussion of this scene, considered from a purely narrative perspective, Fulci uses entirely too much screen time, about six minutes, to kill a minor character. But, of course, simply killing the character is not the point. Mixing close-ups of Paola's beautiful green eye with ones of the splinter it's slowly approaching, Fulci prolongs the buildup to Paola's death in order to emphasize the manner in which she dies.[36] When the splinter finally pierces the eye, it does so very slowly, enabling us to witness fluid oozing from the eye before the splinter completely destroys it, pokes through Paola's eye socket and then breaks off inside her face. By emphasizing the manner in which Paola dies, and then allowing his camera to capture the visceral details of her death, Fulci revels in the violence, and the gore becomes much more sadistic than it would be if it took less screen time to portray.

The other scene for which *Zombie* is best known introduces the silliness that fans and genre critics associate with the Italian zombie film. In this scene, which Thrower calls "a triumph of the ridiculous," an underwater zombie, with waterlogged skin and seaweed growing on his back, attacks a female scuba diver, who escapes by scratching the zombie's face with a piece of coral.[37] The zombie then wrestles a shark. He pokes his hand into the shark's belly, removes an organ and begins eating it while swimming away, but the shark returns and bites off the zombie's left hand, leaving his forearm dangling from his elbow. Contrasting *Zombie* with *Dawn of the Dead*, Totaro notes that "it is far more relentless in its nihilism, lacking any of [*Dawn's*] comic tone or black humour."[38] Instead, it contains nonsensical scenes that add humor to the film.

Zombie grossed around $30 million worldwide, and the next year several more zombie films were produced in Italy, the most significant of which, in terms of the evolution of the subgenre, are Andrea Bianchi's *Burial Ground* (*Le notti del terrore*), Marino Girolami's *Zombie Holocaust* (*Zombi holocaust*), and Umberto Lenzi's *Nightmare City* (*Incubo sulla città contaminate*).

Nothing more than an excuse to show nudity, gore, and an army of rotten, walking corpses, *Burial Ground* is best known among Italian horror fans for its silly Freudian overtones, which build up to a scene in which a zombified boy bites off one of his mother's nipples and a chunk of breast. Bianchi simply recycled the elements that worked so well in *Zombie* and combined them in a film that's much sloppier and sleazier than its predecessor. Totaro calls it a "*Night of the Living Dead* clone, minus the character development and social import."[39] While *Burial Ground* does recycle the basic story of *Night*, it has more in common with Fulci's film than with Romero's. The fact that it's more derivative of an Italian zombie film than an American one shows that by 1980 the Italian zombie film had emerged as a distinct subgenre.

While *Zombie Holocaust* contains all of the elements that Fulci introduced, Girolami and De Angelis, who produced and cowrote the film, did much more than simply recycle them. They added cannibals and a mad scientist to the mix. Throughout the 1970s and early 1980s, Italians made several cannibal films that resemble the living-dead films with their reliance on visceral horror. *Zombie Holocaust* was thus De Angelis's way of exploiting the success of two popular genres.[40]

Like Girolami, Lenzi utilized the basic elements of the Italian zombie film while taking it in a completely different direction with his airplane-flying, knife-, gun-, and axe-wielding zombies in *Nightmare City*. Totaro calls *Nightmare City* "the only true Italian 'zombie-action' film," and one of its opening scenes reveals that Lenzi's zombies, which run after, punch, kick, shoot, and stab their victims, behave more like the zombies that Danny Boyle would later give life to in *28 Days Later* than any that came before them.[41] Later in the film, a scientist explains that exposure to radiation has not only transformed the passengers of a plane into zombies but also given them unnatural strength. Because these undead never died and rose from their graves, their skin is burned rather than worm-eaten. It has a greenish tint, and several zombies look as if their faces have been deep-fried.

In 1981, just two years after Fulci gave birth to the Italian zombie film, it was already starting its gradual decline. As opposed to the six films made the previous year, only three were produced in 1981. But one of these was Fulci's *The Beyond* (*E tu vivrai nel terrore! L'Aldilà*), which Jay Slater calls "one of the most effective horror films of all time."[42] Despite some serious special-effects flaws—a few dismembered faces that are very obviously wax sculptures, several tarantulas that are even more obviously plastic figures, and a shot of a zombie-filled hotel that looks like a cheesy Halloween haunted house—*The Beyond* is more visually intriguing than any zombie film to come before it and most that have come after it.

Not surprisingly, the beauty of *The Beyond* lies in its set pieces. Totaro points out that "as Fulci himself acknowledged [the film is primarily] 'a succession of images' which do not have any direct narrative logic," and Slater refers to the film as "a series of well-crafted set-pieces that seem to have been thrown together at random."[43] A short discussion of one of these set pieces will help illustrate how Fulci utilized his zombie formula to create fascinating visuals that make *The Beyond* more than simply a gorefest with moments of unintentional humor.

Paradoxically, one reason this film is more than simply an object of derisive laughter is because of the way in which Fulci revels in the completely nonsensical and thus gives the film its own interior logic. The best example is the scene in which a beaker of acid spills on a woman's face and kills her. This incident occurs in a hospital morgue where the woman has been dressing her husband's corpse in preparation for his funeral. When she finishes dressing him, she looks across the room and something causes her to scream. The scene then cuts to a shot of her terrified daughter, who's waiting outside. When the daughter enters the room, she sees her mother lying on the floor with a jar of acid dissolving her face. As it sizzles and bubbles into a green and red mess, a large puddle of acid colored red with blood makes its way for the girl's feet. She backs into a wall, opens a door and walks into a freezer, where she's greeted by groaning zombies. We never learn why the woman screams, how she ends up on the floor, or how the acid spills on her face. As a result, the scene makes little sense, but that is the point. It works on a visceral level to show that a world in which the dead walk has its own logic.

De Rossi created the rotten, reanimated corpses for *The Beyond* as well, and in the film's most effective set piece, they zombify a dog, who then rips a gaping hole in the neck of his blind owner. Because the last few minutes of *The Beyond* are so atmospheric and surreal, the film is best known for its bleak closing scene, which shows its protagonists doomed to "the beyond." To the sounds of distant moaning, they walk into a white, foggy wasteland filled with corpses. The cloudy, gray sky overhead contains no sun, moon, or stars. They look in every direction and see the same thing: a landscape that fills them with an overwhelming sense of dread. The film ends with them trapped in this netherworld.

After 1981, the Italian zombie film itself seemed to be trapped in a similar place. Throughout the rest of the decade, only four zombie films were made in Italy, and they all lack the style and charm of those produced between 1979 and 1981. Of these, the most anticipated by horror fans, and especially Fulci fans, was *Zombi 3*, the sequel to his influential classic. But it was also the most disappointing. Its story has nothing to do with the original film; it contains none of the atmosphere or tense set pieces of Fulci's earlier zombie films, and while the zombie makeup works, De Rossi's absence from the crew is very noticeable.[44]

Although a few Italian zombie films were released in the early 1990s, by this time the filone had dried up. But in 1994, Michele Soavi's *Dellamorte Dellamore* showed audiences that the subgenre's potential hadn't been exhausted. Released in the United States as *Cemetery Man*, the film's Italian title, which translates as "Of Death, Of Love," reflects its content much more accurately. Soavi places zombies in the background and focuses on Francesco Dellamorte's failed attempts at love in a world where he finds few distinctions between the living and the dead. Soavi thus approaches this subgenre in a way that's entirely unique. However, he doesn't reject the elements his predecessors seemed to have exhausted; instead, he uses them in very innovative, sometimes ironic, ways.

An example of this irony is in his zombies. By 1994, all zombies looked rotten and worm-eaten, so Soavi made his plant-eaten as well. We see this in one of the film's early scenes when a zombie holding a sapling walks toward Dellamorte saying, "Eat!" Roots sit on top of the zombie's shoulders and cover his upper arms. Other zombies in the film have similar growths, most notably the resurrected corpse of "She," Dellamorte's dead lover. Goddess-like, the she-zombie wears a crown of ivy that grows down her back and arms.

The scene with the sapling-zombie introduces another of the ironic ways in which Soavi uses the zombie formula: some of his zombies speak. Their speech is one of the many ways in which Soavi revels in the ridiculous to add dark comedy to his film. Unlike its predecessors, in *Dellamorte Dellamore*, the humor is intentional. We see one example when the she-zombie hugs Dellamorte and tries to kiss him. He stops her and says, "We can't! I'm alive . . . And you're dead." She answers, "I'm not prejudiced, my love." But this doesn't stop her from biting a gory chunk out of Dellamorte's shoulder and showing us that this film does contain gore, even if it's neither excessive nor sadistic.

Soavi also relies less heavily on set pieces, but the ones he uses are beautifully haunting, particularly the one in which Dellamorte shoots She in the head after she returns from the dead. This takes place in the cemetery's ossuary. It begins with shots of She lying naked on a wooden table, covered only by a white translucent cloth and surrounded by skeletons. When she slowly sits up, Dellamorte covers his eyes with his left hand and raises his gun with his right. She blows the cloth from her face. It drifts toward Dellamorte and covers his face and his gun. He fires, the bullet grazes the left side of her head, and in an overhead shot, she collapses back on the table in slow motion. Dellamorte stands up, covers her with the cloth, and walks away.

While this set piece, like those Fulci used so well, places greater emphasis on spectacle than on narrative purpose, it also adds to the film's love/death motif. Soavi juxtaposes shots of skeletons—images of old, decayed death—against ones of the beautiful, dead body of She—images of recent death, waiting to decay. He thus reminds us of what She's body will soon become, or that her beautiful body, formerly an image of love for Dellamorte, contains and will soon become an image of death.

With *Dellamorte Dellamore*, Soavi seems to ask viewers to take zombie films more seriously and fellow filmmakers to reanimate the subgenre with innovations on elements that worked so well in the past. Unfortunately, fans are still waiting for the revival of the Italian zombie film they had hoped Soavi's film would start. No zombie films have been made in Italy since 1994. However, regardless of whether *Dellamorte Dellamore* marks the end of the Italian zombie subgenre or the new direction it will take, Italians have created a body of living-dead films that continue to fascinate, gross out, and amuse their viewers. Although Fabrizio De Angelis wanted simply to profit from a filone, he inadvertently enabled Fulci and his crew to create a distinct subgenre that's unique in its reliance on rotten zombies, sadistic gore, elaborate set pieces, and moments of utter nonsense. In *The Companion to Italian Cinema*, Geoffrey Nowell-Smith writes, "Considered by some critics as an inferior imitation of American cinema, the Italian horror film is nonetheless remarkably rich and original."[45] Whether they're wrestling sharks, fighting cannibals, skewering eyeballs, or proudly displaying their worm-eaten faces, Italian zombies and the films through which they stumble create lasting impressions on their viewers and add to the richness and originality of Italian horror cinema.

Notes

1. Allan Bryce, "Introduction," in *Zombie*, ed. Allan Bryce (Liskeard, England: Stray Cat, 1999), 5.

2. Donato Totaro, "The Italian Zombie Film: From Derivation to Reinvention," in *Fear without Frontiers: Horror Cinema across the Globe*, ed. Steven Jay Schneider (Godalming, England: FAB Press, 2003), 163.

3. Alan Jones, "Morti Viventi," in Bryce, *Zombie*, 14.

4. Jones, "Morti Viventi," 14.

5. Totaro, "Italian Zombie Film," 161.

6. Tim Lucas, liner notes, *I vampiri* (DVD, Image Entertainment, 2001).

7. Stephen Thrower, *Beyond Terror: The Films of Lucio Fulci* (Godalming, England: FAB Press, 2002), 15.

8. Totaro, "Italian Zombie Film," 162.

9. Thrower, *Beyond Terror*, 25.

10. Totaro, "Italian Zombie Film," 163.

11. One might argue that films like Dan O'Bannon's *Return of the Living Dead* and Peter Jackson's *Braindead* have thousands of fans for the same reason. This is true, but each of these films was made well after the Italian zombie film peaked, and each was clearly influenced by it. More significantly, while these films are overtly comical, most of the ridiculousness in Italian zombie films is presented in a very serious tone. Viewers thus laugh *at* these moments and not *with* them.

12. Ignoring both *The Vampires* and *Hercules in the Haunted World*, Alan Jones begins "Morti Viventi" with Giuseppe Vari's *War of the Zombies* (*Roma contra Roma*), which he claims "is, by popular consensus, the first ever zombie movie to be made in Europe" (14). However, this film contributes nothing to the evolution of the subgenre. Like *Hercules in the Haunted World*, *War of the Zombies* is a sword-and-sandal epic, or *peplum*, as the genre is known in Italy. Vari simply devoted more screen time to the battle between his heroes and the living dead.

13. Kim Newman, "Review of *The Last Man on Earth*, dir. Ubaldo Ragona," in *Eaten Alive! Italian Cannibal and Zombie Movies*, ed. Jay Slater (London: Plexus, 2002), 34.

14. This, of course, is starting to change with twenty-first-century zombie films, such as *28 Days Later* and the remake of *Dawn of the Dead*, whose fast-moving zombies are just as terrifying individually as the slow-moving ones are in groups.

15. Gary Morris, review of *Baron Blood*, *Images*, no. 8 (2004), http://www.images journal.com/issue08/reviews/baronblood.

16. Quoted in Leon Hunt, "A (Sadistic) Night at the Opera: Notes on the Italian Horror Film," *Velvet Light Trap*, no. 30 (1992): 66.

17. Quoted in Maitland McDonagh, *Broken Mirrors/Broken Minds: The Dark Dreams of Dario Argento* (New York: Citadel Press, 1994), 95.

18. Quoted in McDonagh, *Broken Mirrors*, 95.

19. Mira Liehm, *Passion and Defiance: Film in Italy from 1942 to the Present* (Berkeley: University of California Press, 1984), 182.

20. Liehm, *Passion and Defiance*, 186.

21. Lucas, liner notes, *I vampiri*.

22. Gary Johnson, "The Golden Age of Italian Horror," *Images*, no. 5 (1997), http://www.imagesjournal.com/issue05/infocus/intro.htm.

23. Robert Firsching, "Italian Horror in the Seventies," *Images*, no. 5 (1997), http://www.imagesjournal.com/issue05/infocus/seventies.htm.

24. Jones, "Morti Viventi," 16.

25. Luigi Cozzi, *Giallo Argento* (Rome: Profondo Rosso, 2001), 127.

26. One might ask why Argento didn't simply make his own zombie film. But he was less interested in zombies than in the effective ways in which Romero used the zombie subgenre. He explains: "I saw *Night of the Living Dead* and loved it. I liked [Romero's] work and one day we arranged to meet in New York and talked and talked and talked. We thought that maybe we should make a film together, and from that came *Dawn of the Dead*." Quoted in McDonagh, *Broken Mirrors*, 155.

27. David J. Skal, *The Monster Show: A Cultural History of Horror* (New York: Norton, 1993).

28. Christopher Duggan, *A Concise History of Italy* (Cambridge: Cambridge University Press, 1994), 274.

29. Paul Ginsborg, *A History of Contemporary Italy: Society and Politics* (New York: Palgrave MacMillan, 2003), 334.

30. Ginsborg, *History*, 383.

31. Ginsborg, *History*, 384, 383.

32. Thrower, *Beyond Terror*, 13.

33. Quoted in Luca M. Palmerini and Gaetano Mistretta, *Spaghetti Nightmares: Italian Fantasy-Horrors as Seen through the Eyes of Their Protagonists*, trans. Gilliam M. A. Kirkpatrick (Key West, FL: Fantasma, 1996), 119.

34. Thrower, *Beyond Terror*, 32.

35. Thrower, *Beyond Terror*, 32.

36. Totaro, "Italian Zombie Film," 163.

37. Thrower, *Beyond Terror*, 28.

38. Totaro, "Italian Zombie Film," 162.

39. Totaro, "Italian Zombie Film," 168.

40. In an interview that appears in *Eaten Alive! Italian Cannibal and Zombie Movies*, Ian McCulloch, one of the stars of *Zombie Holocaust*, provides an amusing anecdote that helps account for some of the silliness in Italian zombie films. He explains that after Girolami had finished shooting *Zombie Holocaust*, he was called back because the director needed to add ten minutes to the film. McCulloch says the new sequence "was about catching rabbits. . . . Rabbits don't live in jungles—it was insane. I mean, there aren't any, there are no rabbits in any jungle in the entire world. It was so potty! They wrote these two or three rubbish scenes to last an amount of time to allow the film to be sold abroad" (Slater, *Eaten Alive!*, 121). Although this rabbit chase sequence doesn't appear in the film, plenty of other ridiculousness does. The

best example is probably the film's ending, which involves a fight between cannibals and zombies, with their mad-scientist creator caught in the middle.

41. Totaro, "Italian Zombie Film," 168.

42. Slater, *Eaten Alive!*, 170.

43. Donato Totaro, "Review of *The Beyond*, dir. Lucio Fulci," in Slater, *Eaten Alive!*, 166; Slater, *Eaten Alive!*, 170.

44. This film was codirected by Bruno Mattei, and it's hard to tell who was responsible for its many flaws. In an interview published in Palmerini and Mistretta's *Spaghetti Nightmares*, Fulci says, "I finished off an hour and a quarter of film. . . . We were working with a dreadful script, which we couldn't get changed because the second-rate scriptwriter was the [producer's] trusted man. . . . Consequently, I had to modify the script as I went along. . . . When it got to the fifth week, I asked to be relieved of the task of directing the film" (63). In the same book, the screenwriter, Claudio Fragasso, gives his side of the story: "On the set of *Zombi 3* [Fulci] misinterpreted and distorted the script I'd written and in the end, the producer found himself with a film whose duration, after editing, was less than one hour, and so, he [asked] me [and] Mattei to save the film" (56).

45. Geoffrey Nowell-Smith, with James Hay and Gianni Volpi, *The Companion to Italian Cinema* (London: Cassell, 1996), 63.

~

CHAPTER FIVE

The Space of Apocalypse in Zombie Cinema

David Pagano

At least since George Romero's 1968 *Night of the Living Dead*, the cinematic zombie has heralded the end of the world as we know it, and Romero's apocalyptic take on the genre has marked it ever since.[1] Zombie films usually represent the catastrophic end of the human *habitus*, and while it is true that occasionally such an end is narrowly avoided, the contagion of the zombie always at least threatens absolute destruction. As Robin Wood wrote of *Dawn of the Dead*, Romero's thesis seems to be that "the total disintegration of society is the necessary prerequisite for new growth."[2] We might speculate that Romero is guardedly optimistic about the possibility of such new growth, given the qualified utopianism (if such a thing is possible) that concludes *Day of the Dead* and *Land of the Dead*. Yet in these films as well, such optimism grows out of characters and structures situated in opposition to whatever tentative "society" organizes out of the bulk of the narrative (the brutality and misogyny of the underground bunker in *Day* and the oligarchic tyranny within Mr. Kaufmann's tower in *Land*). Therefore, beyond the general diegetic representations of massive and catastrophic sociocultural destruction, Romero's films invoke the particularly apocalyptic paradox that the world must end in order for there to be any future for the world. A more specific examination of apocalyptic assumptions—in particular, assumptions about space and time—can illuminate some of the critical aspects not only of Romero's trilogy but also of some of the more thoughtful films that have followed in his wake.

Apocalyptic Time and Space

The Greek *apokalupsis* means "revelation" or "unveiling," and in the West's most famous apocalyptic text, the Revelation to John that ends the New Testament, John of Patmos recounts truths revealed to him alone (or at least to him as one of God's "servants" [Rev. 1:1]). Specifically, God lifts the veil of *time* from John's eyes, because his received vision consists of events yet to come, events that in fact constitute the concluding era of human history.

Theologically, the violence and strife that turn out to accompany the end of the world (and which tend to color our everyday notions of "apocalyptic") are secondary to the narrative's truth-telling function, its privileged glimpse into a future that normally is withheld from us. This future, moreover, is not merely one yet-to-be moment among others; rather, as the culmination and closure of human time (that is, of *chronos*, or passing time, as opposed to the fullness or ripeness connoted by *kairos*), it marks the definitive and literally ultimate *meaning* of history. There at the end, it is not just that time will have run out but also that the good and the evil will be sorted into their respective axiological and spatial categories, the former judged worthy and therefore admitted into the New Jerusalem, the latter judged unworthy and cast into the lake of fire with Death and Satan. The books will be opened, the records accounted, and nothing will be left hidden. The significance is not merely that John is privileged to behold what is normally not given to humans to see, but that what he sees explains everything that will have come before it—that is, simply, *everything*.

This arrogation of the future necessitates a complex representational negotiation of space and time. Scholars have pointed out that the Book of Revelation, along with many other apocalyptic writings dating from around 250 years on either side of Christ's life, juxtaposes the temporal and the spatial in ways consistent with general Judeo-Christian worldviews. For example, John J. Collins's classic definition of the genre states that these texts "disclos[e] a transcendent reality which is both temporal, insofar as it envisages eschatological salvation, and spatial, insofar as it involves another, supernatural world."[3]

More recently, in the field of literary and cultural studies, the relations of space and time have been explored in their bewildering and even paradoxical complexity. For example, in *Unbuilding Jerusalem*, Stephen Goldsmith has pointed out that not only is Revelation implicitly spatial in that it invokes a supernatural world but the text is also preoccupied with mapping out the precise boundaries of space.[4] At one point, John of Patmos is "given a measuring rod like a staff" and is told, "Rise and measure the altar and those who worship there, but do not measure the court outside the temple" (Rev. 11:1–2). Later, when the New Jerusalem descends from heaven, John writes, "And he who talked to me had a measuring rod of gold to measure the city and its gates and walls. The city lies foursquare, its length the same as its breadth; and he measured the city with his rod, twelve thousand stadia; its length and breadth and height are equal" (Rev. 21:15–17). It is thus important that space be both measurable and perfect, ideally proportioned.

This drive toward the imagination of a perfect space outside of time reflects a rejection of history and its power struggles, including those between John and other early Christian sects. It also infects the text itself, which ends with this admonition: "I warn every one who hears the words of the prophecy of this book: if any one adds to them, God will add to him the plagues described in this book, and if any one takes away from the words of the book of this prophecy, God will take away his share in the tree of life and in the holy city, which are described in this book" (Rev. 22:18–19). At the point where time comes to an end, there is the New Jerusalem; prefiguring that point is the text of Revelation. Thus, as Goldsmith suggests, for John, "the telos of time is space," including the perfect space of the text of Revelation itself, which must not fall victim to future redaction of any kind.[5] And both spaces are proper to John; they compass and protect him, allowing him to lay claim to a stable and unchanging identity under their signs. He can define himself as part of the inside, eternally unshaken and unthreatened by the lost souls outside.

Safety is therefore central for apocalyptic rhetoric. The apocalyptic prophet posits himself as absolutely safe from any risk, contingency, or chance precisely by erasing the futurity of the future, its openness to the unforeseeable. He inscribes a Whole from a position that his critics might describe as unavoidably partial, and this Whole entails his (or his people's, his culture's, or whatever his identificatory community's) knowledge of his own ultimate salvation. The etymology of *safe* can be traced to the Greek and Latin for "entire" or "whole," which points up apocalyptic rhetoric's extreme portrayal of what is perhaps the condition for any sense of safety: a foreseeable future that writes history as completed. In apocalyptic representation, that future is foreseeable all the way to the end of time. And at the end comes space.

As James Berger has pointed out in *After the End: Representations of Post-Apocalypse*, however, this leap from time to space means that "the apocalyptic writer writes as his own ghost."[6] He has already died in a certain way. Often, in biblical fashion, he has been swallowed by a whale or cast into a fiery furnace. But he has *always and necessarily* died insofar as he has been there at, then returned from, the end of all things. His perspective is that of the (imagined) dead, who alone among humans can retrospectively know the whole of their time, having moved beyond it. For the prophet, this end has, in a sense, already happened, yet he persists as "a reanimated corpse."[7] Writing in a post-Romero idiom, therefore, Berger highlights a line of thinking that has always been interwoven with the apocalyptic reassurance that identity and future are secure: the prophet, through his very prophecy, occupies a precariously ecstatic position, standing outside of himself in order to identify himself. Not only has the prophet seen and identified with the eschaton, but he also sees that the world is past being able to choose differently. Apocalyptic predictions generally posit an irredeemably corrupt world, a world so oppressive or evil that only the absolute annihilation of apocalypse can put an end to it. The eschaton is (now) inevitable, already here in a certain way, dwelling within the world as a kind of dark entelechy. Until history blips out of existence, to exist in time means to kill time. Indeed, time itself is dead and gone, but returns in an obscene parody of itself as the prophet braces for the inevitable.

Of course, from the prophet's perspective, this rhetoric of darkness and obscenity entirely misses the point. In Revelation, at least, all returns from the dead are glorious and self-securing: that of John, the judged dead, and Christ. But such glory requires faith in the eternal (never thinkable, it seems, apart from the spatial) and its superiority to the temporal. Now, it has been well documented that the apocalyptic urge is rooted in genuine cultural dismay and persecution and that it can serve tactically to unite the oppressed and instill hope in the despairing. In this sense, it has been deployed in ethical and even socially progressive ways (think, for example, of its role in the civil rights movement, and in the history of African American religion long before that). Nevertheless—even putting aside any skepticism well earned by the last two thousand years of apocalyptically inspired violence, not to mention the apparent failure of the world to have ended at any of the predicted deadlines—even beyond all this, there remains the spatiotemporal violence of traditional apocalypse, its ecstatic need to kill its own prophet in order to redeem him. George Romero, I argue, provides the most explicit warrant for the argument that a prophet is a "reanimated corpse."

Romero's Zombie Films and Apocalyptic Judgment

Romero's zombie films are *meta-apocalyptic*: that is, although they enact a prophetic attempt to claim a true perspective on the present by looking back from the conclusion of history, they emphatically, violently, and gleefully refrain from separating inside and outside, space and time, in the fashion of the apocalyptic prophet. Indeed, if we acknowledge that the apocalyptic prophet *represses* time in favor of space, we can say that Romero stages the return of this repression. Despite the prophet's proclamation, time and futurity always come back, haunting space from the future, as it were. Or we could say, with an eye toward the ambiguously passive-active genitive, that Romero stages a "haunting of the future" by reversing apocalypse's fantasy of invading the future (seeing it in advance and thereby declawing it) such that the risk and unthinkability of the future (the impossible zombies) flood the here and now. Romero represents such futurial haunting by intertwining the apocalyptic future with the apocalyptic present.

Romero's zombie films, of course, contain sweeping ethical condemnations of contemporary America, jeremiads that had not lost force over the decades even before the fourth installment. As has been well documented, the nuclear family, racism, sexism, consumer culture, and the military-industrial complex all come under heavy criticism in the first three films, and "thinly veiled" would fail to convey the intensity of the post-9/11 allegory that is *Land of the Dead*, with its indictment of oligarchic, self-assured, imperialistic authority. The films' central irony is always that, however bad the zombie plague may be, it is only the logical extension of whatever corruption, ignorance, fear, or greed already exist among the living in America today. Hence Romero as prophet: seeing an irredeemable world, he projects its destruction as an inevitable consequence of its own depravity.

What makes him meta-apocalyptic, however, is that he diagnoses our depravity without the aid of any supernatural intermediary. Where the apocalyptic prophet imagines a perfect space that would transcend time to make its judgment, Romero sees judgment as immanent to the order of temporality. Where John of Patmos insists that truth rests on an external, infallible ground, Romero claims a paradoxically contingent-transcendental perspective, both condemning from above *and* plunging into the abyss of human immanence. For Romero, not only our corruption but also our conclusion derives from within humanity, not outside of it. This is partly visible in his insistence throughout on blurring the boundaries between what should be clearly demarcated zones.

Take as an example the narrative strategies of *Dawn of the Dead*. First, even before the protagonists completely secure the interior of the mall, two of the protagonists engage in a delirious shopping spree that mirrors the predations of the zombies. They gleefully pillage the stores, doubling the eternally unsatisfied appetites of the zombies who howl at the gates outside. And their consumption can lead to no familiar sense of gain or satisfaction after the end of its proper economy—it is, in other words, consumption without end, in both senses of the phrase. Second, there is a certain glee in the protagonists' extermination of the zombies; in these scenes, horror becomes slapstick as the zombies become idiotic straight-beings for the elaborately violent antics of our heroes. In addition, when they finally do destroy all the zombies in the mall, they dispose of the bodies not by throwing them outside but dumping them into a freezer inside the mall. Even when the zombies are figuratively exteriorized, they remain literally on the interior.

Moreover, in the final scenes of the film, the barrier that the walls of the mall represent is broken not by zombies, but by a living biker gang that has survived the plague and has come to raid the mall. The gang is eventually driven out by the protagonists, but not before it has destroyed the security of the mall by allowing the zombies to come streaming inside. Before the bikers go, however, they engage in the same kind of shopping spree we had seen earlier in the film; this spree is presented as slightly more degenerate, more like looting than shopping, but the similarities to the main characters' behavior are more striking than the differences. They also partake of the same kind of slapstick violence, though even more literally, using seltzer bottles and cream pies against the zombies. In short, the mall is finally breached not by what is properly exterior, Other, or outside, but by a version or repetition of the heroes themselves—which is all it had contained in the first place, in the form of the consumptive zombies.

Narrative features such as these have been observed by previous critics of the film, and they appear, *mutatis mutandis*, in the other three as well (e.g., the all-too-human posse that kills Ben at the conclusion of *Night*, the violence of the soldiers and the questionable ethics of the scientists in *Day*, the single-minded brutality of Mr. Kauffman in *Land*). Indeed, as Frank Kermode famously observed in *The Sense of an Ending*, apocalypse above all is a narrative articulation; it appears at the end of a chronological sequence of events as a closure that would tie up loose ends and account for all previous details.[8]

It is therefore not surprising that an even more fundamental aspect of Romero's meta-apocalyptic stance becomes clear where his films work *against* narrative. This contranarrative movement appears primarily in the figure of the zombie itself: the shambling, insatiable insistence of a corpse that refuses to be still. Returning from death with no revelation and no insight beyond whatever rapacious desire had been immanent within humans all along, Romero's zombies are both autopoetic and insignificant. The structure of contagion they embody both alludes to and undermines apocalyptic dualism, since their infernal danger is precisely the transubstantiation of "us" into "them."

Steven Shaviro comments brilliantly on the kind of temporality the zombies' threat engenders:

> Romero gives the blank time of anticipation a value in its own right, rather than just using it to accentuate, by contrast, the jolt that follows. . . . The slow meanders of zombie time emerge out of the paralysis of the conventional time of progressive narrative. This strangely empty temporality also corresponds to a new way of looking, a vertiginously passive fascination.[9]

Shaviro is writing a polemic against psychoanalytic film criticism and is drawing on the writings of Gilles Deleuze and Félix Guattari to articulate this zombie time; however, one can also frame these ideas in terms of apocalyptic temporality. The zombie continues on after the end, outlives the temporal project of its life, both embodying and parodying the apocalyptic impulse to find rest in a safe space beyond the exigencies and traumas of time.

The ruptured body that only superficially hampers purposive movement defines Romero's zombies, who do not need closure (of the skin). Whatever regions of their bodies remain covered by skin stand only as signs of the superfluity of any particular somatic functions that those regions once performed. Like the homogenous space of the New Jerusalem, the zombies' bodies contain parts that are functionally undifferentiated, "perfect" in their absolute reduction to hunger. Moreover, the films' (compulsive) repetition of the attack scene—in which the bodies of the living are eviscerated or transgressed in the service of the zombies' unending hunger—tends to blur the line between the living and the dead, as the bodies of both parties become fragmented or incomplete. This fragmentation causes the living time of memory and anticipation to converge with the zombie time of empty motion.

In *Land of the Dead*, in a line that acts as a CliffsNote to Romero's entire zombie oeuvre, one character observes that a building's barriers were meant to keep people safe, but that those same barriers will now trap and doom them. The slow and shambling zombie body has always been thus, embodying an eerie lag time that determines life as a bracing for an inevitable end. *This is what it is like when you know the end of the story*, Romero suggests; *you may be secure in one sense, but that very security cannot help but return to bite you.*

In addition, as Shaviro's rhetoric of "fascination" suggests, Romero highlights the inevitably visual biases of apocalyptic thinking. A fundamental source for the well-established Western tradition of associating vision with truth, the apocalyptic prophet *sees* (the truth is unveiled, revealed). The structural precision of Revelation and other apocalyptic texts accords with their emphasis on the stability that vision engenders (John sees the truth, and even when he does hear it in speech, that speech exhorts him to spatialize: measure the temple; do not alter these words). Indeed, it is only when one imagines time as somehow visible that any pretension to claim its completion is possible; John has cognitive command of time's line, its alpha through its omega, as if viewing it from the standpoint of eternity. Romero's excessive and shocking mise-en-scène captures our vision, rather than allowing our vision to master it. We may read the visual signs in the manner of the prophet, but any epistemic quest such legibility would imply must fail, because (apart from the brief and, in retrospect, strikingly insignificant allusions to the Venus probe in *Night*) the films' diegesis discloses no first cause of or fundamental reason for the zombies. They simply exist.

It is interesting to note that, in his anthropological study of folklore and physiology, *Vampires, Burial, and Death*, Paul Barber suggests that ideas of the undead may have originated with the misinterpretation of signs.[10] Because of ancient associations of physical movement with intentional purpose or will, the phenomenon of a decomposing corpse—which, as Barber observes, evinces both movement and change—may have invited the impression that some kind of purposiveness remained in the body.[11] It would not have been an unthinkable step from the observation that many bodies are far from inert (especially when death was violent) to the idea that some kind of life continued to force itself on death, and indeed that some bodies were perhaps even more mobile when not pinned down by the anxious gaze of the survivors. What we moderns take to be the physiological signs of decomposition (e.g., shifting of the body, changes in color, sudden bleeding, bloating), our ancestors could have read as signs of vampirism or witchery.

For us, death marks the absolute end of something—variously describable as life, consciousness, personality, will, agency, and so forth—which no longer finds itself subject to time, change, or movement. No continuation, no going back, the life can now be called whole or complete. Although Barber does not use the term, one can say that in this sense, the life has been spatialized. Any subsequent observable movement pertains to something else, something ornamental or parergonal to the essence of life. Such movement is completely determined by physical laws and merely plays out in time what one could have predicted (within a certain margin of error) in advance. It cannot be the index of any choice or intention.

Barber does presume that some version of these modern assumptions about death would have been seen as the general rule in premodern ages as well. However, he suggests, these ancestors would have noticed that some bodies seemed to alter in anomalous or dramatic ways and they might well have wondered whether such signs meant that the bodies could be moving about causing trouble, having somehow retained their will and resisted the absolute rupture of death. Some people, they suspected, managed to retemporalize themselves and disrupt the proper spatialization of their lives. They continued after the end, not as mere physiological process but as intentional, purposive agents.

However valid Barber's thesis may or may not be as an etiology of ideas about vampires, it certainly highlights the ways in which the undead and the apocalyptic can be seen to intersect. The former continues on after its proper end, the latter imagines an end that has not yet properly arrived, and we are back to Berger's observation that the apocalyptic prophet is his own reanimated corpse. What Barber can add, however, is a perspective on how Romero uses his zombies apocalyptically. While we are on the "inside" of his ethical pronouncements, we remain on the "outside" of the zombie plague. That is, Romero invites us to participate in his truth-telling about the present; we are encouraged to make the connections to a degenerate contemporary America. We therefore join Romero in standing in a certain position of mastery of, a distance from, the habitus Romero critiques—hence a measure of comfort, assurance, control, and stability.

Yet we also find ourselves in the position of our credulous ancestors, staring, fascinated and horrified, as the dead (seem to) walk. The power that derived from standing within the New Jerusalem of judgment simultaneously evaporates as we lose any sense of how we might corral or control the zombies (Shaviro writes that Romero stages a "politics of mimetic debasement, as subtle and never-completed opening to abjection").[12] It is as if we are confronted with Immanuel Kant's mathematical sublime: we experience the zombies not as mighty or powerful but as overwhelming and infinite in their contagious, metonymic quasi-progress. Indeed, the formlessness that Kant associates with the sublime informs the zombies' persistent breaching of boundaries and their fundamental insistence on their own immeasurability (their unstable somatic borders, their always-increasing numbers). Rather than nevertheless reassuring us that our reason exceeds our imagination (as Kant argues the sublime does), however, the zombies infect space's comforting reassurance of mastery with time's discomforting refusal of stability.

Each film in Romero's tetralogy ends on a progressively less bleak note, although in no case does he project any kind of transcendent *kairos*-space in order to compensate for his previously unruly spatiotemporality. The island paradise that concludes *Day* could be read as a kind of New Jerusalem, a safe space beyond the zombie threat, but the final shot of the calendar insists on the continuation of time toward a precisely indeterminate future.

For the remaining protagonists, life will have been one X after another, until the X's stop. Indeed, Romero's last word in that film seems to be an ethical pronouncement not just on contemporary America in general but precisely on the straining toward apocalyptic closure that has constituted our corruption in the first place (think, for example, of the racial-spatial purification projects that constitute the end of *Night* and the first quarter of *Dawn*). In *Land*, the immigration to Canada underneath ironically placed fireworks is an obvious nod toward many citizens' despair over George W. Bush's America. Yet in the context of his zombie films, it strikingly promises no determinate home toward which the protagonists might be safely retiring. The emphasis is on movement rather than destination—in this case, movement away from the closed and homogenous tower of Mr. Kauffman.

The Apocalypse after Romero

Much post-Romero zombie cinema has repeated some of these same apocalyptic and anti-apocalyptic tropes. However, two in particular have toyed with the avant-garde in their deployment of these tropes, placing these spatiotemporal issues outside of any particular social context or even coherent diegesis, while retaining the meta-apocalyptic reflection on the idea of permanent closure as such. Both Lucio Fulci's 1981 *The Beyond* and Michele Soavi's 1994 *Cemetery Man* (*Dellamorte Dellamore*) end with what we might call a *dis*establishing shot that renders space literally incalculable. Each film leaves behind the kinds of ethical pronouncements Romero makes through narrative, while picking up on and even radicalizing his antinarrative tendencies.

In these films, the concluding mise-en-scènes are themselves anti-apocalyptic. In *The Beyond*, the protagonists wander out into the undifferentiated plain of Hell on Earth, and in *Cemetery Man*, the protagonists' attempted journey of escape leads only to a dead-end overhanging a gaping chasm. Without even the vague hope of futurity found in Romero, these films transform the comforting fantasy of a space that would exist beyond or after time into a nightmare—indeed, they reveal that the films' diegeses have *all along* been circulating within such an anti-apocalyptic space. In each case, the narrative conclusion is simultaneous with the characters' finding their own progress thwarted by an impossibly static environment, captured in a long shot that marks not the space of an anticipated action, but the end of the possibility of action, beyond even the release of death. The "body" of the narrative itself is thus wounded, but not unto death. Its conclusion fades out into no imaginable future, not even silence or void (i.e., the protagonists are not exactly eliminated, but are stripped of the means by which we might project any possible *next step* for them).

Start with the more recent, though less radical, *Cemetery Man*. As has been observed, the film unfolds like a collaboration between Romero and Samuel Beckett. Francis Dellamorte is the groundskeeper of the Buffalora cemetery, a job that includes destroying what he calls "returners": the flesh-eating corpses that for no clear reason rise after seven days in their graves. The familiar zombie mayhem of the genre gets an absurdist twist here, as the pointedly named Dellamorte quips about the emptiness of existence, falls in love with six different incarnations of the same woman, and sees his buffoonish assistant, Gnaghi, pursue a romance with the decapitated head of a zombie. It is not too much to say that Beckett's Godot haunts these undead, for while it is true that if one waits long enough the zombies do eventually arrive, the film emphasizes the extent to which their arrival makes no difference in the lives of the protagonists, who exist in a state of enigmatic stasis where goals are unreachable and desire unfulfillable.

Indeed, as Donato Totaro has suggested, *Cemetery Man's* narrative seems to unfold within the psychology of the protagonist, rather than in any conventionally objective, diegetic reality.[13] Pointing out the film's several allusions to *Citizen Kane*, Totaro reads the film as an exploration into the mind of one man, with Dellamorte paralleling Charles Kane, and where the absurd town of Buffalora is itself Dellamorte's pointless existence. When Dellamorte and Gnaghi reach the edge of town, having attempted to escape their Sisyphean responsibilities by escaping Buffalora, they find a border not between here and there, but between here and nothingness. When one's town is existence itself, one of course cannot escape it, at least not in life; to do so literally would be "beyond imagination," as Dellamorte suggests Gnaghi says. Hence, the lengthy passage through the tunnel that seems to promise a new world beyond ends only in broken pavement overhanging an abyss, and the revelation that "the rest of the world doesn't exist" (as Dellamorte says, acknowledging that he "should have known" as much). The flash of brilliant white light that envelops the end of the tunnel marks Dellamorte's blinding enlightenment: shocked and pained, he sees that there simply is no beyond. The light at the end of the tunnel stands not for prophetic hope but for the negative revelation of the impossibility of transcendence. Dellamorte and Gnaghi change roles, and they take up their arbitrary places in the claustrophobic space of the snow globe. To return "home," then, is also to stand still.

The Beyond's narrative discourse is even more disjointed and disorienting— indeed, at least Dellamorte and Gnaghi are literally allowed a fixed orientation in space: the untraversable chasm is inaccessible to them, and although they stand rooted and fixed, they nevertheless do stand. Even this much is robbed of Fulci's characters. Where Soavi defines his characters by placing them at the edge of the possible, Fulci plunges them directly into the *impossible*, and thereby annihilates them. (Fulci has in fact said that the film comprises a series of "absolute" images and is not based on traditional narrative coherence.) In this movie's final scene, our protagonists find themselves beneath the hotel that marks one of the gates to Hell. It is in this space—the ostensible "beyond" of the title (*L'aldilà*, "afterlife")—that Fulci stages a dynamic and somatic conflict between stability and contingency.

The protagonists find themselves in an undifferentiated, dun-colored plain, a kind of moonscape, marked only by what appear to be occasional coffins, rock formations, and human corpses. Light filtering down from a hazy sky does not penetrate far into the surrounding darkness. Now so far, this is bad for them, but still within the bounds of a conventionally Euclidean (if supernatural) diegesis, in which characters might stand as capable subjects against a world of objects (that is, leaving aside the "impossibility" of this space existing under the hospital). The shot, therefore, allows for the possibility of character agency: our protagonists in fact step purposively into the center of the frame, modeling the epistemic quest of traditional narrative as they move forward to investigate their surroundings. Moreover, the camera in this shot echoes and heightens the characters' controlling point of view, beginning with a medium close-up, over-the-shoulder framing, then tracking out and craning up to a long shot, so that both audience and protagonists might better apprehend the scene.

However, in the final seconds of the shot, the composition of the frame associates the protagonists with the corpses, as the living and the dead become strikingly similar in both size and color. Hence we have a disestablishing shot, because as the characters begin to visually fade into the landscape, the possibilities of subjectivity and agency begin to fade as well.

We then cut to a conventional two-shot of their horrified reactions, their eyes scanning left to right. This shot (and several more like it which appear in the remainder of the scene) represents a moment of tension between possibility and impossibility: the framing has returned the protagonists to a privileged discursive position above and beyond their surroundings, even as the staging registers their panic.

The next cut, though, removes them again from the possibility of action. We return to a long shot of the landscape, which at first we might assume represents the characters' point of view; given the homogeneity of the space, we might have forgotten the few features (the calculable relative locations of corpses, coffins, and rocks) that had made the space (defined earlier through the long shot) a *particular* space. And the particularity of any space is what any establishing shot first of all establishes. That is, we might initially assume that we are now seeing that stretch of landscape *beyond* the characters—we might even hope this, insofar as the low angle would imply that they (and we) had reached some level of mastery over the space. In fact, however, the camera has returned to precisely the same long shot, only now absent the protagonists' bodies. There where we expect them to stand (since the narrative has not suggested that they have shifted positions), they simply are not. So either they have disappeared (impossible, if we are to take the hints of the intervening frontal medium shots, which imply that they continue to stand there) or they *are* both standing in and gazing out upon the same space; that is, that they are inhabiting their own *beyond* (geometrically impossible).

The impossibilities multiply as they wheel around to look behind them (presumably for some egress from this impossible space), where they are horrified to discover (if verbs like "discover" can have any sense here) directly behind them the very *same* landscape, now in its third iteration in the narrative. The tunnel through which they had crawled to enter the space is gone. Flipping back around to the front, they see before them (that is, are also still within) the same precise space. It is as if the editing does the work of a Cubist painting, where point of view becomes unmoored from any privileged perspective. But this is a particularly nightmarish Cubism—not one in which different points of view are juxtaposed within the frame, but one in which the very possibility of different points of view is eliminated.

In their last attempt at agency, our protagonists break into a run, which the camera records in a reverse of its earlier mobility, by tracking in and craning down. But it is this final camera move that completely severs them from the possibility of action, as their few half-hearted steps are halted by the realization that they are blind. Throughout the film, blindness and deoculation have been the primary marks of the undead; it is not fortuitous, then, that the character's final revelation is their own blindness, their eyeballs' particularities fading into a homogenous haze. They then do what any subject must who is not just pushed to the edge of, but in fact plunged into, the beyond: they disappear. But they also remain, in a certain sense, as their graphic doubles—the corpses—not only remain in the shot but also appear as foci in the following long shots.

Shaviro is correct to invoke Julia Kristeva when he writes of Romero's "opening to abjection." Kristeva says that abjection is "the breaking down of a world," "death infecting life," "a land of oblivion," and "the edge of non-existence and hallucination, of a reality that, if I acknowledge it, annihilates me."[14] We can see Fulci's final staging of radical passivity as a kind of narrative abjection, where blindness paradoxically marks the characters' "acknowledg[ment]" of stepping past their own edges.[15]

Hence, neither of these films even allows its characters a proper death. Indeed, Fulci's and Soavi's last turn of the narrative screw is to figure into their final shots these nightmarish impossible spaces as artworks (painting and snow globe), as if Keats's Grecian urn, where art captures movement forever, were not so much a heavenly New Jerusalem as an artifact from Hell. In each film, the suspended temporality of the zombie spreads as if by metonymic contagion to the protagonists, who occupy a new kind of liminality. Zombies—Romero's zombies especially—were already neither living nor dead, and now these characters stand as neither zombie nor nonzombie. In these experimental, fragmented, and antirealistic narratives, the characters begin as properly alive humans, run the gauntlets of zombie mayhem, and end up marked as neither properly human nor properly zombie. Their states of final passivity and powerlessness, isolated from the films' contexts, would not necessarily bespeak zombification, but in the circumstances they stand as zombiesque above all. And this is primarily because they inhabit impossible spaces, living on without *telos* or *arche*, purpose or history. Dellamorte turns out (possibly) always to have been trapped (somehow), and Fulci's protagonists simply disappear as if they had never been there (or had always only occupied the painted landscape of Hell). Like zombies, they exit time without existing in a proper space.

Simon Critchley has suggested that the philosophy of modernity "begins in disappointment," specifically a postreligious disappointment in the apparent failure of anything external, for example, God, to provide "a meaning for human life." He writes that this philosophy's "peak experiences—Hegel, Nietzsche, Heidegger" think through "the death of God in terms of the problem of finitude."[16] In a similar way, and for similarly complex historical and sociocultural reasons, zombie cinema reflects a disappointment in apocalypse. Apocalyptic thinking was already, one could argue, a response to disappointment, if "disappointment" can be broadly applied to various catastrophic and meaning-wrenching traumas of history that seemed to call for an eventual redemption if the universe were to be imagined to hold any justice or order. Apocalyptic rhetoric has held (still holds, of course, for many) the promise of security and identity through space and stasis.

But Romero no longer accepts this answer to disappointment, and he opens the way to a zombie cinema that reacts violently to the breaking of a specific apocalyptic promise: a New World or an America that was meant to be a just and righteous city on a hill. Romero responds to an impossible by marshalling a new impossibility and outfitting infinity in the body of the finite. What had been timeless now becomes compulsive repetition, like the death drive that Freud situated beyond the pleasure principle. Indeed, what had been "beyond" in traditional apocalypse now becomes immanent, stasis perversely taking up residence within time (or vice versa) via the body of the zombie. Romero uses this structure to castigate the power structures and unthinking habits of late twentieth- and early twenty-first-century America, hypothesizing an already dead country but allowing for the possibility that a certain lack of closure, or perhaps an ethics of movement, may revive us.

Themselves drawing from Romero, Soavi and Fulci nevertheless situate their films *beyond the zombie*. There is no revival in these films because there is nothing to be revived, no identity or coherence to be saved from the jaws of the mendacious soothings of apocalypse. There is no cultural critique because there is no ideal that has been betrayed. It is not fortuitous that my discussion above tends to deal with Romero in broad narrative strokes and with Fulci and Soavi in smaller details of image and cutting; Romero presents a relatively traditional narrative, within which lurks the suspended temporality of the zombie, while the others explicitly deploy an unresolved suspension as their narrative principle. Romero offers us allegory, in which zombies turn out to be all too human; Fulci and Soavi, in their final scenes, question the grounds on which allegory might be founded (it is now too simple even to say that zombies *represent* humans). Romero gives the lie to apocalypse from the outside; Fulci and Soavi, in staging a deliberately meaningless apocalyptic stasis, work from within to disperse the very possibility of identity on which any apocalypse could be based.

Notes

1. There is a prehistory to Romero's zombie apocalypse that includes 1959's *Invisible Invaders* and 1964's *The Last Man on Earth*. For overviews of these and other pre-Romero zombie films, see Peter Dendle, *The Zombie Movie Encyclopedia* (Jefferson, NC: McFarland, 2001). Romero's social and existential engagements, however, are decisive for the genre's later apocalyptic tendencies.

2. Robin Wood, *Hollywood from Vietnam to Reagan* (New York: Columbia University Press, 1986), 61.

3. John J. Collins, "Introduction: Toward the Morphology of a Genre," *Semeia* 14 (1979): 9.

4. Stephen Goldsmith, *Unbuilding Jerusalem: Apocalypse and Romantic Representation* (Ithaca, NY: Cornell University Press, 1993).

5. Goldsmith, *Unbuilding Jerusalem*, 43.

6. James Berger, *After the End: Representations of Post-Apocalypse* (Minneapolis: University of Minnesota Press, 1999), 18.

7. Berger, *After the End*, 17.

8. Frank Kermode, *The Sense of an Ending: Studies in the Theory of Fiction* (Oxford: Oxford University Press, 1967).

9. Steven Shaviro, *The Cinematic Body* (Minneapolis: University of Minnesota Press, 1993), 97, 99.

10. Paul Barber, *Vampires, Burial, and Death: Folklore and Reality* (New Haven, CT: Yale University Press, 1988).

11. Barber, *Vampires*, 91.

12. Shaviro, *Cinematic Body*, 105.

13. Donato Totaro, "Review of *The Beyond*, dir. Lucio Fulci," in *Eaten Alive! Italian Cannibal and Zombie Movies*, ed. Jay Slater (London: Plexus, 2002), 231–35.

14. Julia Kristeva, *Powers of Horror: An Essay on Abjection*, trans. Leon S. Roudiez (New York: Columbia University Press, 1982), 4, 8, 2.

15. Kristeva's notoriously enigmatic articulation of abjection deserves more attention than I can give it here. There is no question that *Powers of Horror*, with its thematics and stylistics of boundary-crossing and its discussion of Céline's "laughter of the apocalypse," deserves a place in any thorough consideration of contemporary apocalyptic rhetoric. See chapters 2 and 3 of Megan Becker-Leckrone, *Julia Kristeva and Literary Theory* (New York: Palgrave Macmillan, 2005) for a careful study of Kristeva's abjection.

16. Simon Critchley, *Very Little . . . Almost Nothing: Death, Philosophy, Literature* (London: Routledge, 1997), 2.

CHAPTER SIX

~

Zombies without Organs:
Gender, Flesh, and Fissure

Patricia MacCormack

In this chapter, we will theorize the flesh of zombies as one example of how the body can alter its signification and hence the way it is "read" as a textual surface. The affect of images of gore, impossible situations of the dead-be-come-living, and disheveled flesh remaining ambulatory will be discussed as catalysts for transformation of psychoanalytic film theory and horror paradigms. The pleasure the spectator finds in gruesome zombie gore films can challenge the way in which the spectator watches, beyond the description and subsequent "meaning" of what is watched.

Italian horror cinema compels thinking such a body for two reasons. Italian horror cinema is insensible while encroaching on all senses. Two films in particular, both by Lucio Fulci, form the main axes of analysis in this chapter. Fulci's two "Gates of Hell" films, *Paura nel città dei morti viventi* (*City of the Living Dead*, also known as *Gates of Hell*) and *E tu vivrai nel terrore! L'aldilà* (*The Beyond*), have been widely criticized for narratives described as rudimentary to incoherent.

Paura is a Lovecraftian tale of parish priest Father William Thomas (Fabrizio Jovine), who, by hanging himself, opens a gateway of Hell. After his death, he reappears as an apparition and kills various townspeople in bizarre ways—even his basilisk gaze causes death—upon which they, in turn, return as zombies with similar profane drives. Investigating this phenomenon is Mary Woodhouse (Catriona McColl) and Peter Bell (Christopher George), but far from resolving the problem, the film ends ambiguously, suggesting that truncating this "infection" is impossible.

L'aldilà is the story of Liza Merril's (McColl again) inheritance of a hotel where an alchemist was crucified in the bowels of the building sixty years previously. When his body is discovered, one of the gates of Hell is opened and a series of gory corporeal transformations through zombification occur. Within this situation is Emily (Cinzia Monreale), a blind woman from whom Liza seeks answers to the incomprehensible situation. Later we discover Liza herself has escaped from Hell and is a zombie who is compelled to return. The investigation of the events by Liza and John McCabe (David Warbeck) leads not to resolution but to the pair left wandering in the landscape of the beyond which is Hell.

On the surface, the two narratives are both weak and similar. However to subjugate the success of these films to traditional systems of narrative fails to acknowledge that these films, like many gore films, are films that rupture *outward* rather than along a narrative axis. Although they are essentially a series of dreamlike, often lyrical and beautiful, baroquely gory scenarios, these moments are the purpose of the films rather than their apology.

These two films are not to be analyzed as purely textual objects, a dialectic that ascertains the distance between the observer and the observed. They take as their primary aim the ability to *affect* their audience, causing transformations of pleasure and disgust, using the spectacle of the opened flesh to challenge the spectator's ability to read the film as a meaningful text. Affection describes a bodily experience that calls into question both the rigidity of binarized conceptions of subjectivity and the ability to conceive of "a body" at all without attending to the constant differentiation and flux of the flesh. We are less concerned with who these bodies are than with what happens to them. The why (Why have the gates of Hell opened? Why is she doing that?) is forsaken for the how—How are these bodies configured differently? How do these images affect the spectator?

The gap between viewer and viewed is less a space than a folding that sees each bleed into the other. Images of gore open up fissures in the viewing flesh as fissures open up in the bodies on-screen. We are not comfortable viewers, safe in our own bodies and their ability to read the images, thus containing them through affirming what they signify. We split, between horror and pleasure, desire and disgust, and are therefore viewing *as* fissure.

Fulci's zombies differ from the frozen, dammed-up consumer zombies of the Romero films who can no longer demarcate the consumption of people and items (a loss of demarcation that reflects the capitalization of sexuality and desire in general). Fulci's zombies have not become robotic but excessive, they are reconfigured body become flesh. Flesh refers to the body that has lost its significations as a hermeneutic entity where markers of gender, race, and even sexuality can be read on the body as a text.

In these two films, Fulci's zombies are not Afro-Caribbean or other racial minorities whose subjugation is defined by their alterity to the powerful, colonizing white. The zombies in *Paura* and *L'aldilà* are formed of all subject types—male, female, old, young. But more important, they are all physically ruptured, where the inside of flesh turns outward, where brains protrude, eyes become white egglike orbs, faces melt, and skin rots. Similarly, these zombies don't eat people; they are driven by a desire to rupture the bodies of others, which leads not to death but to a transformation where the victim's flesh similarly refolds and reconfigures. This drive is nontranscribable, unable to be annexed to established desires, be they sexual or alimentary. The body as flesh, far from the body as a continual reiteration of the subject, is here opened up, folded back, driven by desires for acts that defy rather than affirm automatic consumption and patterns of reified subjectivity and sexuality. Fulci's zombies behave not like each other but in bizarre and unique ways. The incoherent nature of the gory acts that they inflict on the living suggests they do not consume so much as transform.

In *Paura*, Father William seduces teenager Rose Kelvin (Daniela Doria) to weep blood and vomit up her entrails simply by staring at her. He tears the back out of Tommy Fisher's (Italian horror director Michele Soavi) skull, squelching the brains between his fingers. Town idiot Bob (the wonderful Giovanni Lombardo Radice) has phantasms of a writhing, maggot-infested baby corpse, and in spite of his death being at the hands of patriarch Mr. Ross (Venantino Venantini) rather than Father William—by pneumatic drill through the head—he returns as a zombie nonetheless. The zombies' torment of their victims incarnate in similarly strange acts.

L'aldilà's deaths are more colorful—various characters are melted by acid, a face is eaten by spiders, Emily's throat is torn out, and handyman Arthur (Ginapaolo Saccarola) has his eyes gouged out and kills his wife in an equally gruesome way in a marital parody, showing that interest in corporeal reconfiguration (the body, literally "beyond") has replaced sexual patterns. It should be noted here that the violence in these films is entirely devoid of aggression, with the exception of Mr. Ross's murder of Bob. This is a key point, as violence equivocated with aggression evokes issues of power and subjugation, even in reference to the biting drive of cannibal zombies. The bodies in *Paura* and *L'aldilà* are transformed by violent acts, or passive gazes, but as one transforms, one infects other victims through violent acts as a means by which that body will also go beyond—beyond signification and subjectivity.

Bodies in *L'aldilà* and *Paura* exist to be disorganized, not to organize a story. These films are not about death equaling termination but about re-creation of self.

"We want to see frigid, imprisoned, mortified bodies explode to bits, even if capitalism continues to demand that they be kept in check at the expense of our living bodies."[1] The criticism that Fulci has forsaken ideas for gratuitous gore can be leveled only by those who see the films as imprisoned by the frigidity of narrative, usually psychoanalytic film theory. Our viewing bodies cannot directly mimic these ruptured, splayed bodies, so they must be something else. Or, more correct, they must become something else that defiantly resists definition. We don't know how, in what way, or why, but our bodies are affected by images of horror. The desire to know is not enough to begin to explore the pleasures, pains, and eventually propulsions caused in our viewing bodies when we watch these films. In this chapter, using Gilles Deleuze and Félix Guattari's notion of the "body-without-organs" (BwO), we analyze Fulci's films and their affects through what Deleuze and Guattari call "schizoanalysis," which acknowledges cinema's capacity to seduce, dissipate, pervert, and transform the viewer by exploring different and differentiating configurations of the signified body, of gender, of desire, disgust, and pleasure.[2]

Horror's force of rupture is a feminist force because it compels the constant and renewing creation of bodies of difference—not one or two but endless differences within and between bodies. The horror of gore films comes from the horror of viewing the "human body," sewn up to be all it can be before it exists, destroyed. Simultaneously, everyday urbane horror of corporeality comes from our own body's incapacity to be controlled, complete, and, for those bodies that occupy minority positions (in terms of power more than demographics), to fulfill the basic structure of what being a "human body" means. Deleuze and Guattari call these minority bodies "minoritarian" to describe not simply that these bodies differ from the white male but that to be minority can be an ideological or philosophical position, whereby all bodies are called to become minoritarian so as to multiply subject positions available and valued for all subjects. Our body exceeds its own potential to be defined.

For many, horror of the body is born of a political inability to fulfill "the human" body along majoritarian—a state of ideological or corporeal majority—axes through a failure of skin (to be white) or genitals (to be male). For all, the body's uncontrollability and its possibilities is the force of desire that cannot be contained within such a tightly sewn shell. Desire to become otherwise takes, as its first step, the body itself as simultaneously self and Other, acknowledging its irrefutable potential to be more than itself and certainly more than "that" body. The blown-apart body on-screen is *not* the viewer's potential to be dead, but instigator of the viewer's propulsion through the affect of the image.

In Italian gore, the image is not what it *says* but what it *does*. Gore says nothing; what it does similarly resists language and meaning, thus affect and its resulting body can never be theorized, only desired. If our relationship to the image is neither predictable nor "readable," then our relationship with and as our bodies is even further undetermined. What the zombies in these films show is that bodies are always more than we can bear and are capable of configurations beyond the few available and acceptable in culture. Of course, we cannot mimic these dead-alive bodies, but to navigate and negotiate such images asks us what is at risk and what is subversive about addressing bodies beyond legibility and, indeed, taste?

Beyond Psychoanalysis: The Affection Image

"Reading" reduces corporeally disruptive and excessive images to logical signs commensurable with the thinking subject who views them. These interpretations are indexed purely on psychoanalysis's closed concepts of available subject possibilities. Women identify with objectified women on-screen, men with active gazing male figures. The identificatory positions available to women in horror have been reduced by psychoanalytic film theory to the victim, the monstrous mother, the monster itself, and virgin tomboy survivor, known as the "Final Girl."[3] Because psychoanalysis supposes the brain in the body, through psychological problems as symptoms, rather than a constant oscillation traversing brain and body simultaneously, it is unable to offer a truly corporeal reading of film.

Although it has been widely argued against since its inception, even by its author, Laura Mulvey's "Visual Pleasure and Narrative Cinema" has informed most attempts to theorize cinema through psychoanalysis, and for most laypersons it represents a common understanding of watching practices—that pleasure is felt in the coherence of the narrative with established subjects in the "real."[4] One can only believe and enjoy a film if one can identify, whether transvestitically or literally, with the character on-screen. While the male gaze replaces the audience's male bodies, the female viewing body must be theorized as either body-object or transvestitic gazing subject. Implicit in this reading is the exclusion of female cinematic identification outside of traditional configurations of "woman." Lacan's "What do women want?" has become cinema's "How do women gaze?" Whether psychically, phenomenologically, or (whole) bodily incarnated,[5] women's desire to gaze as something otherwise to the essential nature of the phallic look continues to fascinate film theory. The question has been dealt with ad nauseum, but remaining is the enigmatic nature of the question. That there is such a question to ask, and that the question is, like Lacan's, both unanswerable and answerable in multiple ways, fails to account for images and the bodies watching them that resist concepts of reading and meaning by actively affecting.

Horror film itself emphasizes the ambiguous and problematic nature of desire as longing. We could just as easily ask, "What does the horror fan want?" We certainly do not want pleasure, defined in its traditional sense, and if we are now moving beyond psychoanalytic theory, we do not want shock purely for catharsis, nor violence born of aggression. We want to *feel otherwise*, where all former definitions of pleasure, power, violence, and desire are troubled in the face of the spectator's cerebral-corporeal submission to these images that challenge, disgust, delight, confound, and horrify. The power of horror is that it forces us to submit to images that destabilize our sense of self, and the gorier and less coherent the film, the more this destabilization is activated. Affection is not identification. Affective nonreading is available for all bodies and is undefinable due to the specificity, in time, space, and taste, of all viewers. The confounding nature of Fulci's nonracialized, degendered, and perversely acting zombies that offer irrefutable pleasure beyond identification show psychoanalytic film theory to be a fiction. Consequently, the rigid subject positions within this system must also be fictive. This is not to say that it is a fiction against the "truth" of affect, but rather that it is one spectatorial fiction among many that could possibly be available. By multiplying the ways in which spectators can variously take pleasure in the cinematic act, the definitions of the meanings and desires of those bodies that watch may simultaneously be multiplied.

Deleuze, in his *Cinema 2*, points out that affect cinema is precisely about this constant traversal:

> There is as much thought in the body as there is shock and violence in the brain. There is an equal amount of feeling in both of them. The brain gives orders to the body which is just an outgrowth of it, but the body also gives orders to the brain which is just a part of it: in both cases, these will not be the same bodily attitudes nor the same cerebral gest.[6]

Put simply, the body is always present in cinematic pleasure, by virtue not of what it *is*, but of what it *experiences* viscerally, thoracically—through nerve, muscle, gritted teeth, and the brain's forced negotiation of bodies on-screen beyond the spectator's ability to identify. Here the cerebral becomes visceral and the visceral, or sensuous, sensorial. Similarly, the libidinal, usually oriented around gender, when incarnated in corporeal excavative acts between nongendered zombies, transforms for the viewer to the delights of disgust.

Horror film, especially Italian gore film, is derided as "low," seen in the direct-to-video marketing of these films—when they are not outright banned (which in Australia and the United Kingdom, at least, is a strong possibility). The body, too, is the lower aspect of subjectivity in discursive systems that privilege the male, the white, rationality, and logic. As Deleuze points out, traditionally the brain gives orders to the body, the brain houses the subject while the body stands as a plastic version of everyone else; the body is our sameness, while the brain houses our individuality.

Against this, feminist body theory has located the body as the primary site of phallologic's indifference to differences between bodies, which ironically represents itself as only interested in difference as it relates to aberration. Aberrant bodies are any bodies that do not fulfill the rigid criteria of the white male majoritarian body. *The* matter of bodies is their failure to fulfill majoritarian axes, while successful majoritarianism carries with it the luxury of bodily transcendence. Only if a body passes can it be said to be a generic "human" body—otherwise it is a black body, a female body, an insane body, a criminal body.

How can we locate the ways in which the spectator "identifies" with Fulci's zombie bodies? When the characters in the films are transformed into zombies, they confront us with a series of questions rather than a series of signifiers of both body as object and as acting subject. What gender are these zombies after their transformation? Does their gender matter? What do the things that happen to them *mean*? How do we read Rose vomiting her entrails? What desires do we see in Father William giving Bob gruesome hallucinations, or Emily haunting Liza with the unnerving gaze of her white eyes? How can we explain these bodies returning from the dead when the very concept of a living corpse is an impossible paradox? Such theorization of viewing is made possible through Deleuze's affection-image.

We watch the film *expecting* viscerally shocking things to happen, and thus we are able to explain their inclusion. But what we cannot explain is any necessarily causal affect these images will have on us. Deleuze calls the image that subjugates movement to time, where affect is event independent of or privileged over narrative, a *time-image*:

> The before and after are no longer themselves a matter of external empirical succession, but of the intrinsic quality of that which becomes in time.

> Becoming can in fact be defined as that which transforms an empirical se-
> quence into a series: a burst of series.[7]

The assemblage of these images and our bodies are intrinsic and indeterminable quality. The assemblage literally describes the beyond—beyond
reading, beyond dialectics, beyond comprehension, beyond being and the
body organism to becoming and the BwO. Donato Totaro sums up the time-
image thus: "Deleuze does not propose neat or rigid classifications [for the
time-image.] . . . The time-image moved beyond motion by freeing itself of
the 'sensory-motor' link to a 'pure optical and sound' (tactile) image."[8]

We can either force the images in L'aldilà and Paura to represent what we
know (majoritarian power defining the minoritarian), thus immobilizing cre-
ativity, possibility, and affect, or allow the tactility rather than the meaning
of the image to affect and hence propel our bodies into becoming undetermined and indeterminable new zones. Due to the fantasy of images always
being intentional, film constantly resists a repudiation of comprehensibility.

What I find attractive about reading the body in its relationship to an affection-image is that both the image as being only in relation to its affect of
the flesh, and the body affected confound any claim to the absolute tran-
scribability of meaning. In order to become, we must sidestep the binary of
readability and nonreadability and fall into the interval between "this means
this" and "I don't get it." Brian Massumi states that "rather than looking per-
pendicularly up or down, one moves sideways toward another position on the
grid for which one was not destined, toward an animal, a machine, a person
of a different sex or age or race, an insect, a plant."[9]

We must move sideways when watching L'aldilà and Paura. The only other
alternatives are to read meaning in the films, closing off their affective potential by surmising it as one meaning, or to turn the film off, which is a response many viewers make to gore film. The irreparable fissure the shock of
the visceral images in L'aldilà and Paura causes in the viewing flesh is the in-
stigation toward the becoming flesh beyond age, sex, or race. More than becoming something else, however, these images simply cause an undetermined
process. We need not know (indeed we should not even ask) *what* we are becoming. The least and best we can do is accept the absolute divisibility
within ourselves, the fracture at the very essence of being, the more-than-
one we are already but are made viscerally aware of through the affection-image.[10] The affection-image makes aware the brain in the body and the body
in the brain—we look at the gore of L'aldilà and Paura and the thought of our
flesh makes our stomachs rumble and our throats gallish, while our brains becomes pure viscera from the affect of the raw saturation of the red of blood,

the sound of the squelching of organs, the sizzle of the flesh melting under acid, the hollow rattles that emit from the zombies replacing language. Our brains cannot read these images, and our bodies cannot react to them empathically (we cannot literally empathize with evisceration, like we can in other "body genres" such as coming in porn and crying in melodramas). Our flesh reacts sensorily, reading the images corporeally, while our brains think the inability to think the images sensibly.

Sensuousness is not enough, though. As a move from mind to embodied self, sensuous affect values the body as maker of meaning—as many bodies as there are, as many meanings may be. But more than this diversification of meaning as resultant from affect, as many unknown conditions of my body may be perceived when affection images jolt my brain into body and my body into brain. A double transformation takes place: the self becomes embodied, refusing and exceeding Cartesian subjectivity, while also becoming otherwise; an Other to itself through a perception of the foreignness of its own body to its self. Watching these films makes us sick, and when we are sick, we feel the absolute alterity of our body to our sense of volition and willful power over subjectivity. When the body and self are merged together as force, all we become is alterity—to the moment before, to the concept of singular self, and indeed to the concept of all as knowable. We are the same body but suddenly realize that body is never the same as itself. This is why becoming need not be a grandiose project, but can be a becoming of the foreignness and excesses of the everyday body through cinema.

Interestingly, Fulci claimed of *L'aldilà* that he wanted "to make a completely Artaudian film out of an almost inexistent script."[11] Antonin Artaud is the inspiration behind Deleuze and Guattari's body-without-organs:

> It is true that Artaud wages a struggle against the organs, but at the same time what he is going after, what he has it in for, is the organism. . . . [The BwOs] are opposed to the organism, the organic organization of the organs.[12]

Fulci, too, has it in for the organization of the organs, (di)splaying flesh in a number of increasingly gruesome ways—spiders chew out eyeballs, crucifixions and acid baths abound, Emily's throat and ear are ripped out by her guide dog in a more bloody homage to Dario Argento's *Suspiria*. In *Paura*, brains extrude from scalps, eyeballs bleed, heads have holes through their apex, intestines emerge, bodies are punctuated by clusters of writhing maggots. The body in *L'aldilà* and *Paura* is only successful in disarray; those bodies that remain organized end up wandering the empty wasteland of the beyond of the title. Fulci's message is, "Destroy the organized flesh or be relegated to a land of pure nothingness."

Body-without-Organs

If we are to create another option against psychoanalysis by which to theorize cinematic pleasure, we cannot simply resist without offering suggestions toward possible future ways of thinking (without reifying) these zombie bodies. Deleuze and Guattari's body-without-organs is one way by which Fulci's zombies can be thought. The images in *L'aldilà* and *Paura* declare war on organizations and organizing principles—of narrative, of causal movement and result, and of the body. Both the narrative and the on-screen bodies in the films are BwOs: "In other words [they resist] a phenomenon of accumulation, coagulation, and sedimentation that, in order to extract useful labor from the BwO, imposes upon it forms, functions, bonds, dominant and hierarchized organizations, organized transcendences."[13]

The BwOs on-screen form BwOs off-screen through reorienting and creating new opportunities—violence creates pleasure; pleasure is no longer toward things that preserve but rather those that destroy and transform the body. Disgust is desire, and the real world is exchanged for the world beyond, which forces a reorientation of all the laws of reality; this confounding is its own form of pleasure through confusion, the death of the psychoanalytic spectator.

> You invent self-destructions that have nothing to do with the death drive. Dismantling the organism has never meant killing yourself, but rather opening the body to connections that presuppose an entire assemblage, circuits, conjunctions, levels and thresholds, passages and distributions of intensity. . . . Actually dismantling the organism is no more difficult than dismantling the other two strata, significance and subjectification.[14]

By repudiating the possibility of the spectatorial body mirroring the on-screen body, the viewer must form an assemblage with the image so that intensities rather than actual acts are catalysts for refoldings of the flesh and desire. Horror impinges on and creates new thresholds of intensities and undulates as durations and events of corporeal dismantling. The term *zombie* guarantees that any dismantling cannot lead to death and thus must lead to something else postdeath. Viewing zombies hence leads to fear not of death but of its own "something else." Viewing flesh is redistributed by opening up to horror. Far from a sadistic gaze, this requires an actual opening up of the viewing flesh to being dismantled and reorganized in continually new and foreign formations through conjunction with the images. It is a risky project, indeed.

The BwO is not a new kind of body: it describes the project of resistance to the ways in which our flesh is organized and regimented both in form as meaningful anatomy (genitals fix gender; skin color, race) and function (gender infers sexuality; organs are either appropriate or inappropriately used for pleasure). It is not an object but a project. *L'aldilà*'s and *Paura*'s zombies are not literally without organs—indeed one of the primary ways in which they affect the viewer is through their provocative display of internal organs—but without bodily organization. That is, the bodies of the film's characters are not mutilated specifically according to the matter of their flesh. The gender of the victims is equally distributed, unlike films such as Sergio Martino's *I corpi presentano tracce di violenza carnale* (*Torso*) and all women-as-victim films. The race of the zombies is irrelevant, demarcating them from the invariably black Haitian zombies of older, more traditional zombie films, including Fulci's own *Zombi 2*.

The bodies in *Paura* are not born monstrous, a frequent device in order to vindicate gory deaths in monster movies. The bodies are not signified as objects of perversion through abject sexuality, like the body and object of desire of the necrophiliac in *Buio omega* (*Beyond the Darkness*) and *Il mostro è in tavola* (*Flesh for Frankenstein*) or the cannibal sex-crime in *Anthropophagus*. The acts of the zombies do not mirror sexual acts or transfer the sexual to the alimentary, which is vaguely suggested in *Apocalypse domani* (*Cannibal Apocalypse*), where Charles (Giovanni Lombardo Radice) bites the breast of a girl whose boyfriend is sucking her nipple.[15]

These films all show interesting configurations of perversion, renegotiating the way bodies and pleasure become disorganized and challenge traditional corporeal and sexual paradigms. Much of their interest occurs as a result of the proximity of the perverse sexuality in reference to or annexed around these norms, though, which means they still rely to an extent on reading the acts, albeit often in delirious and different ways. But the acts of violence in *Paura* and *L'aldilà* are aimed at no one in particular and are perpetrated by zombies, who have no moral, sexual, or pathological agenda, except perhaps that the living are alive and the zombies are dead. Their zombie state ablates gender, which thus ablates definable sexuality through object choice, and their zombification occurs independent of Caribbean lore.

Form does not drain them of organs, but destratifies anatomical possibility and traditional organ function—instead of digestive function, Rose vomits her organs in a perverse libation to Father William; the priest uses

Tommy's brains for digital pleasure; Arthur's eyes are for pushing in, not looking out, yet this blinding does not stop him from "seeing" his wife in order to elicit her zombification; skin is for melting, not for integrating the hermeneutic body. Similarly, Emily's white eyes, although signifying pathology through blindness, are a beautiful, engaging, and uncanny part of her aesthetic appeal; her throat being torn out does not kill her, but rather launches her on her journey back to the world beyond.

More saliently, these acts launch *us* toward the beyond. Tommy's brain is taken out of his head, disrupting his corporeal strata, and this brain becomes *our* organ, not of cerebral physiology but of affect as we are affiliated with its squelch, its vulgarity, its beauty, the pleasure of disgust, shock, and confusion. We receive a brain as a fine segment between us and the image, and its reference to Tommy is arbitrary as to what it means but affective for what it does to us. These acts of violence are acts of corporeal experimentation, not destruction.

> The body without organs has replaced the organism and experimentation has replaced all interpretation, for which it no longer has any use. Flows of intensity, their fluids, their fibers, their continuums and conjunctions of affect, the wind, fine segmentation, microperceptions, have replaced the world of the subject.[16]

I must reiterate, however, that these violences to the body are violences toward signification of their form and function, *not* violences born of aggression and a desire to kill subjects. What these violences do kill is subjectification through signification of flesh, where we are subject *to* the signifying systems that organize and regulate our bodies. The zombie bodies are not replacement bodies, but flesh unbound. Beyond the threat of death as absence of any form of life or self, the living dead in the films almost point to the living flesh, which is dead to the laws and rules of corporeal signification. While this of course cannot be literally mirrored in the world outside of cinema, the affective nature of the images puts end to the stratification and significations of the demand that we "read" images by deferring them to their meanings and possibility of existence in the real world. Horror is all about exploiting—not bodies, but the impossible in the real becoming possible through cinema.

Baroque Bodies

Although I have pointed out that the BwO is a body in permanent shift, beyond this body we can see spectatorial pleasure through gore as catalyst toward a becoming-otherwise. Deleuze and Guattari describe the dismantling body as a body in process that enters into alliances with other elements to continually transform. Gore cinema refolds our bodies within the bodies on-screen, and as they open up, *we* must open up to receive their affect. The screen and self form a symbiosis of affect, a becoming-otherwise. Far from describing Gothic worlds, Fulci's two films are Baroque.[17] While *Gothic* refers to alienation found in a space—relevant to Fulci's films as both are nomenclatured within a relatively tight environment—it entirely ignores the aspect of Fulci's films that both defines them away from generic horror toward pure gore and has been the very reason for their being cut, banned, and described as offensive.

Baroque, according to Deleuze,

> invents the infinite work or process. The problem is not how to finish the fold [through thought or act] but how to continue it. . . . It is not only because the fold affects all materials that it thus becomes expressive matter with different scales, speeds and different vectors . . . but especially because it determines and materializes form. It produces a form of expression.[18]

Gore makes thought matter; gore image is the force of image materially able to transform viewer. Representation, which defers image to preconceived referent, does not acknowledge the transformation affect forces through the materiality of these images. Gian Lorenzo Bernini's quickening of Baroque architecture to the sculptural architecture of the affective body that affects its viewer—St. Theresa in ecstasy, St. Jerome's contemplation, Proserpine's rape—seems a more appropriate genealogy than Gothic for this fellow Roman director and disciple of flesh transformed through affect.

While Bernini's religious figures achieve Baroque rapture through God, their God is one of infection, contagion, and corporeal invasion, not of law or regulation. Similarly, Fulci's images affect via invasion "for the affect is not a personal feeling, nor is it a characteristic; it is the effectuation of the power of the pack that throws the self into upheaval and makes it reel."[19] Effectuation-as-pack seems appropriate in reference to zombies, as they rarely appear as individuals. Zombies are plague and infection; in these films, transformation comes through contagion, not biological but through perversion of the desire to act otherwise.

The zombies in *Paura* and *L'aldilà* use action upon flesh as their mode of contagion. The force of the zombies incarnates as their unfolding flesh refolding the flesh of other bodies and of the spectator, deforming matter/flesh. These zombies are "form that reveals its folds [which] becomes force."[20] The act of pack with these zombies both multiplies forms but also multiplies forces so that minor transformations that continually occur within bodies also ripples transformation through the pack. "The multiple is not only what has many parts but also what is folded in many ways."[21]

Zombies as pack contagion exploit contagion's transformation within as well as between bodies, yet these symptoms are not the predictable cannibalistic impulses of many other zombie films. Each zombie expresses its symptoms differently and also draws exterior, noncorporeal elements toward facilitating their becoming-zombie: Bob's hallucinations, Emily's dog Dicky ripping her throat out, Martin (Michele Mirabella) having his face ripped apart by a cluster of spiders, even Father William's use of the hanging rope. Propagation through "unnatural participation" is in direct repudiation of familial production, the supreme structure of psychonalaysis. Deleuze and Guattari ask, "How can we conceive of a peopling, a propagation, a becoming that is without filiation or heredity production?"[22] The simple answer is zombies!

Often zombification produces a perversion of the Oedipal or familial, swapping incest for alimentary desire, seen explicitly in Andrea Bianchi's *Le notti del terrore* (*Burial Ground*) when the child Michael (Peter Bark) bites off his mother's breast instead of suckling. This is also hinted at in *Paura* when Emily (Antonella Interlenchi) pays night visits to her little brother John-John (Luca Paisner), who is apparently ripe for pedophilic pickings as earlier his disappearance is blamed on Bob, whose history includes doing an unnamed "thing" to a schoolgirl. It is impossible to reduce Fulci's situations to Oedipal-gone-awry acts because the knowledge of precisely what these zombies will do is never available to us. Filiation is now both heredity and contagion, another Baroque folding, here of family and pack, desire as both incest and infection (remembering that St. Theresa's invasion by God was a libidinal experience by her Holy Father but was not reducible to incest). Act and resultant form are not incest for mental trauma but a visceral folding event toward material and infinite transformation. Emily does not abuse her brother, she infects him. Power is contagion through affiliation, not hierarchical force.

It is not the body per se that is destroyed and disheveled in horror films; it is the majoritarian body and its identifiable desires. Satisfaction is not the product of the affection-image. We become production. Dorothea Olkowski claims that "Deleuze and Guattari argue, however, that desiring-production does not produce hallucinations; it is a material process of production, the production of what might otherwise be called bodies but might better be called becomings."[23] *L'aldilà*'s and *Paura*'s signs are not metaphors, they are real, and our relationship to them is material. Their powers of affect can take cinema beyond the screen to rethink, through affect, the ways in which the viewing body is organized and the filiations it may form with images of gore and horror that take the paradigms by which we think the body toward the beyond.

Notes

1. Félix Guattari, "In Order to End the Massacre of the Body," in *Soft Subversions*, trans. Jarred Becker (New York: Semiotext(e), 1996), 31.

2. Gilles Deleuze and Félix Guattari, *A Thousand Plateaus: Capitalism and Schizophrenia*, trans. Brian Massumi (London: Athlone Press, 1987).

3. For the monstrous mother, see Barbara Creed, *The Monstrous-Feminine: Film, Feminism, Psychoanalysis* (New York: Routledge, 1993). For the monster itself, see Linda Williams, "When the Woman Looks," in *Re-Vision: Essays in Feminist Film Criticism*, ed. Maryanne Doane, Patricia Mellencamp, and Linda Williams (Los Angeles: University Publications of America, 1984), 67–82. For the "Final Girl," see Carol J. Clover, *Men, Women and Chainsaws: Gender in the Modern Horror Film* (Princeton, NJ: Princeton University Press, 1992).

4. Laura Mulvey, "Visual Pleasure and Narrative Cinema," *Screen* 16 (1975): 6–18.

5. These three perspectives are described, respectively, in Mulvey, "Visual Pleasure," among others; Vivian Sobchack, *The Address of the Eye: A Phenomenology of Film Experience* (Princeton, NJ: Princeton University Press, 1992); and Linda Williams, "Film Bodies: Gender, Genre and Excess," *Film Quarterly* 44, no. 4 (1991): 2–13.

6. Gilles Deleuze, *Cinema 2: The Time Image*, trans. Hugh Tomlinson and Robert Galeta (London: Athlone Press, 1989), 205.

7. Deleuze, *Cinema 2*, 275.

8. Donato Totaro, "Gilles Deleuze's Bergsonian Film Project," *Offscreen* 3, no. 3 (March 1999), http://www.horschamp.qc.ca/9903/offscreen_essays/deleuze2.html.

9. Brian Massumi, "Realer than Real: The Simulacrum According to Deleuze and Guattari," *Copyright* 1 (1999), http://www.anu.edu/hrc/first_and_last/works/realer.html.

10. This is different from Lacan's *spaltung* because it lacks an ideal model against which it fails.

11. Quoted in Luca M. Palmerini and Gaetano Mistretta, *Spaghetti Nightmares: Italian Fantasy-Horrors as Seen through the Eyes of Their Protagonists*, trans. Gilliam M. A. Kirkpatrick (Key West, FL: Fantasma, 1996), 60.

12. Deleuze and Guattari, *Thousand Plateaus*, 158.

13. Deleuze and Guattari, *Thousand Plateaus*, 159.

14. Deleuze and Guattari, *Thousand Plateaus*, 160.

15. This theme was to be enhanced with the inclusion of a cannibal fellatio scene where a nurse bites the penis off a doctor whom she is fellating; for details,

see my interview with Giovanni Lombardo Radice: "Male Masochism, Male Monsters: An Interview with Giovanni Lombardo Radice," in *Alternative Europe: Eurotrash and Exploitation Cinema since 1945*, ed. Xavier Mendik and Ernest Mathijs (London: Wallflower, 2004), 106–16. See also Patricia MacCormack, "Masochistic Cinesexuality: The Many Deaths of Giovanni Lombardo Radice," in Mendik and Mathijs, *Alternative Europe*, 117–23.

16. Deleuze and Guattari, *Thousand Plateaus*, 162.

17. Steven Jay Schneider and Michael Grant, in *The Couch and the Silver Screen*, both discuss *L'aldilà* in reference to its Gothic expression. However, both entirely avoid discussions of bodies, referring to the space and place of the film rather than the flesh which inhabits it. It seems troubling that in order to give these gore films academic value, their "lower" aspects seem to be repressed in favor of placing them within the more respectable horror genealogy. See Steven Jay Schneider, "Notes on the Relevance of Psychoanalytic Film Theory to Euro-Horror Film," in *The Couch and the Silver Screen: Psychoanalytic Reflections on European Cinema*, ed. Andrea Sabbadini (London: Brunner-Routledge, 2003), 119–27; and Michael Grant, "Cinema, Horror and the Abominations of Hell: Carl-Theodor Dreyer's *Vampyr* (1931) and Lucio Fulci's *The Beyond* (1981)," in Sabbadini, *Couch and the Silver Screen*, 145–55.

18. Gilles Deleuze, *The Fold: Leibniz and the Baroque*, trans. Tom Conley (London: The Athlone Press, 2001), 34–35.

19. Deleuze and Guattari, *Thousand Plateaus*, 240.

20. Deleuze, *The Fold*, 35.

21. Deleuze, *The Fold*, 3.

22. Deleuze and Guattari, *Thousand Plateaus*, 241.

23. Dorothea Olkowski, "Flows of Desire and the Body-Becoming," in *Becomings: Explorations in Time, Memory, and Futures*, ed. Elizabeth Grosz (Ithaca, NY: Cornell University Press, 1999), 114.

~

CHAPTER SEVEN

Cannibalizing Gender and Genre: A Feminist Re-Vision of George Romero's Zombie Films

Natasha Patterson

While much work in feminist film theory has been directed toward the conventionally "female" genres of melodrama (i.e., "weepies"), there is a small but lively body of research in films that appear to have no positive space for female viewers, specifically horror films. Much of the feminist literature in this area suggests that horror films are culturally dominated and consumed by men, produced by a subindustry that narratively victimizes and punishes women over and over again. Feminist psychoanalytic film theory has informed much of the gender/genre debate surrounding women and horror filmdom, often reinforcing essentialist assumptions about women (e.g., that they are passive or masochistic).[1] Typically, genre has been thought to construct readers into neat gender categories, from which critics try to theorize male and female readers (and their responses) by examining a popular text. Feminists' employment of psychoanalytic theories in the early criticisms of horror films reinforced mainstream assertions that horror was no place for women, giving little recourse for those women who do not experience horror film consumption negatively or masochistically.

Feminist literature of the late 1980s and early 1990s began to question whether the apparent misogyny of horror films was the whole story, focusing instead on the possible "feminist" pleasures to be had for viewers within the genre. These later works employ what Stuart Hall and others call a "negotiated reading strategy," which argues that viewers, far from simply accepting or rejecting a narrative "message," can organize elements in order to constitute a meaning and use that allows them to partake in the pleasures of a given text—in this case, horror film—even as they recognize the social problems that on another level make this genre far from unproblematic.

Significantly, the majority of feminist film criticism of the horror genre is comprised of examination of Gothic horror and the slasher film. Little attention has been paid to the zombie film, a subgenre of horror that is quite different from some of these other categories. In particular, George Romero's *Dead* series has brought to the fore some interesting problems and questions for feminist critics of the horror film, suggesting that the predominant tools available for theorizing horror films (i.e., structural analysis) are insufficient to an understanding of the zombie subgenre. In fact, the development of an alternate approach may reopen analytic questions about the genre as a whole.

As a preliminary reevaluation of possible feminist approaches to horror films, I will analyze Romero's *Dead* trilogy, the genre-breaking zombie films *Night of the Living Dead, Dawn of the Dead,* and *Day of the Dead.*[2] Romero's films are a useful place to reassess feminist approaches because the zombie monster sets up an alternative film narrative structure that does not follow the same logic as classic horror films or other horror film subgenres (e.g., slasher films). Moreover, unlike most critics' assertions that the (classic) horror film reinstates the symbolic social order at the end of the film, Romero's zombies defy this narrative closure—there is no return to order in these films. By the end of the trilogy the "living dead" have outnumbered the "living."

Because Romero's zombie films defy (horror) narrative conventions, they suggest that we may want to reevaluate our assumptions about the gender/genre debate, as the "gender question" has been so central to the constantly growing body of work on the horror film. In this chapter, I will therefore explore Romero's zombie films through the feminist gender/genre debate, showing the ways in which his films provide rich textual spaces in which to consider the relationship between gender and genre, but also to suggest that his narrative solution may actually offer a more "radically democratic" vision of the gender/genre system.

Horrific Insights:
Feminist Film Criticism and the Horror Film

There have been ongoing scholarly debates among feminists about the horror film since the early 1980s. It is only recently that these debates have attempted to address issues outside the film text, looking at the horror film as cultural practice as it pertains to women. Moreover, there has been a shift in criticism over the years, from women as victims of the horror film narrative to how and why women find pleasure in horror films.

Feminist interest in the horror film seems initially to have coincided with social concerns over the impact of violence in young people's lives. Obviously, horrific imagery and literature have been in circulation for a long time, but the contemporary horror film became increasingly violent and explicit in content after the 1960s. Indeed, many critics and fans cite Romero's classic zombie film *Night of the Living Dead* as being the first of its kind to graphically depict the "gory" dismemberment of its victims; some refer to this type of film as "splatter."[3] All of these social concerns over who would subject themselves to such grotesque violence seemed to cast a shadow over the place of the female viewer. Essentialist and sexist notions about the horror genre presumed that women were neither a desirable nor a targeted audience for horror films, reinforcing the idea that the horror film industry is male-dominated terrain. Thus it is crucial to provide some review of feminist literature on horror to pay homage to some of the key moments in the evolution of debates about gender/genre and horror.

One of the earliest writers on women and horror, Linda Williams, took up Laura Mulvey's theory of the gaze by examining classic horror and "psychopathic" horror films. Williams proposes that the female spectator fears the monster because she recognizes in it her own subordinate status in patriarchal culture—they are both "freaks."[4] The woman sees her reflection mirrored back by the hideousness of the monster, and ultimately this affinity illustrates that woman's sexual difference is indeed a threat to the patriarchal social order and must be suppressed, or else "horrible" things will ensue. Thus, the female must look away in horror—her subordination is too much.

Similarly, the psychopathic horror film (e.g., *Peeping Tom*) is used to further support Williams's claim that it is the woman who does not look that is saved from death and thus survives the narrative. This reinforces the binary system for females (i.e., "good girl" vs. "bad girl"), dictating which women will be punished for looking and which will not. Therefore, according to Williams's early account, the horror film works narratively to suppress and punish women because they are a threat, inherently Other to man.

For Barbara Creed, woman is not so much *like* the monster as she *is* the monster.[5] She coins the term *monstrous-feminine*, which she examines across several horror films, paying special attention to filmic representations of the horror of the female body. The monstrous-feminine is a visual manifestation of patriarchal fears and anxieties about women's bodies and bodily functions (e.g., lactation, menstruation), identifying films such as *Aliens* and *The Brood* as narrative spaces where these patriarchal fears uncover themselves. In terms of psychoanalytic theory, she argues that this fear suggests maybe it is not women's (Freudian) *lack* that is so terrifying, but rather her ability to remove the phallus, thus reducing the patriarch to a lack as well. In short, it is the *castrating* woman that is the threat, not necessarily the *castrated* woman.

Carol Clover's work on gender and the slasher film has been widely referenced and continues to be a point of discussion for many horror film critics. Clover looks at slasher films from the 1960s and 1970s and concludes two things: women are not predominantly the victims, and almost always there is a lone woman who survives the narrative, which she dubs the "Final Girl."[6] Clover concludes that the Final Girl is a bigendered character; she changes roles during the course of the film, moving narratively from potential (female/feminine) victim to triumphant (male/masculine) hero/survivor. Similarly, Creed also suggests that it is men in horror films who are "feminized," as men are often asked to identify "with a male monster that is feminized."[7]

These types of readings assume that there are clearly demarcated lines between the genders in horror films—that is, that we can easily identify the male as victim/monster, or else the female as victim/monster, and therefore the spectator can oscillate between identificatory positions. Zombie films do not subscribe to such readily available transparencies, and in fact, Romero's films make no differentiations at all, as we will see in the next section. These female writers believe that sexual difference is at the root of horror's violence, but we should bear in mind that it is not always so explicitly laid out for us with every horror film.

Alternately, later approaches to reading horror films adopt a cultural studies perspective, heavily influenced by the early works of writers such as Hall and Annette Kuhn. This (feminist) cultural studies approach to reading film texts bears several names, which indicates their own particular theoretical heritages—such as reading the "progressive text," the "negotiated" reading, and even "resistant" reading.[8] Feminist critics utilize such textual approaches to focus on the pleasures of popular film genres for women. Traditionally, cultural studies critics theorized pleasure as a function of ideology: pleasure masks ideology and makes the audience complicit. Conversely, feminist critics have argued that pleasure is more contradictory and complex, thus triggering the move toward looking at women's popular genres, such as the soap opera. Much of this research attempts to show that pleasure can be a form of resistance to the ideological patriarchal underpinnings of a popular text. Specifically, this reader response approach allows critics to elucidate multiple readings of the horror film text, while acknowledging the role of the social audience and the female spectator in circumscribing valuation to the horror text.[9]

These criticisms often reflect on and revisit highly contested horror films, such as *Night of the Living Dead* and *Silence of the Lambs*, as feminist writers re-vision these film texts as more than one-dimensional depictions of patriarchy run amok. Instead of inciting psychoanalytic feminist film theory to explain the appeal and significance of horror films, these writers—while still relying on textual analysis—employ alternative interpretative strategies to "reread" particular films through a more positivistic lens. These rereadings further refute the notion that women are only *ever* victims in relation to violent film texts.

The emphasis in these kinds of writings is often on female pleasure and the reclamation of mass-produced genres. Feminist scholars especially narrowed in on the pleasures to be had for female viewers of women's genres, such as romance fiction (e.g., Janice Radway), often arguing that there was indeed pleasure to be had for readers of "feminine texts." In particular, fantasy and realism have been identified as sources of pleasure for female viewers.[10] Conversely, an overcelebratory focus on female pleasures of popular genres can be problematic, because when feminist scholars limit their interests to mainly "women's genres" and pleasure, they are "in danger of an essentialist reconstruction of gender and [reproducing] a stereotypical view on the gendering of the reception process."[11] I, too, share these sentiments, yet I find it curious at best, and negligent at worst, that few substantial studies have been undertaken that examine women's relationship to genres traditionally coded as "masculine," such as horror. There has been some promising scholarship in the area, such as Brigid Cherry's work on female viewers of horror and Annette Hill's on women and violent films, but there is still much that needs to be done.[12]

Most important, none of these aforementioned critics writes specifically about the zombie film. Often the zombie film will be included among a wide range of horror subgenres, like slasher films and vampire films, but I wonder, Why not the zombie film as a focus of its own? Again and again, we see feminist scholars speaking mostly about those films in which women are explicitly the narrative victim. This poses problems when adopting those same arguments for examination of the zombie film, especially Romero's *Dead* trilogy. To continually speak about "the tortured women" of horror films only serves to perpetuate and reinforce the notion that horror films are notoriously antiwoman.[13] Changes in genre conventions over time also begs the need for further discussion of these issues, especially in light of more recent horror films such as *May* and *Ginger Snaps*, whose stories center around the problems of their female characters. This is not to say that classic horror film texts are passé, but rather that, as feminists, we need to look at changes in genre in relation to broader cultural and social changes toward women. More young women than ever before embrace horror films, and I believe that the horror film is starting to reflect this as well. Thus, while feminists have written little about the zombie film per se, they have no doubt contributed a great many insights into the relationship between women and horror.

Now I would like to turn our attention to what has been said about the zombie film, complementing my review of Romero's *Dead* trilogy, in order to further illuminate my discussion of gender and genre. The way we currently approach horror films as feminist critics is not sufficient to account for films like Romero's zombie films, which are somewhat ambivalent in their treatment of the issue of gender, as everyone is capable of becoming a zombie. Indeed, zombies seem the least gender-specific creature of all horror film monsters.

Romero's *Dead* Trilogy: A Feminist Investigation

Horror films frequently have been deemed a debased or low-status genre within film, as well as within the broader popular cultural realm. While I do not have the space to get into the full extent of these debates about the cultural merit, or lack thereof, of the horror film, it must be stressed that "genre wars" are integral to the construction and maintenance of definitions of the horror film. According to Williams, horror films have often been lumped in with pornography as the lowest of the low, as both genres make visual the "excesses" of our bodies.[14] Similarly, these "body genres" have often been coded as masculine—films that are solely intended for a (sadistic) male audience. As Mark Jancovich contends, the question of genre boundaries is still a critical issue within genre studies, despite scholarly works that dispose of genre as something "modern."[15] Jancovich uncovers in his own research that the question of genre, particularly among horror film fans, is still a continually contested area as different groups debate "good/high" versus "bad/low" horror.

According to critics like Williams, the horror genre is characterized by excess, specifically, bodily excess. As well, with a "low" body genre such as this, it is assumed that the audience mimics the screen body, and depending on how well it provokes real bodily response will determine how successful the film is according to genre conventions.[16] Moreover, the horror film is preoccupied with issues of sexual difference and sexual identity, but as Williams suggests, genres such as the horror film cannot always be seen or dismissed as "evidence of monolithic and unchanging misogyny."[17] Indeed, genres thrive on both the problems they address and the ways in which they attempt to deal with those problems. They are not always passively perpetuating or celebrating problems between men and women, but at times actively or not so actively create alternative visions of gender relations. Here I would reiterate that Romero's zombie films actively attempt to address broader social and cultural dilemmas, including gender (issues). As both a fan and a critic, I find it quite interesting that Romero chose the zombie as the primary creature from which to tell his stories and to depict his apocalyptic visions.

Critics and fans have credited Romero with changing the face of the zombie film from the earlier renditions of voodoo-inspired tales of the living dead and creating the splatter film.[18] Romero's zombies envision a whole different take on the living dead, monsters more "human" (yet not) than ever seen before—creatures who feed on the flesh of the living.

There is a strange evolution that takes place over the course of the first three *Dead* films. Romero has stated in past interviews that, through his zombie films, he was attempting to construct a New World Order, one that would come to be ruled by the living dead.[19] Indeed, the fourth installment, *Land of the Dead*, visualizes a world completely run by zombies. By *Day*, we see that the zombies are beginning to come to some kind of consciousness with Bub, a zombie kept by Logan ("Dr. Frankenstein"), who is trying to prove that they do have memory and memories. There is an extremely unsettling moment in the film where Bub is interacting with some cultural artifacts (a toothbrush, a razor, and a copy of Stephen King's *Salem's Lot*) and we see pangs of recognition overcoming his zombified face—an odd moment, surely, in a film where people are trying to protect themselves from these flesh-eaters, yet here the audience is compelled to feel something other than disdain or horror for these creatures.

There is another, similar compelling moment with Fran in *Dawn*. We find Fran inside the department store, guarding the glass; all the while, a zombie stands right outside in front of her. Fran seems to have a "moment" with the zombie, and you really wonder what she is thinking. She almost seems to sigh, like she feels something for the zombie. Or maybe she is just sighing with exasperation. It is moments like these that point to the uneasiness of the viewer, between fear and sympathy for these cannibals functioning on "instinct." The audience must share in the burden of uncertainty and anxiety presented by the zombies.

Romero makes it more and more difficult with each *Dead* film to feel disgust or pleasure in watching bodies ripped open and torn inside-out, despite the fact that with each film there is more explicit and gory zombie violence. There is a sense by *Day* that it is not only about zombies taking over the world but also about them taking over the narrative. It is like they come to saturate the narrative to such an extent with their all-encompassing pres-ence—there are just so many—that it becomes inescapable even for the viewer. There is nowhere for any of us to go. And if there is ultimately nowhere to escape to, then we must accept or submit to this figurative can-nibalism. There is simply no way that we are left with any kind of narrative reconciliation, which seems counter to the finale of most trilogies, wherein all the loose ends and worries of the previous films are dealt with and drawn to a close. Romero's *Dead* films harbor contradictions like these for both the viewer and the characters within the film, and it is these contradictions that make the question of gender one worth discussing.

With regard to gender, there is no question that Romero refrains from nar-ratively victimizing any of his female characters in the *Dead* trilogy. Indeed, the lead female characters in both *Dawn* and *Day* survive the end of the film, but Barbara in the original *Night* does not (although it is worth noting that the black male character Ben survives the narrative).[20] Barry Keith Grant has addressed Romero's cinematic treatment of gender representation(s) in a comparative piece on *Night* (both the original and the remake), in which he suggests that Barbara's ability to survive in the *Night* remake and to enact agency within the diegesis of the film indicates Romero's empathy toward women. In fact, Grant argues that Romero is empathetic to all his female characters in the *Dead* trilogy, whereas his male counterparts tend to be writ-ten as inadequate and idiotic.[21] Grant states that "the new *Night*, then, at-tempts to reclaim the horror genre for feminism, and for all those female vic-tims in such movies who attempt to resist patriarchal containment."[22]

While I do not totally embrace Grant's sentiments, I do not eschew them altogether, either. On the one hand, I agree that the presence of strong fe-male characters are important in mainstream film genres, but on the other hand, I do not think that merely inverting gender roles is exactly the answer female viewers are seeking. Moreover, who is to say that the original Barbara is a totally negative image of womanhood for women?

I see Barbara One, if you will, as symbolic of everything that is wrong with patriarchy and male-defined notions of femininity and womanhood. She is reminiscent of Catherine Deneuve's character in Roman Polanski's *Repul-sion*; at some point, both women become catatonic, as they find themselves increasingly unable to deal with their respective situations. As well, neither character survives the end of the film, suggesting that the "good girl" is not always exempt from a violent or even cannibalistic demise. Indeed, the as-sertion that so many feminist critics make about the narrative treatment of good girls versus bad ones does not hold any weight with these visual texts.

It is ultimately the symbol of patriarchy that destroys Barbara One, as she is unable to distinguish between living Johnny and zombified Johnny, and her lack of participation and awareness in the face of danger (i.e., behaving in ways appropriate to her gender) ultimately causes her death. Therefore, in the face of zombification, patriarchy in terms of its ideology and political domination is essentially useless, despite Barbara Two's narrative transition to hero. Her "status" does not force us to question as much as the destruction of Barbara One does, because the original film disrupts any fixed notions we have about women (in film), as one by one each archetypal female figure and what she represents is annihilated (i.e., "wife/mother," "virgin," "good girl," "daddy's girl," and "lover").

In terms of gender and genre, it would be easy to take the position that Romero's films are so clearly empathetic to women because they are progressive, or female-friendly, and therefore feminist. But it goes beyond that. His zombies do something quite different. It is their presence in the films that enable his female characters to be so demonstrably aggressive and unapologetic. In *Dawn*, once the men find out that Fran is pregnant, there is considerable change in their behavior toward her—a chauvinistic attitude that seems oddly out of place and somewhat ridiculous in light of the circumstances surrounding them. Fran questions the men and thereby patriarchal definitions of femininity, telling the men:

> I'm sorry you found out I'm pregnant because I don't want to be treated any differently than you treat each other . . . and I'm not going to be den mother for you guys and I want to know what's going on, and I want to have something to say about the plans. There's four of us okay?

Fran also insists on learning how to fly the helicopter, which comes in handy when she becomes the only person able to escape (besides Peter, again the only black male lead character).

It seems that the construction of a zombie narrative calls into question everything we ever believed in, everything we ever thought to be true about the Other, whether a racialized or gendered Other. Therefore, the zombie narrative in particular makes possible alternative visions of femininity, opening up spaces for the female viewer that do not rely significantly on gender stereotypes that anticipate the passivity or masochism of the female viewer.

American film scholar Robin Wood argues that the zombie film specifically exposes and attempts to destroy what the horror genre embodies.[23] For Wood, the zombies take issue with the dominant social structures: the family, capitalism, and patriarchy. The specificity of these attacks is of great interest, as well—in each film, we find the living taking refuge in very gendered spaces: first the home, then the shopping mall, and last in a bunker that appears to be a masculinized space due to the overwhelming occupation of "science" (i.e., Dr. Logan) and the military.

For example, Romero's decision to set the story of *Dawn* within the confines of an abandoned shopping mall is still interesting to viewers and critics to this day. In a way, the mall setting allowed Romero to be quite critical (if campy at times) of gender relations. It is a contradictory space, where male and female are clearly designated through department store layouts (i.e., "men's clothing," "women's clothing"). The four characters attempt to live a "normal" life under the constant threat of zombie annihilation. They even go so far as to "set up house" after Roger's death. But it all seems so artificial and pointless. This becomes quite clear when Stephen proposes to Fran at a make-believe romantic restaurant dinner, and she says, "We can't. . . . Wouldn't be real." Zombie apocalypse makes everything devoid of meaning, yet the living are not absolved of responsibility or complicity. As Fran so poignantly remarks, "What have we done to ourselves?" One is compelled to wonder, What *have* we done to ourselves?

The gendering of these spaces and places is of no consequence for the zombies, though, as their cannibalistic drives sweep over the cultural landscape. Admittedly, I am rather drawn to these destructive images; I feel that there is something to be said for the complete destruction and utter ignorance of the zombies toward these places. Indeed, the more I watch *Night* and *Dawn*, the more I find something quite exhilarating and, dare I say, empowering in the abolishment of home and consumer culture. Even money no longer has any meaning; it is simply paper, a reminder of days gone by. Despite these self-indulgences, the question remains: What does Romero's apocalyptic vision mean for the viewer? Furthermore, in what way does the *Dead* trilogy open up "democratic" or pleasurable spaces for feminist viewers? Finally, how might these cinematic treatments of the body relate to issues of gender/genre?

Genderless Bodies, Genderless Spectators?
Romero's Genre Apocalypse

The question of pleasure and spectatorship is an interesting one for the viewer of the zombie film. The exploration of the two as they relate to the body have intriguing consequences for the study of gender and genre, because zombies are essentially expressions of the uncontrollable body. As

Patrick Fuery asks of the body in cinema, "In what ways is it *uncontrollable?*"[24] Indeed, as the last section revealed, zombies come to take over the narrative as well as Romero's filmic world. Romero's films leave the spectator completely anxiety-ridden (or bored?), providing little opportunity to rejoice in Ben's survival in *Night*, or Sarah's escape from full zombie takeover in *Day*. Pleasure resides in the utter avowal of chaos, and in the uncertainty of the zombie landscape.

As Steven Shaviro comments, "Our anxieties are focused upon events rather than characters, upon the violent fragmentation of cinematic process rather than the supposed integrity of any single protagonist's subjectivity."[25] Thus, if we are to address the question of gender, this might suggest that Romero's films refute any notion of a "gendered gaze," if, as Shaviro's remarks suggest, we are incapable of really taking up any standpoint or any point of identification. This destabilization and categorical meltdown is exacerbated by the zombies' presence, pulling our attention away again and again from the living, as they steal the spotlight and delight us in their total disregard for humanity. We are discouraged from becoming too attached or concerned with any protagonist's identity or cinematic treatment when they stand to be expelled at any moment. Why invest anything then? Viewer attention is directed toward survival above and beyond categories of gender or race, because once abjectified, identification is dissolved and spectatorial neutrality comes into play. Thus, it can be contested to what degree the viewer can identify with anything or anyone. As Tania Modleski suggests, the horror film elicits a kind of "antinarcissistic identification" as we take pleasure in the destruction of the very thing we support.[26]

Using my own viewing experiences and attraction to the zombie film may provide a textual place from which we may begin theorizing this viewing position, thus shedding some light on the complexities and disjuncture between gender and genre. The process of cannibalism resonates within the film, as well with the position of the viewer. Following the trajectory of the zombie narrative, "I" too would not be exempt from processes of cannibalism, due to my simultaneous feelings of fear and fascination. It is in this state of spectatorial ambivalence that I find a *democratic textual viewing space*, in which I am able to question things, even as I recognize my own complicity with social inequities. I can see myself in the zombies, as I too yearn for destruction of everything I know, yet part of me fears the apocalypse and what this destruction may bring forth.

Zombie cannibalism serves to provide me with a space to revel in the unthinkable, in the undesirable, in the unspoken—a place where my body, as a thing, and not necessarily as a *gendered* body, is so evidently vulnerable. Romero's zombie films enable me to imagine revolution outside the context of my oppression, the things that always remind me of my Other status—breasts, hips, and so on, in short, my femininity. I can take pleasure in my own destruction safely, and from a distance. Zombification is not about hunting me (Woman) down and killing me. It is not about using my body as a metaphor for pain, or for politics, either. The zombie desire for flesh is beyond me; many say it is something so primal, so abject. It reflects back to me my own cannibalistic desire for images—any images that express something other than hatred of women. It is my own passion for consuming those images that brings me back to the horror.

Ironically then, the viewing position I take up in relation to the zombie spectacle is ultimately one of self-annihilation as I participate in my own ideological destruction as Woman and Feminist, because these categories are meaningless when confronted with zombie invasion. Thus, the pleasure I derive from viewing Romero's *Dead* films is like embracing my own abjection; it is the pleasure of seeing myself (ourselves) turned inside out. Shaviro also comments on the viewer's relation to Romero's zombie films, as I share many of his visceral reactions and emotional responses: "I find myself giving in to an insidious, hidden, deeply shameful passion for abject self-annihilation."[27] This "shameful passion" that Shaviro speaks of is exacerbated by the narrative structure and plot formation of Romero's *Dead* films.

These images force a recognition and awareness of the body that is often denied in patriarchal classic-liberalist rationality, which asks us to deny the body pleasure, or to separate bodily pleasure from mental pleasure.[28] One of the contributions of Shaviro's work is the way in which his zombie article values the relationship between the mind and the body, forcing the reader to acknowledge the importance of the body while watching film. Even as we pretend to ignore it while engrossed in the zombified bodies on-screen, our very bodies are expressing a reaction to these images. Indeed, his unapologetic visceral reactions defy modernist sensibilities about "bodily correctness" and have implications for both male and female viewers. The zombie film restores pleasure to the female viewer through the zombie's ambivalence toward gender (and genre), while the male viewer has a space opened up for him that allows for a relationship to the body that may not otherwise be realized with other kinds of horror films. The eating of flesh is beyond male or female, though—it seems beyond human. Thus, the function of the zombie film as a genre does not seem contingent upon reinvoking gender binaries, or boundaries, for that matter. Binaries are subject to annihilation in the zombie film;

distinctions such as good/bad, black/white, man/woman, body/mind, and so on are not easily identified in the zombie creature, and these categories become increasingly futile.

The new world order that Romero has created with the *Dead* trilogy makes the maintenance and struggle for the old world order (i.e., capitalist patriarchy) problematic and even undesirable, and by implication makes the maintenance of certain (horror) genre conventions outmoded. Therefore, feminist extractions about gender premised on genre are insufficient, as subgenres critique prevailing genre codes, making generalizations of any kind about horror or its female viewing audience problematic. Cannibalizing gender and genre may ignite much needed change, and further the study of women and horror films in new and exciting ways.

Conclusion

As I have demonstrated, the ambivalence of Romero's *Dead* trilogy to gender and genre begs the need for newer and alternative frameworks for feminist examinations of horror and its female audiences. The two main approaches to studying gender and genre have come from psychoanalytic feminist film theory and within feminist cultural studies. While both fields employ very different models for looking at the issue of women and horror filmdom, both have tended to reinforce stereotypical views about women's viewing habits. As well, feminist writers have tended to focus on particular eras or genre cycles of horror (e.g., 1970s slasher films). A continual preoccupation with these subsets of horror film comes at the expense of other interesting and intriguing films, particularly the zombie film.

These particular zombie films open up narrative and visual spaces that create genderless identificatory viewing positions. Thus it seems that the need to seamlessly align gender with genre (e.g., feminine texts with female viewers) is somewhat problematic, pointing to the need to dismantle gender/genre frameworks in favor of more open-ended models. This is not to say that, as feminist critics, we should dismiss gender/genre systems altogether, but rather that the "system" is much more contradictory and complex than previous analyses sought to prove or demonstrated. Romero's zombie films offer one such textual space from which feminist critics may begin to rethink our understandings of gender and genre, by offering up a viewing space that deconstructs gender through cannibalism. Indeed, these films can be reclaimed for feminism, as they offer feminists another way to think about the complexities of film viewing for women and call into question tensions over politics and genre tastes (i.e., fan cultures). These tensions cannot be easily answered by assuming that certain genres revolve in "feminine" orbits and others in "masculine" ones.

This rereading/re-vision does, however, beg the need for further theorizing of, and empirical research on, "actual" audiences, particularly female audiences of horror. As Philippe Meers points out, studying audiences has not been an easily defined field of study.[29] Indeed, audience research has remained a largely speculative area of research, straying little from its intellectual and theoretical moorings. Yet these early debates are important, as contestations over theory and analysis have contributed to an interesting and dynamic area of study. Moreover, it is necessary and crucial to the vitality of feminist studies of gender and genre to utilize varying discourses and methodologies, as studies of women and film are not confined to one discipline or community. By looking at audiences' affinities for certain subgenres of popular genres, we may be able to get a better idea of how genre interacts with gender, rather than trying to generalize gender through genre.

Notes

1. As Annette Kuhn writes: "It might be argued that the *options* on offer to spectators in cinema are basically either to take up a masochistic subject position as . . . is proposed by the huge number of films in which the enunciating instance is male/masculine; or to submit to a masochism of over-identification, as is evoked, for example, by the Hollywood 'woman's genre'"; Annette Kuhn, "The Body and Cinema: Some Problems for Feminism," in *Grafts: Feminist Cultural Criticism*, ed. Susan Sheridan (London: Verso, 1988), 15.

2. *Editors' note:* At the time of this writing, *Land of the Dead* was just being released.

3. Michael Arnzen, "Who's Laughing Now? The Postmodern Splatter Film," *Journal of Popular Film and Television* 21, no. 4 (1994): 176–85.

4. Linda Williams, "When the Woman Looks," in *Re-Vision: Essays in Feminist Film Criticism*, ed. Maryanne Doane, Patricia Mellencamp, and Linda Williams (Los Angeles: University Publications of America, 1984), 67–82.

5. Barbara Creed, *The Monstrous-Feminine: Film, Feminism, Psychoanalysis* (New York: Routledge, 1993).

6. Carol J. Clover, *Men, Women and Chainsaws: Gender in the Modern Horror Film* (Princeton, NJ: Princeton University Press, 1992), 77.

7. Creed, *Monstrous-Feminine*, 156.

8. Yvonne Tasker, "Having It All: Feminism and the Pleasures of the Popular," in *Off-Centre: Feminism and Cultural Studies*, ed. Sarah Franklin, Celia Lury, and Jackie Stacey (London: HarperCollins Academic, 1991), 90.

9. Sarah Trencansky, "Final Girls and Terrible Youth: Transgression in 1980s Slasher Horror," *Journal of Popular Film and Television* 29, no. 2 (2001): 63–73; Barry Keith Grant, "Taking Back the *Night of the Living Dead*: George Romero, Feminism, and the Horror Film," in *The Dread of Difference: Gender and the Horror Film*, ed. Barry Keith Grant (Austin: University of Texas Press, 1996), 200–212.

10. Barbara O'Connor and Elisabeth Klaus, "Pleasure and Meaningful Discourse: An Overview of Research Issues," *International Journal of Cultural Studies* 3, no. 3 (2001): 380.

11. O'Connor and Klaus, "Pleasure," 380.

12. Brigid Cherry, "Refusing to Refuse to Look: Female Viewers of the Horror Film," in *Identifying Hollywood's Audiences*, ed. Melvyn Stokes and Richard Maltby (London: British Film Institute, 1999), 187–203; Annette Hill, "'Looks Like It Hurts': Women's Responses to Shocking Entertainment," in *Ill Effects: The Media/ Violence Debate*, 2nd ed., ed. Martin Barker and Julian Petley (New York: Routledge, 2001), 135–49.

13. Linda Williams, "Film Bodies: Gender, Genre, and Excess," in *Feminist Film Theory: A Reader*, ed. Sue Thornham (New York: New York University Press, 1999), 272.

14. Williams, "Film Bodies."

15. Mark Jancovich, "'A Real Shocker': Authenticity, Genre and the Struggle for Distinction," in *The Film Cultures Reader*, ed. Graeme Turner (New York: Routledge, 2002), 469–80.

16. Williams, "Film Bodies," 270.

17. Williams, "Film Bodies," 280.

18. See Steven Beard, "No Particular Place to Go," *Sight and Sound* 3, no. 4 (1993): 30; Arnzen, "Who's Laughing Now?" When questioned by Rod Gudino, in the July/August 2003 issue of *Rue Morgue* magazine, about whether he was responsible for splatter films, Romero said, "I don't remember coining that term. . . . I'm pretty sure it was around."

19. In a 1975 interview with Dan Yakir of *Film Comment*, Romero explained that the zombie trilogy was a story dealing with a "new world order" represented through the formation of a "zombie take over."

20. The only black character in the film, Ben is also the strongest, the smartest, and the most efficient in warding off the zombie attack on the house. Much work needs to be done in the area of race and horror, and to my knowledge, it is still a largely absent area of study.

21. Grant, "Taking Back the *Night*," 206–7.

22. Grant, "Taking Back the *Night*," 210.

23. Robin Wood, *Hollywood from Vietnam to Reagan* (New York: Columbia University Press, 1986), 115.

24. Patrick Fuery, *New Developments in Film Theory* (New York: St. Martin's, 2000), 72.

25. Steven Shaviro, *The Cinematic Body* (Minneapolis: University of Minnesota Press, 1993), 91.

26. Tania Modleski, "The Terror of Pleasure: The Contemporary Horror Film and Postmodern Theory," in *The Film Cultures Reader*, ed. Graeme Turner (New York: Routledge, 2002), 272.

27. Shaviro, *Cinematic Body*, 103.

28. See Modleski, "Terror of Pleasure."

29. Philippe Meers, "Is There an Audience in the House? New Research Perspectives on (European) Film Audiences," *Journal of Popular Film and Television* 29, no. 3 (2001): 138–44.

~

CHAPTER EIGHT

Hybridity and Post-Human Anxiety in *28 Days Later*

Martin Rogers

Le mort saisit le vif!

—Karl Marx

See the movies from the point of view of the disease.

—David Cronenberg

We live in a post-human age. Our traditional ideas about the relationship between the human body and human consciousness have been redefined through advances in a variety of technologies. Elaine L. Graham is one of many contemporary critics who uses the term *post-human* to describe these advances in science and culture, including the technologization of nature (via genetic manipulation/modification, digital models of living systems, etc.), the blurring of species boundaries (via new reproductive technologies and advances in cloning), the technologization of the human body (via implants and microchip integration), and the creation of new personal and social worlds (via virtual/electronic spaces, communities, and identities).[1] These changes, argues Graham, produce a "widespread anxiety about the diminishment of uniqueness in the face of new technologies" and can best be understood through their visualization in popular films.[2] As an illustration, Graham offers David Cronenberg's *eXistenZ*, which, she claims, appears to be a science-fiction thriller but is "perhaps better viewed as a horror film for the digital and biotechnological age."[3]

The split identity of *eXistenZ*—apparently a science-fiction text but perhaps something more horrific—is not unique in its generic ambiguity.[4] In the world of genre criticism, it is often difficult to distinguish between horror and science-fiction films. Furthermore, critics of both generic camps often claim sovereignty over certain films that fulfill the requirements of either one. For instance, films like Ridley Scott's *Alien* and Danny Boyle's *28 Days Later* become narrative sites claimed by both genres. Boyle's apocalypse film in fact exemplifies this hybrid or "cross-pollinated" genre.[5]

And while we bicker over terms, it should be mentioned that the word *zombie* never appears in Boyle's film, although that does not stop George Romero's *Night of the Living Dead* (which also omits the term) from being conceived as a zombie film. Nevertheless, Boyle's "infected" perform the role of the zombie in recognizable patterns.

28 Days Later appropriates a conventional horror scenario—the zombie film—to explore the aftereffects of personal and physical trauma and the various drives such traumas provoke, namely, the desire to consume and the desire to reproduce. The desires or drives coincide on-screen with anxieties and conflicts that arise from physical trauma—disgust with the body and suspicion of its "fluid" productions. However, *28 Days Later* "embodies" these fears not in a conventional mode of transmission—the "zombie"—but in an altogether different kind of host: the "infected."[6] By applying the medicinal/scientific term rather than the monstrous one, *28 Days Later* modifies the traditional concern of the horror film over human bodies and their vulnerable processes into a concern over disembodiment and the transference of virulent reprogramming via the human information stream. By examining *28 Days Later* as a zombie film (and therefore a subgenre film subordinated to horror) and a representative hybrid of science fiction and horror (subordinated to both), I hope to demonstrate that the dissolution of generic boundaries of content and structure mirrors our shifting and anxious conceptions of human embodiment in the post-human age.

Substrates and Subgenres

The term *post-human* derives from the fields of cybernetics, artificial intelligence (AI), genetic research, and indeed almost all contemporary biological sciences. Post-human can be taken, quite literally, to mean "after human": a point when humans are in immediate danger of becoming extinct or obsolete in favor of superhuman biological species or mechanically created yet self-replicating "artificial" life-forms. *Post-human* and the condition or "era" that term describes can generally be viewed as science fiction turned actual science—that is, the scientific *fictions* of cyborgs, AI, and genetic manipulation, which were often a cause of great anxiety in the so-called golden age of sci-fi, have become science *fact*.

Of course, this anxiety over man–machine symbiosis is not new—it is something of a tradition that has existed in the great philosophical discussions of the last two hundred or so years since the Industrial Revolution and the advent of "modern" warfare. Both modernism and futurism have previously engaged the tenuous relationship between man and machine, and the dehumanizing effect of machinery on the landscape, on art, on systems of power and control, on industry, and on the human body itself. Should the current post-human condition come to be called a revolution, then the roots of this evolution would be far-reaching and interdisciplinary.

It is a different revolution—the so-called Information Revolution—that turned this scientific and philosophical discourse in the direction we now call post-human. Some scholars trace the origin of this current phase of the man/machine dialectic to the essay "The Technological Society" by Jacques Ellul; the theoretical work of Jürgen Habermas, as well as that of Francis Fukuyama, is also a part of this technocultural critique.

The term *post-human* is an evolved version of the *cyborg*, a hybrid life-form both biological and mechanical. *Cybernetic* has also come to describe a certain epistemology or method of reading, often related to science-fiction studies, but also in social and cultural studies as a whole; the post-human "movement" has been characterized by Donna Haraway in her book *Simians, Cyborgs, and Women* as operating at the point or from the space of the "boundary breakdowns between animal and human, organism and machine, and the physical and non-physical."[7]

The cyborg is no longer only the stuff of science fiction, of course; researchers around the globe have already experimented with microchip implants and other electronic augmentation of the human body—the pacemaker, an electronic device to regulate the heart, stands as an early example of such augmentation. A professor of cybernetics at the University of Reading, Kevin Warwick, sees these biological amplifications and implants as the key to human enlightenment, immortality, and evolution: "Linking people via chip implants directly to [supercomputers] seems a natural progression. . . . Otherwise, we're doomed to a future in which intelligent machines rule and humans become second class citizens."[8] Warwick's either/or scenario indeed sounds as if it came from the script of a late 1970s or early 1980s science-fiction film, but he is, quite literally, walking the walk: as of 2002, he had had microchips implanted into his left arm twice, the first time in 1998 (removing that chip after nine days of experiments with it) and again in 2002. The chips communicated directly via radio waves with a computer network in his Reading labs. He has stated that his next goal is to have a chip implanted directly into his brain. Warwick sees this technologically accelerated evolution as a way to set the human conscious free of the limitations of the biological: "I was born human," Warwick has stated, "But this was an accident of fate. . . . I believe this is something we have the power to change."[9]

In this respect, Graham's assertion that the post-human condition is manifest in popular film appears most evident. Indeed, zombie films exemplify these fantasies of disembodiment because their generic identity is so slippery: they look very much like a horror film but are often motivated by anxieties over science and technology. Though zombie "flicks" are considered a subgenre of horror, they often feature science-fictional elements—visualizing both reawakened graveyards and "radiation from the Venus space probe" à la *Night of the Living Dead*. The cause of the walking dead often turns out to be scientific in nature.[10] Zombie plagues erupt as chaos both social and personal, a trespass of science that affects the individual as well as the communal body.

Perhaps, however, the generic confusions that plague zombie films are a result of the more systemic confusions between the genres of horror and science fiction.[11] Films such as the seminal *Alien*, the regrettable *X-tro*, and Cronenberg's generic deviant *Videodrome* make any clean differentiation between horror and science fiction, well, *messy*. The editors of the journal *Sight and Sound*, for instance, have recently released a collection of essays simply titled *Science Fiction/Horror*, which includes essays on genre-benders like *Alien* as well as more controversial selections (e.g., *Fight Club* and *It's a Wonderful Life*). Kim Newman, the editor of the anthology, claims that the aim of the collection is to

> move away from topicality, towards the controversial pantheon-building necessary as an adjunct to the map-making impulse that drives us to draw boundaries of genres or compose Venn diagrams that allow for such subsets as the science fiction horror movie . . . or the teenage postmodern slasher picture.[12]

Newman goes on to speculate that, since the two genres are often considered together, that the science-fiction "establishment" feels disrespected by such "Siamese twinning":

> Sci-fi writers and filmmakers like to think of themselves with their eyes on the stars, alive to the possibilities of science and exploration. . . . Meanwhile, the

misshapen lump of the horror genre clings to their backs, dragging them down into a neurotic morass of doubts and fears . . . intent on seeing decay and collapse and death to the exclusion of rationality, progress and credibility.[13]

Vivian Sobchack, in her seminal *Screening Space: The American Science Fiction Film*, identifies the site of this twinning: "The films which most typify what is considered by some to be the 'miscegenation' of the two genres are what we commonly call the Monster or Creature film."[14] Sobchack goes on to differentiate between the cold and impersonal Creature of science fiction and the sympathetic and fascinatingly libidinal Monster.[15]

The important item to note in these two critics is their insistence on this connection being discussed as embodied, and monstrously so: the intersection between the genres is figured in terms of blood (miscegenation), reproduction (conjoined twins), and virulence (the cancerous "lump" on the back of science fiction).

So an intersection between the two genres, though easily spotted, is often explained away by observations like Sobchack's or by emphasizing the hybridity that has come to mark the postmodern condition. For our purposes, I would like to emphasize not only this hybridity but also the idea that a genre can somehow adapt or assimilate the conventions of another genre to accomplish its particular narrative goals—that is, to successfully execute its generic programs. This position can bring to light the particular habit of science fiction to (almost) seamlessly integrate other generic substrates into its narrative modus operandi. Horror and science fiction—both concerned with the body—have managed to treat these particular concerns as information that cannot be entirely separated from its typical generic substrates. One cannot simply remove the data from the medium in which they are carried, though perhaps those data can be translated; there is no such thing as "pure information." And in this respect, we should not expect to have "pure" genre films either, though film genres exist as a sort of social contract between the film makers and the audience wherein adherence to certain generic conventions is at least implied.[16]

Concerns over embodiment nevertheless seem to be registered in both horror and science fiction—making their hybridization necessary rather than aesthetically pleasing or satisfying. It is the peculiar nature of the science-fiction film to assimilate other genres to accomplish its goals, providing itself as an example of one of its own typical visualizations: the assimilating hive or collective that augments its body (or bodies) through cybernetic amplification. The "future noir" of *Blade Runner* or the gunfighting robots of *Westworld* offer particularly salient examples. Much like the

Borg from *Star Trek*, science fiction assimilates other genres—including, very often, horror—into its genetic makeup. The horror/science-fiction hybrid has proven to be a rather successful specimen.

This term—*hybridity*—is apt because it not only seems to evoke the conventional topic matter of both genres and their intersection (hybrid machines, hybrid mutations/half-breeds, hybrid "super species," etc.) but also draws on a genetic metaphor, one involving the *chimera*: a genetic hybrid organism and, of course, the multiple-headed monster of Classical myth and philosophical dilemma. The science-fiction/horror hybrid chimerically stands guard over those liminal spaces between rationality and irrationality (human vs. creature) and between control and chaos (man vs. monster).[17]

But the hybrid often manifests as a subgenre of science fiction, just as the zombie film is considered a subgenre of horror films. The zombie film appeals to audiences because it visualizes many instinctual anxieties and social conflicts through the exhibition of animated corpses: death, corporeality, mechanization, the supernatural, and science, among others. In this way, the zombie film is a chimerical subgenre: both in the genetic sense of the word *chimera* (a hybrid organism) and in the mythological form of the monstrous chimera: zombie films hybridize science fiction (technological anxiety), horror (body anxiety), and paranoia (social or individualistic anxiety). So one problem is to address just what the anxieties of *28 Days Later* are, where its ideological tensions resonate. These anxieties are perhaps better served with a discussion of their alleged source—that is, the audience who would be drawn to such sci-fi horror. The computer-identified post-human subject is the core of this spectatorship.

Digital Fantasy and Data Made Flesh

In *How We Became Posthuman*, N. Katherine Hayles discusses the literary, theoretic, historic, and scientific senses of the phrase *post-human*.[18] The post-human subject, according to Hayles, "is an amalgam, a collection of heterogeneous components, a material informational entity whose boundaries undergo continuous construction and reconstruction."[19] This "point of view" is characterized by certain assumptions: the post-human privileges informational patterns over material instantiation; embodiment in a biological substrate is seen as an accident of history rather than an inevitability of life; consciousness is an "epiphenomenon" of human of information and life and is "an evolutionary upstart trying to claim that it is the whole show when in actuality it is only a minor sideshow."[20] The view is further characterized by an understanding of the body as the "original prosthesis we all learn to manipulate," and augmenting the body with other prostheses appears as "a continuation of a process that began before we were born." Finally, the post-human being is configured to be "seamlessly articulated" with intelligent machines.[21]

28 Days Later appears to be a text that appeals to all or most of these criteria, though its screen image is not populated with intelligent machines or cybernetic assassins. *28 Days Later* does not explicitly seem to visualize cybernetic organisms, though we can perhaps give in to the temptation to read the images of Jim, naked and connected to intravenous devices, as a depiction of this seamless augmentation. Such intravenous drip systems are machines, and no matter how simple they appear, they are in fact a wondrous technology of intercession, allowing doctors to "jack in" to a formerly closed portion of the circulatory system and manipulate the information it transports—blood and its various components. Jim "wakes up" to this state, perhaps visualizing the anxiety over this form of emergence into post-humanism, or perhaps into its wonder. The seamlessly articulated human subject will in fact exist in a world quite different than its previous physical environments, and this will be the source of great terror—or pleasure.

The subtle encoding of the film's events and mise-en-scène in this post-human view needs some unpacking, but ultimately shows the film to be more fully integrated into this worldview than perhaps the robotic fantasies of *The Matrix* or perhaps *Terminator*, which might otherwise seem to be obvious examples of the phenomenon. For instance, Graham uses the films *Terminator*, *Blade Runner*, and the AI of the television series *Star Trek: The Next Generation* as examples of the cinematic post-human; Hayles concentrates on the dystopian fiction of Bernard Wolfe (*Limbo*, 1952) and Phillip K. Dick (*The Simulacra*, 1964; *Do Androids Dream of Electric Sheep?*, 1968). The plot of *28 Days Later* may not overtly deal with the post-human subject or a post-human audience, but the film betrays its post-human orientation in the desire of the survivors, whose struggles to meet basic human drives are entangled with new drives that are more complex.

28 Days Later grounds the zombie apocalypse scenario in the viewer's reality by visualizing the characters as being in a realistic world: modern-day London and Manchester, specifically. The film accomplishes this by demonstrating the physical needs of the survivors (the uninfected). For instance, a great deal of screen time concerns the acquisition of basic biological needs— food and shelter. When Jim first awakens in the hospital, he comes upon a soda machine that has ejected cans of soft drinks and the like. He takes several of these and puts them in a bag to take with him, obviously aware that he will be forced to "fend for himself." While he walks along the streets of London, he also picks up pound notes that blow by (although they are now useless) and stashes them as well. Selena carries with her cans of Pepsi and candy bars—as well as painkillers and other pharmaceutical booty. More than simple product placement shots, these meager, "technologized" provisions realistically demonstrate the instinctual drive for nourishment and highlight the difficulty in achieving these needs in a social collapse: the fantasy of eating candy and junk food without moderation couples with the nightmarish reality that these substances will not, in fact, keep a human body alive in any productive way—as Jim's near-collapse on the stairwell at Frank's flat demonstrates.

The scene in the abandoned grocery store further emphasizes this conflict of drives: the survivors take a break from terror and flight to frolic in a grocery store, hoarding provisions without paying for them. But the reality of food acquisition is again brought to the forefront, as Jim and the others are simultaneously faced with an abundance of luxuries (e.g., rows of single-malt Scotch) but also with bins of rotten fruit. Once again, the pleasure of plentitude must coincide on-screen with the terror of decay and famine, a strange combination of visualizations echoed in the shots of the formerly congested city of London that is now a plentitude of open space—though decaying bodies and scraps of paper litter the streets.

But equally important to the search for food is *information*, clearly a valuable commodity for the subjects of an "information society." Jim begs Selena and Marc, when they rescue him, to tell him "what's going on," to feed him back into the informational loop. This desire is also visualized at the first site of catastrophe Jim experiences, the kiosk in downtown London where survivors have posted fliers searching for their missing loved ones. After all, it is information—*data*—that started the apocalypse in the first place, as the chimps who have been infected with rage have been so in an effort to "understand" the virus: they are living information stores, or as William Gibson puts it in *Neuromancer*, "data made flesh."[22]

The insidious mirror image to the chimpanzee test subjects is Major West's own test subject, Mailer, the infected soldier who has been chained down and contained to be observed by the soldiers. West explains that Mailer will provide important answers to the behavior of the infected—among them, how long it takes for the infected to starve. The formerly "human" entity is refigured as living information. This experimentation is not unlike the training of the zombie Bub by the mad scientist Dr. Logan in Romero's *Day of the Dead*. The difference here is that West's experiment will end simply with data, while Logan's taming of Bub is an attempt to "rehumanize" the animated corpse. Mailer functions here as a kind of modeling program, making the body the data, while Bub represents the desire to put the "human" back into the "body."

Obviously, the drive to procreate in the face of species survival appears in the film as well: Major West's "answer to infection" is to promise his soldiers women with which to breed. This drive functions on-screen as a source of horror (in the threat of rape) as the troglodyte soldiers fight over the bodies of Selena and Hannah. Earlier in the film, Selena sarcastically asks Jim if his plan for survival is to "fall in love and fuck," further devaluing the procreative drive in the economy of the film.

The horror of the rage virus, aside from the physical violence enacted upon the survivors by the infected, is its ability to quickly replicate and travel—to reproduce. Clearly, biological reproduction is problematic in the economy of *28 Days Later*; while Jim and Selena rather happily integrate into Frank and Hannah's "family" (Jim, waking from a dream, calls Frank "Dad"), the system of the family unit has clearly undergone a change. What is important is the system itself, not the biological creation of one. The system Jim and Selena integrate into is not so much a family as a *network*, a social unit of interdependence and connectivity.

Jim's own family network provides one of the more tender scenes of the film, which appears as a kind of digital fantasy when Marc, Selena, and Jim spend the night at the family house. Wandering through the abandoned home, Jim fantasizes about seeing his parents again: the audience is shown a subjective camera shot, which represents Jim's perspective. His parents come into the kitchen and unload groceries. Jim interacts with this vision, talking to the phantoms and picking up a carton of orange juice and "drinking" it (though he tells the vision of his father that it is empty). When the shot reverses to see Jim reacting to his vision, he is still in the post-zombie room, but the audience sees his arm enter the frame of the parent vision as he reaches for the orange juice. The overwhelmingly "digital" nature of the vision (which seems to have had distortion added to heighten the effect, as the film image was already shot on digital film) and the phantom actions of Jim's hand in this shot create a virtual experience for him in which the audience participates.[23] Jim's interior thought processes are visualized as being digital virtual reality—phantom hands and all—with which he can interact. Paul Virilio argues that virtual or "cyber" space is, more accurately, an "augmented" or "accelerated" reality.[24] Maybe this is why Jim's fantasy of the past involving the virtual bodies of his parents erupts in an accelerated encounter with reality, as the sequence explodes into a confusing frenzy of the infected crashing into the house and being dispatched by Selena. The bloodbath is frenetic.

Perhaps the most apparent inflection of the post-human into the film's signifying practices can be experienced through all of this bloodletting. Horror films are often concerned with or marked by the presence of the abject—that which the body must repulse in order to survive. This concept so marks the horror film—especially in the depiction of the body's data stream, blood—that its presence in *28 Days Later* ought to dispel some of the film's generic hybridity. The abject is "that which does not 'respect borders, positions, rules' . . . that which 'disturbs identity, system, order.'"[25] Julia Kristeva associates the abject with biological functions, expulsions, and secretions, as the abject is that which must be expelled from the body: images of

> blood, vomit, pus, shit, etc. are central to our culturally/socially constructed notions of the horrific. . . . These images of bodily wastes threaten a subject that is already constituted, in relation to the symbolic, as "whole and proper." Consequently, they fill the subject—both the protagonist in the text and the spectator in the cinema—with disgust and loathing.[26]

In *28 Days Later*, the infected not only voluminously produce a black vomit-like substance—presumably infected blood—but also themselves personify the abject, at least to the old social order. The infected are socially "dead" (as Marc tells Jim regarding his family) and, as corpses, function as the ultimate in abjection.

The abject threatens life and therefore must be "radically excluded" from the place of the living subject. Consider the city of London for a moment in biological terms—as a body. When Jim's network of survivors escape London, they are actually expelled from the body of London. The survivors literally burst out of a tunnel to leave the city limits, repeating the act of expulsion of waste from the human body via any number of its orifices.

The infected have taken over the city, as zombies often do in the genre, and this new social order has no place for the human subject. This nightmare vision of London is one of an urban system independent of human presence. The great metropolis has finally become a nonbiological machine: the traffic lights continue to blink, but for no one; car alarms fulfill their programming, but protect the car for no one from no one. The dead city continues on purely in its machine functions, itself a spatial/national automaton not unlike the walking dead that now haunt its streets.

This catastrophe reverses all conceptions of the human subject because it is now the human *abject*. What once ordered, now disorders: we now shit where we eat and there are no boundaries for the survivors that would allow them to continue in any "human" state, observing human laws and taboos or preserving standing orders of property, entitlement, or social order. Worse, however, is the acceptance in the reality of the film that human bodies—clean, uninfected, living human bodies—have become waste to be expelled: the survivors as well as the phantom radio voices agree that the only way for the human to survive is to leave the city that has come under the "control" of infected. Thus, the human element has become a variable of disorder, an error to be adjusted through elimination. The tables have turned: the dominant human animal becomes synonymous with shit, vomit, detritus. The human body has become obsolete; viral, nonhuman, or formerly human substrates are the new order, and it is the nonviral that is forcibly expelled. This aspect of the film perhaps represents a more pleasurable aspect of disembodiment: the release from a purely biological—and therefore impure or unclean—substrate into one where infection becomes a distant threat.

Which brings us back to David Cronenberg, a director who frequently dramatizes the effects of viruses and other infections upon human bodies.[27] Cronenberg once reflected, regarding viral life: "Perhaps some diseases perceived *as* diseases which destroy a well-functioning machine, in fact change [that] machine into a machine that does something else. . . . Instead of having a defective machine, we have a nicely functioning machine that just has a different purpose."[28] We see here the desire to compare the human body to a machine, or to at least attach a system of values wherein machines are not unlike humans, and viruses are not unlike either. In this quote, infection functions as an agent of transformation—a catalyst for change rather than a vehicle for degeneration. If viewers take Cronenberg's advice from the epigraph of this chapter and see the movie from the point of view of the disease—in this case, the disease as an agent of cognition, not unlike (in fact, similar to) AI—then the film produces an entirely different set of meanings. And just as infection in *28 Days Later* transforms humans into machine-like bodies, noting these "viral" interpretations can help us delineate, explore, or discuss the transformations occurring in the generic or subgeneric conventions of the science-fiction/horror hybrid.

What would the robotic subject think of the human subject? Humans are filled with blood, a good communication system but rather messy and prone to acquiring viruses and contagions due to its permeable embodiment. The human subject is fundamentally wet and meat-like. It behaves like a lower-level primate (perhaps the chimpanzees of the opening shots). It incessantly consumes, to the point where it must consume itself. And human subjects are always breeding, very much like viruses. In fact, bodily reproduction becomes horrific in this film, not only via the zombie's method of reproduction (infection through contact with fluids, biting, etc.) but also in the forced breeding of the soldiers at the camp. And the happy ending—wherein humans are able to survive this plague and reestablish their mastery dominance of consciousness—would indeed seem apocalyptic to an artificial agent of consciousness, which would not necessarily be rooting for the humans. In this reading, *28 Days Later* is not science fiction: it is a horror film for computers.

The Cure for Infection

The question of the zombie film and its generic status (horror or sci-fi?) is a question about genre specificity, which is really a question of taxonomic specificity: it is concerned with classifying the subgenre as one *species*—a term that grows ever more archaic as otherly bodied forms of intelligence are given more recognition. If viewers can accept that consciousness might not still be rooted in a mind/body split—that we have already begun to think of ourselves as humanly embodied information, and of other species as otherly bodied information with the same claims on consciousness—and that we are collectively coming to terms with the futility and obsolescence of the biological (nonamplified) body, then they can reconfigure the zombie film as reflecting anxiety rooted in an altogether different source: the technologized or computer-oriented mind. What anxieties, then, does *28 Days Later* offer this hypothetically post-human subject, this alternative agent of consciousness? The answer is troubling: the film visualizes machine intelligence worrying about its formerly biological substrate: the human body. *28 Days Later* depicts a fantasy of humans without active agency, and the pleasurable expulsion or rejection of the human body as a material substrate.

Graham, discussing the changes in monstrous representation, writes that just as "monsters of the past marked out the moral and topographic limits of their day, so today other similar strange and alien creatures enable us to gauge the implications of the crossing of technological boundaries."[29] The zombie—masquerading as "the infected"—offers just such a gauge for the technological boundary, leading us to a post-human condition. Furthermore, it allows for the visualization of the convergent or retrograde crossing of the machine toward sentience in the form of embodied viruses.

Science fiction, in the form of *28 Days Later*, has infected horror (and produced a virulent strain of film) so that technological intelligence—on the brink of being considered an agent of conscious or autonomous being—can deal with its anxiety over human bodies, their tenacity, and their persistent, bloody corporality. Our film genres have become unstable because our conception of the body is unstable: it is so thoroughly confused and implicated in the technological that body-horror and medical- or science-horror have become the same thing. Human consciousness is no longer solely figured through bodies. In this post-human world, the horror/sci-fi hybrid will visualize these transformational anxieties. Just as soldiers experience sensations from limbs long since amputated, the human body, amputated from its biological-consciousness, will haunt the living information of self-aware technology.

Notes

I would like to acknowledge Andrew Cole for his extensive and thoughtful suggestions for this work and without whom this essay would not be possible.

1. Elaine L. Graham, *Representations of the Post/Human: Monsters, Aliens, and Others in Popular Culture* (Manchester: Manchester University Press, 2002), 2–4. The term has some variations; some use the unhyphenated "posthuman," while some hyphenate; Graham herself uses the "and/or" strategy of the solidus: "post/human." For the purposes of clarity, the hyphenated phrase is used in this chapter.

2. Graham, *Representations*, 22.

3. Graham, *Representations*, 22.

4. I opt for the term *text* here rather than *film* in an attempt to bridge the various media wherein these post-human moments are enacted and perceived. For the sake of this chapter, I view post-humanism as a particular way of encoding information, and the various bodies—biological and otherwise—that carry that information as texts.

5. Anthony Lane of the *New Yorker*, for instance, refers to *28 Days Later* as a "horror flick" ("Days of Plague," *New Yorker*, 30 June 2003, 102), while Owen Gleiberman of *Entertainment Weekly* calls the film "a swankly austere piece of jeepers-creepers sci-fi" ("*28 Days Later*," *Entertainment Weekly*, 27 June 2003, 114).

6. The salience of this term in lieu of our discussion here can be quickly understood by recalling another type of zombie of the Information Age: computers afflicted with a "virus." For instance, on February 25, 2004, the *Washington Post* posted an article about a computer virus, titled "Latest MyDoom Outbreak Spreading, Deletes Files" (http://www.washingtonpost.com/wp-dyn/articles/A4354-2004Feb25.html). The article, from Reuters, claimed that computer viruses "have instead evolved over the years to turn unsecured computers into 'zombie' machines capable of carrying out the virus writer's commands." It postulated that the MyDoom worm "*surfaced* in January and is considered the most virulent outbreak ever, infecting millions of computers around the globe" (emphasis mine). This vision of infected computers that "surface" echoes the signature zombie image of such films as *Evil Dead* (1982) and *Horror Rises from the Tomb* (1972): an undead, reanimated arm clawing up through earth and soil under which it had been buried.

7. Donna J. Haraway, *Simians, Cyborgs, and Women: The Reinvention of Nature* (London: Free Association Books, 1991), 149.

8. Kevin Warwick, "Cyborg 1.0," *Wired* 8, no. 2 (2000): 151.

9. Warwick, "Cyborg 1.0," 143. Consider also the more recent case of Matt Nagle of Massachusetts, a C4 quadriplegic man, paralyzed from the neck down, who had microelectrodes inserted into his brain that transmit signals to a microcomputer. Through this interface, Nagle is able to move a cursor on a computer screen and execute all of the ensuing functions that result from pointing and clicking. Richard Martin, "Mind Control," *Wired* 13, no. 3 (March 2005).

10. Though it is equally as often the machinations of voodoo, as in *The Serpent and the Rainbow*, or some supernatural intervention, as in *Tombs of the Blind Dead*.

11. For a discussion of the confusions between science fiction and horror, see Carlos Clarens, *An Illustrated History of the Horror Film* (New York: Capricorn Books, 1967); John Baxter, *Science Fiction in the Cinema* (New York: Paperback Library, 1970); Michel Laclos, *Le Fantastique au Cinema* (Paris: J. J. Pauvert, 1958); and Vivian Sobchack, *Screening Space: The American Science Fiction Film* (New York: Ungar, 1987).

12. Kim Newman, ed., *Science Fiction/Horror: A Sight and Sound Reader* (London: BFI Press, 2002), vii.

13. Newman, *Science Fiction/Horror*, vii.

14. Sobchack, *Screening Space*, 30.

15. She writes that both genres "deal with chaos, with the disruption of order, but the horror film deals with moral chaos, the disruption of natural order (assumed to be God's order), and the threat to the harmony of hearth and home; the SF film, on the other hand, is concerned with social chaos, the disruption of social order (man-made), and the threat to the harmony of civilized society going about its business" (Sobchack, *Screening Space*, 30).

16. For more on this "social contract," see Thomas Schatz, *Hollywood Genres* (New York: McGraw-Hill), 1981.

17. The chimera as a monstrous creature—equal parts lion, goat, and snake, and possessing the head of each—symbolizes a system of information that disrupts the human sense of "natural" and social order (the two defining concerns of horror and sci-fi, respectively), for the chimera is, literally and allegorically, many things: the creature is natural order disordered, a body driven by outlandish and horrifying desires.

18. N. Katherine Hayles, *How We Became Posthuman: Virtual Bodies in Cybernetics, Literature, and Informatics* (Chicago: University of Chicago Press, 1999). It is Hayles's definitions and conceptions of the post-human viewpoint I will use to talk about film, and it is Hayles's work to which any reader not satisfied with my glosses should turn.

19. Hayles, *How We Became Posthuman*, 3.

20. Hayles, *How We Became Posthuman*, 3.

21. Hayles, *How We Became Posthuman*, 3.

22. William Gibson, *Neuromancer* (New York: Ace Books, 1984), 16.

23. The penetration of Jim's hand into this camcorder fantasy echoes the interactive video hallucinations of *Videodrome*, as in the infamous shot of James Woods's hand reaching into the bulbous and elastic television screen.

24. Paul Virilio and Sylvère Lotringer, *Crepuscular Dawn* (Los Angeles: Semiotext(e), 2002), 80.

25. Julia Kristeva, quoted in Barbara Creed, "Horror and the Monstrous-Feminine: An Imaginary Abjection," *Horror: The Film Reader*, ed. Mark Jancovich (London: Routledge, 2002), 69.

26. Creed, "Horror," 70.

27. See, for instance, *Rabid* and *The Brood*.

28. This is also the concluding remark of Cronenberg's epigraph at the beginning of this chapter; quoted in Kim Newman, *Nightmare Movies: A Critical History of the Horror Film, 1968–88* (London: Bloomsbury, 1988), 116.

29. Graham, *Representations*, 30.

~

CHAPTER NINE

Can't Sleep When You're Dead: Sex, Drugs, Rock and Roll, and the Undead in Psychobilly

Annelise Sklar

Deep inside the gardens of soul a riot has started in vein [*sic*]
Rioting from the places unknown the night carries secrets of pain
A zombie riot is coming an army of unhuman eyes
From every yard they're strolling with no less value to die
Chaos people who never won they come out of the shiny dust
Be grateful to know what you've done cause they're coming for
    some teenage lust
A zombie riot is coming an army of unhuman eyes
I'm gonna get me a coffin to sleep one night to survive
A zombie riot is coming an army of unhuman eyes
From every yard they're strolling with no less value to die
Chaos people who never won they come out of the shiny dust
Be grateful to know what you've done cause they're coming for some
    teenage lust
A zombie riot is coming an army of unhuman eyes
I'm gonna get me a coffin to sleep one night to survive

—Batmobile, "Zombie Riot"

Psychobilly is a mutant mixture of rockabilly, punk music, and subcultures, with a hearty dose of horror genre kitsch thrown in for good measure. Although psychobilly appropriates many visual aspects of the horror genre and standard monster-movie types, zombie imagery is by far the most prevalent.

Zombies turn up in band names, song titles and lyrics, visual artwork, and theatrical costuming. This chapter will briefly discuss the zombie as it is used in the psychobilly subculture.

Psych-Psych-Psycho! A Brief Primer on the Subculture

Tracing the history and development of psychobilly as a definitive subculture, as with most subcultures, is a tricky undertaking.[1] The term *psychobilly* itself is attributed to a Johnny Cash lyric: he refers to a "psychobilly Cadillac" in the chorus of his 1976 song "One Piece at a Time," in which the song's character puts together a car from pilfered factory parts over several years. The inception of psychobilly coincided with the popularity in the early 1980s of neo-rockabilly bands like the Stray Cats and the second wave of British punk. "Mutant rockabilly," as psychobilly has also been called, hybridized both the rockabilly and punk subcultures. The combination might initially sound odd, but, as Ted Polhemus, author of *Streetstyle*, explains, the two subcultures have the same nonconformist roots, and

> the thumping beat, the in-your-face sexuality, the deliberate shunning of prissy sophistication and the greasy quiffs of the early Rockabillies were in tune with Punk's gutsy spirit of raw rebellion. The Punks simply added a stylistic extremism, an assumption of gender equality and a fetishistic trashiness which could not have conceivably existed in Memphis in the mid-fifties.[2]

In addition to its parent subcultures, psychobilly also draws heavily on the related styles and subgenres of teddy boy, rocker, garage, psychedelic, surf, Goth, ska, and, later, alt-country and heavy metal—in short, any and all music-based, working-class, youth subcultures, especially those associated with the pompadour and/or juvenile delinquency and particularly those white subcultures that had already appropriated elements from and melded with earlier subcultures primarily populated by minorities.

Early punk bands such as the Cramps, the Misfits, and their predecessors were obviously influential to psychobilly music and style, but the consensus is that the Meteors, founded in South London in 1980, were the first true psychobilly band, and that the subculture grew up around the West London Klub Foot venue before spreading through Europe to Japan and the Americas. Some of the better-known psychobilly bands include Demented Are Go, King Kurt, the Klingonz, and the Frantic Flintstones (United Kingdom); the Guana Batz, the Quakes, and Tiger Army (United States); Batmobile (Netherlands); the Nekromantix (Denmark); Mad Sin (Germany); Os Catalepticos (Brazil); the

Meantraitors (Russia); and Mad Mongols (Japan). Typically, these bands, among psychobilly bands, differentiate themselves from their punk rock cousins with the addition of an upright bass (although many bands have used an electric bass effectively as well), and from their rockabilly brethren by the adoption of punk visual aesthetics—hair dye, leather jackets painted and patched with band logos—in general, anything designed to shock, offend, and/or titillate.

Like both punk and rockabilly, psychobilly is fashion-conscious, and, as with its music, psycho style incorporates pieces of its parent subcultures into spectacular, cartoonish costumes. Again blending rockabilly and punk aesthetics, psychos are often found in denim, leather, metal-studded accessories, and a variety of animal prints never found on any natural pelt. Popular footwear ranges from work boots to the ever-impractical creepers (platform-soled dress shoes often decked out in a variety of colors, patterns, and designs) to more comfortable canvas sneakers, also available in basic black or a variety of colors and designs.

Some psychobilly fashionites sport the rockabilly pompadour or the punk mohawk, but typical psycho hairstyles combine elements of both: the "quiff" is a tall, gravity-defying flattop; the aptly named "fin" is molded into the shape of a shark fin on the top of the head. Some psychobilly women have feminized these hairstyles or appropriated the retro styles popular with rockabilly girls, but the most common female cut is reminiscent of pinup queen Bettie Page's classic style: long black hair with bangs straight across. All of these hairstyles are frequently dyed or streaked with fluorescent colors, and the more adventurous ones incorporate designs, such as leopard spots, as well.

Skin art completes the psycho look, and visible tattoos often depict popular psychobilly iconography such as devils or demons, pinup girls, pirates, skeletons, popular horror-genre monsters, or any combination of these. Unlike most punks and rockabillies, psychos may even don theatrical makeup for special occasions. It is not uncommon to see a psychobilly band or audience member in paleface horror-movie-style makeup, fake blood dripping strategically from the mouth or temple.

For much of its existence, psychobilly has been very much an obscure underground subculture, undifferentiated from its parent subcultures to outsiders. In the early twenty-first century, psychobilly has become slightly more popular, with formerly hard-to-find music, clothing, and accessories now available not only through small, independent record stores and online mail-order websites but also at malls across America in chain stores like Hot Topic and Torrid.[3] While many subgenres of punk promote an anticapitalist dogma critical of the popularization of their subculture, psychobilly does not. In fact, even though psycho, like both rockabilly and punk, has obvious working-class roots, it has no official political stance at all. Surpassing affairs of state, psychobilly instead delights in all the pleasures of trash culture, from custom cars to tiki bars to very bad B movies. Psycho worships the trinity of excess: sex, drugs, and rock 'n' roll.

Sexuality is celebrated in an openly hedonistic and often humorous fashion. Psychobilly songs give audiences a laugh with lyrics like, "I'll be pumping my rise/between your thighs" (the Frantic Flintstones' version of "Blue Christmas") and the blunt chorus of "I like big titties" (the Barnyard Ballers' "Silicon City"). At the same time, though, like the Goth subculture, psychobilly embraces the slightly darker side of sexuality, as manifested in the fetish/BDSM (bondage, discipline, sadomasochism) scene and its sensibilities and garb, maintaining a strong tie to dominatrices and fetish models, as rockabilly does with burlesque performers. Necrophilia, or love for an alluring (un)dead temptress like those found in urban legends, makes for popular song themes (e.g., the Meteors' "Meet Me at the Morgue"), as does seduction by vampires (e.g., the Sharks' "Love Bites"). Psychobilly, with its appreciation for flamboyance and shock value, is also partial to other fringe sexualities, such as transvestitism (e.g., Demented Are Go's "Transvestite Blues") and bestiality (e.g., Barnyard Ballers' "Grease Up That Pig"). Psycho sexuality is playful, however. The dungeons and acts of torture of BDSM go hand-in-hand with monster movies and psychological thrillers in which serial killers are often motivated by psychosexual disorders, but the motivating factor is less misogyny than a fondness for social deviancy. After all, the fascination is manifested more in masochism than sadism (e.g., Demented Are Go's "I Wanna Be Your Slave"). Psychobilly sexuality should be framed, then, as a parody of the snuff film rather than akin to it.

The subject of mind-altering substances is likewise addressed with a mixture of bluntness and ironic self-awareness. Substance (ab)use is common in most music-based counterculture subcultures, rockabilly and punk among them, and psychobilly is no exception. Most bands poke fun at their immoderation, such as Demented Are Go's straightforward tribute "Marijuana" (with the chorus "I like marijuana, you like marijuana, we like marijuana, too") and Godless Wicked Creeps' self-explanatory "Too Drunk to Drink."[4] Psychobilly music frequently substitutes traditional lyrics in old spirituals with drug references, such as the Frantic Flintstones in their variant of "Peace in the Valley," "Drugs in the Valley," and Demented Are Go with "Old Black Joe," where the line "I'm coming home" is replaced by "I'm gonna get stoned." Doing so juxtaposes self-styled immoral psychobilly life with historic religious mores in a postmodern acceptance of and expansion on these poles.

Psychobilly, however, is more than a simple fusion of sex, drugs, and mutated rockabilly and punk music. The sound of psychobilly runs the gamut from rockabilly to loud, fast punk, and clothing and lifestyle choices vary tremendously among individual psychos. The primary cohesive element is the fascination with iconography of the horror genre. Psychobilly draws on imagery from all eras of horror, from Gothic novels and classic films to schlocky cold war flicks to psychological thrillers and splatter films. Psychobilly celebrates slashers (as in the Meteors' "Michael Myers"), serial killers (e.g., the Frantic Flintstones' "Jack the Ripper"), aliens (e.g., Godless Wicked Creeps' "Little Green Man"), and pop culture monsters of all kinds (e.g., 12 Step Rebels' "Curse of the Pentagram" or Mad Sin's "Where the Wild Things Are").[5]

The Psychobilly Zombie—Seriously

While Frankenstein's monster, vampires, the Creature from the Black Lagoon, werewolves, and mummies are all well represented in psychobilly music and imagery, by far the most prevalent psychobilly icon is the zombie. With psychobilly's attraction to the horror genre and related spectacle, it is little wonder that the psychobilly zombie is more akin to the modern cinematic zombie than to either traditional Haitian zombies or the types of zombies discussed among philosophers of the mind. In psychobilly, zombies are not only favored subjects for song lyrics (Demented Are Go's "Zombie Stalk" and the Meteors' "She's a Zombie Now," to name just two) and album artwork (for example, the Os Catalepticos' *Zombification* cover, which depicts a blue-tinted psychobilly on an autopsy table with glowing yellow eyes) but also the personas adopted by fans and bands, with "zombie" being a common adjective on psychobilly Web pages and in Internet screen names as well as popular dress for stage shows and album covers (as the Frantic Flintstones did when they posed in the woods for the cover of their *Nightmare on Nervous* LP). Martin Millar, in his *NME* review of an early Guana Batz show, describes members of the audience as "braindead soulless psychobillies with tattoos on their foreheads and bloodlust in their eyes all hunting for live brains to nourish their rotting flesh," "mutant flat-top monsters," "malevolent deathwalker[s]," and finally "zombies" who eat both his girlfriend and his foot, though "it's a small price to pay. The Guana Batz were fab."[6]

Polhemus contends that subcultural fashion is primarily about attitude, and that the superficial—the clothing and other visible characteristics—is merely "the visible tip of something much greater. And encoded within its iconography are all those ideas and ideals which together constitute a (sub)culture."[7] He describes the connection of this iconography as a "language" and the stylistic choices as "simple 'adjectives'" which, as new subcultures are formed by combining older ones, are blended into a single fashion statement.[8] He compares the process to the pop music process of "'sampling & mixing'—taking little snatches ('samples') from the past and mixing them together."[9] Polhemus argues that those "who shop at the Supermarket of style know full well that every garment (a 'target' T-shirt or one with Queen Elizabeth II sporting a safety pin through her nose) and every accessory on offer (Hippy beads, Psychedelic plastic rings) comes as part of a complete semiological package deal."[10]

As previously noted, the psychobilly zombie appears in song titles and lyrics, screen names, and visual artwork such as album covers, tattoos, and logos and is generally in evidence in psychobilly culture. In short, the zombie functions as a mascot for the subculture. To analyze the psychobilly zombie thoroughly, the subculture must first be deconstructed into its component parts: rockabilly style, horror-film imagery, and punk aesthetics. Each area, in turn, offers its own favored methodology for analysis—among them, genre studies, psychoanalysis, subcultural and fashion studies, retro culture and nostalgia as a commodity, and postmodern negationist ideology.

The psychobilly zombie can be read as a cinematic archetype, a fashion statement, and/or a self-conscious manifestation of ideological stance. Like members of most subcultures, the psychobilly is both *auteur* (creator/producer) and *spectator* (participant/consumer) of zombie images, and each role allows for a multiplicity of simultaneous meanings (having to do with genre conventions, psychoanalytic archetypes, ideology, nostalgia, and camp, among others) to be associated with the single icon. It can be a monster that connotes fear, the unknown, and Otherness. More specifically, though, the zombie can be read as part of a specific group of monsters—the partially human and the undead—that have their own body of associated folklore, mythology, and popular culture, including associated parody and camp value. The zombie itself is a monster unique among monsters, with its own significance.

The psychobilly performance incorporates many images and icons from rockabilly, punk, and the horror genre, all of which somehow fall under the "retro" rubric. As a phenomenon, Paul Grainge suggests that nostalgia lies somewhere on the scale between a mood, in which it is "understood as a socio-cultural response to forms of discontinuity, claiming a vision of stability and authenticity in some conceptual 'golden age'" and a stylistic mode that "satisfies a desperate craving for history."[11] As a commodity, Grainge explains, nostalgia creates a new context for something old (for example, reruns or "oldies" hits) while often "repackaging" it in a playful, campy way.[12] As replay technology has evolved, media outlets have been especially successful, "recycling" old songs, artists, and films through box sets and reissues on new formats (CD, VHS, DVD), allowing spectators "to access, circulate, and reconfigure the textual traces of the past in new and dynamic ways."[13]

On the surface, rockabilly epitomizes this retro-hip way of thinking, obsessed as it is with authenticity of 1950s "classic" sound, fashion, and automobiles. Like rockabilly, psychobilly embraces and revamps postwar popular culture, favoring hearses with tail fins, buxom and tattooed Marilyn Monroe look-alikes, bowling shirts decorated with flames and skulls, and similar commodities. However, Scott W. Renshaw explains that postmodern rockabilly and swing culture is itself a fusion of rockabilly, ska, and punk into a "modern attitude" of "rebelliousness fused with the excitement and resurgence of Swing music, Swing dance, tavern socializing, vintage clothing and style, and thrift store shopping."[14] Likewise, psychobilly is the "reconfiguration," or pastiche, of rockabilly, punk, and horror, as is most evident in the fashion and musical styles.

In the case of the horror-film element, psychobilly especially embraces the iconography of postwar horror films, particularly those, such as those made by Hammer Films, first released in the 1960s and early 1970s but repopularized and recast as camp through afternoon and late-night television in the 1970s and 1980s. Younger psychobillies grew up with horror films strongly embedded in the segments of mainstream popular culture favored by hipsters and replicated in equally popular artistic derivatives like *From Dusk till Dawn*.

Like punks, rockabillies, and, of course, psychobillies, horror fans are their own particular breed. Horror fandom takes many forms. Robin Wood notes that the

> horror film has consistently been one of the most popular and, at the same time, the most disreputable of Hollywood genres. The popularity itself has a peculiar characteristic that sets it apart from other genres: it is restricted to aficionados and complemented by total rejection, people tending to go to horror films either obsessively or not at all. They are dismissed with contempt by the majority of reviewer-critics, or simply ignored.[15]

Popular culture and film scholars have attempted to explain the appeal of the horror genre with mixed results. Polhemus, in his analysis of the Goth subculture, explains that "there always seems to be a minority—especially

among angst-ridden youth—who are comforted by and attracted to a roman-
ticized, stylish vision of life in the shadow of death."[16] Andrew Tudor considers approaches that "'explain' horror by reference to seemingly immutable
characteristics of the genre or its consumers" to be "reductive," assuming that
all fans enjoy the same things for the same reasons or that "they harbour basic repressions, they are driven by fundamental, bestial needs; their given nature is routinely to take pleasure in transgressive representations."[17] He explains that horror is multifaceted:

> Like all popular genres, horror appeals to people for as many reasons as its con-
> sumers can find ways of making use of genre products. For some, no doubt, hor-
> ror may be a source of titillation. For others, a fount of salutary warnings, and
> for yet others, an occasion for collective hilarity. Some horror fans relish and
> rely upon the stigma that attaches to such officially undervalued culture. Some
> experience going to horror movies as an essential element in sustaining indi-
> vidual identity within a distinctive peer-group context. And across cultures,
> variations multiply and deepen in the context of radically different cultural
> practices.[18]

However, he also suggests that the appeal of the horror genre lies in both the
"narrative tension" and the presence of outright monstrosity, be it inferred or
an outright graphic representation.[19]

The narrative formula associated with the horror genre, Wood explains,
begins when "normality is threatened by the Monster."[20] Wood considers this
normality to be "in general boringly constant: the heterosexual monogamous
couple, the family, and the social institutions (police, church, armed forces)
that support and defend them."[21] Note that this is the same status quo—often represented by suburbia—that so many punks and post-punks have re-
belled against. The monsters themselves are not scary, Steven Jay Schneider
insists. Instead, he proposes, the very appeal of horror films is the fact that
the monsters are "depictions of monsters, representations of monsters" and
that they have the potential to horrify because "they metaphorically embody
surmounted beliefs."[22] The actual success in horrifying viewers, however, is
due to "the manner in which they embody surmounted beliefs is invested
with cultural relevance."[23]

Noël Carroll claims that "the locus of our gratification is not the monster
as such but the whole narrative structure in which the presentation of the
monster is staged."[24] Likewise, Schneider differentiates between "the most
disturbing *images* of horror cinema . . . and the most frightening *narratives*," a
consequence of which is that "the overwhelming majority of horror film
monsters turn out to be not so much literal manifestations of paradigmatic

uncanny images as metaphorical embodiments of paradigmatic uncanny metaphors."[25] The primary pleasure of the horror genre, then, horrific or not, Carroll asserts, is discovering the unknown as the plot unfolds: "The real drama in a horror story resides in establishing the existence of the monster and in disclosing its horrific properties. Once this is established, the monster, generally, has to be confronted, and the narrative is driven by the question of whether the creature can be destroyed."[26]

Of course, the psychobilly zombie has already been revealed, at least to those in the subculture, and functions within the narrative of everyday life. Neil Gabler suggests that the postmodern public learns how to behave—the appropriate gestures, poses, attitudes, expressions—in certain situations by watching movies and that everyday objects, such as fashion, function as props in the performance of life.[27] He suggests that each personal identity is a role, and that life, rather than a series of frontstage and backstage scenes, has a plot with a beginning, provisional middle, and provisional end. In this process, he explains, "one saw a life genre to which one aspired and with which one felt comfortable, and one started easing into the role that fitted the plot."[28] Psychobilly zombiedom, then, can be read as an intentionally se-lected role. Like punk and other counterculture currents, horror films teach us the shortcomings of normalcy, but the only other option they offer, if one chooses to reject conventional Western reality, is the antithetical character of monstrosity.

As a character, the monster in horror films is usually more interesting than the world it attacks. Paraphrasing Wood, Barry Keith Grant remarks, "That horror films are progressive to the extent that they refuse to depict the mon-ster as simply evil seems clearly borne out by these films."[29] Barbara Creed applies Julia Kristeva's concept of the abject,[30] suggesting that

> it is relevant to note that several of the most popular horrific figures are "bod-ies without souls" (the vampire), the "living corpse" (the zombie), and the corpse-eater (the ghoul). Here the horror film constructs and confronts us with the fascinating, seductive aspect of abjection. What is also interesting is that such ancient figures of abjection as the vampire, the ghoul, the zombie, and the witch (one of whose many crimes was that she used corpses for her rites of magic) continue to provide some of the most compelling images of horror in the modern cinema.[31]

Carroll elaborates: "Obviously, the anomalous nature of these beings is what makes them disturbing, distressing, and disgusting. They are violations of our ways of classifying things and such frustrations of a world-picture are bound to be disturbing." At the same time, he explains, "anomalies are also

interesting. The very fact that they are anomalies fascinates us. Their deviation from the paradigms of our classificatory scheme captures our attention
immediately. . . . One wants to gaze upon the unusual, even when it is simultaneous repelling." Thus, monsters "are curiosities. They can rivet attention and thrill for the self-same reason that they disturb, distress, and disgust."[32]

At the same time, Wood notes that the manifestation of the monster is
"protean, changing from period to period as society's basic fears clothe themselves in fashionable or immediately accessible garments—rather as dreams
use material from recent memory to express conflicts or desires that may go
back to early childhood."[33]

Zombies have certainly evolved since their cinematic debut. Zombies
come to popular culture through Haitian folklore, where it was thought that
a *bokor*, or Voudou practitioner, could enchant a person into a coma-like
state, steal their soul, and then revive the victim—now without soul, memory, personality, or speech—to be a slave. This is more or less the modus
operandi of Bela Lugosi's zombie master character in the first zombie film, the
1932 *White Zombie*. In cinema, the zombie evolved, and today's most familiar zombies are corpses who have been reanimated through scientific (usually
chemical or nuclear) experimentation, an alien force, or black magic. The
popular-culture zombie, as a text and character, is constantly evolving, starting in Caribbean folklore but no less "authentic" in its popular movie role.
Just as Paul O'Flinn noted about the Frankenstein story, "History demonstrates clearly the futility of a search for the 'real', 'true' meaning of a work.
There is no such thing as *Frankenstein*, there are only *Frankensteins*, as the
text is ceaselessly rewritten, reproduced, refilmed and redesigned."[34] Like
most other nostalgic icons, the zombie is actually a simulacrum, the often-
replicated image of an artifact that never was, and, although most popular-
culture zombies share common archetypal elements, each zombie is, in the
end, a manifestation of its creator's aesthetic vision.

The most analyzed zombies in particular are those from George Romero's
films, *Night of the Living Dead*, *Dawn of the Dead*, *Day of the Dead*, and the
Night of the Living Dead remake. Wood suggests that these

> zombies can be read as representing the heritage of the past from which the
> protagonists must struggle to free themselves. Their most obvious characteris-
> tic is their need—apparently their sole need—to consume. They represent,
> that is, the logical end-result, the reduction ad absurdum and ad nauseum, of
> Capitalism; the fact that they consume flesh is but a literal enactment of the
> notion that under Capitalism we all live off other people.[35]

Likewise, Grant maintains that

the zombie becomes as crucial a metaphor of social relations for Romero as the prostitute for Goddard. . . . *Night*, which David Pirie calls 'probably the only truly modernist reading of the vampire myth,' has been read variously as a critique of the Nixonian 'silent majority,' of American involvement in Vietnam, and of the family under capitalism. *Dawn* self-consciously uses the zombie as a conceit for macho masculinism and conspicuous consumption, 'the whole dead weight of patriarchal consumer capitalism' as Robin Wood puts it. (Romero's own description of the film as 'a satirical bite at American consumerism' is equally apt.) *Day* shows the extent to which society has collapsed five years later, concentrating the political connotations of zombiedom on the issue of sexual politics. Men in the film are consistently shown to be as much of a threat to life as the zombies that are forever surrounding the band of human survivors.[36]

In short, as Grant explains,

Where, say, R. H. W. Dillard finds the original *Night* to be so effectively frightening because it articulates a fundamental nihilism and negation of human dignity, it is more accurate to say that all four zombie films are so powerful because Romero's undead demand the suspension of normal (bourgeois) values, particularly those of patriarchy.[37]

The same can be said about many (post-)punk subcultures, like psychobilly, which create spectacle as a means of upending normalcy. In a common reading of horror films, then, the monster represents a startling, frightening, foreign Other that upsets the status quo. Citing Roland Barthes, Wood explains that "Otherness represents that which bourgeois ideology cannot recognize or accept."[38] This zombie Otherness is not racial or gendered, although psychobilly, with its American and European rock-and-roll roots, is, like most Western youth subcultures, subject to hegemonic whiteness and most visibly populated by white males (and white male zombies).[39] Psychobilly zombies exist in all races and genders and are above discussing such things, but again are, as are most popular culture zombies, predominantly white as well.[40] Instead, the Otherness embraced, the other half of this "us/them" divide, is youth culture—psychobillies—alienated from hegemonic culture's mainstream society.

Greil Marcus, in *Lipstick Traces*, explains that punk—and thus its postmodern children such as psychobilly—was about not nihilism and complete annihilation but negationism and refusal to accept mainstream norms. "Negation is always political: it assumes the existence of other people, calls them into being. Still, the tools the negationist seems forced to use—real or symbolic violence, blasphemy, dissipation, contempt, ridiculousness—change hands with those of the nihilist."[41] With the introduction of punk, Marcus explains, "there was a reversal of perspective, of values: a sense that anything was possible, a truth that could only be proven in the negative. What had been good—love, money, and health—was now bad; what had been bad—hate, mendacity, and disease—was now good."[42] With its "new set of visual and verbal signs . . . punk made ordinary social life seem like a trick."[43]

As a mascot, the zombie provides a single rallying point, a symbol readily recognizable as an Other to anyone with even a bit of Western popular culture education. Monsters and monster imagery are a part of our common culture, and many popular creatures, including the zombie, have roots in folklore. As Joan Hawkins explains in her discussion of Eurohorror films, creators and users of this imagery "draw on what Pierre Bourdieu would call a 'cultural accumulation' that is shared by paracinephiles and Eurohorror aficionados, a 'cultural accumulation' that accrues from both 'high' and 'low' culture."[44]

Becoming the Other, or defining oneself as someone outside of the mainstream—a member of one of Polhemus's styletribes—through fashion or iconography, is, as Polhemus notes, "to put oneself on the firing line. But if such stylistic commitment brings a sense of group solidarity and comradeship, then, for many, it is worth it."[45] Embracing monstrosity—be it by putting a safety pin through the queen's face or by aligning oneself with zombies—has the same effect. Seen through the punk-tinted gaze of psychobilly, then, the zombie—as ideologically interpreted by scholars of Romero's works—epitomizes psychobilly values: as previously noted, consumption and hedonism (fashion, sex, drugs, rock and roll).

Each popular-culture monster has its own familiar symbolism derived from its associated "cultural accumulation" of history, folklore, and popular culture. For instance, in popular-culture analysis, werewolves are generally considered to embody teenage angst, witches harbor unharnessed female power, and vampires are pretty, deep, charming, and oh-so-fashionable. The psychobilly zombie is the archetypal monster: it devours, infects by biting, and is sensitive to sunlight like vampires and werewolves. It plods and shuffles like Frankenstein's monster. Compared with the other undead, though, zombies are especially inelegant and brutal. Peter Dendle goes as far as to call the zombie the vampire's antithesis.[46]

The stereotypical zombies, unlike some of their monster counterparts, are dirty from their time in the cemetery, eat brains, are missing limbs, and grunt ineloquently rather than narrate novels. Zombies are visually grotesque; they dress in funeral finery (which may be shredded with wear and tear in a manner similar to fashionably diced punk garments), but it is typically coupled with an open wound or a missing limb, a pairing that provides a postmodern aesthetic simultaneously contrasting and embracing beauty and terror. This low-key, angst-free, persistent attitude and vulgar physical nature makes the zombie the blue-collar monster of the horror movie world (perhaps appealing to the psychobilly subculture for this reason).[47] Like missionaries, zombies travel en masse in motley packs and take no prisoners; anyone they encounter is either killed (eaten for lunch, if you will) or themselves converted into a zombie.

Marcus reminds us that the original punks were ugly, too.

> Today, after more than a decade of punk style, when a purple and green Mohawk on the head of a suburban American teenager only begs the question of how early he or she has to get up to fix his or her hair in time for school, it's hard to remember just how ugly the first punks were.[48]

They "were not just pretty people . . . who made themselves ugly. They were fat, anorexic, pockmarked, acned, stuttering, crippled, scarred, and damaged, and what their new decorations underlined was that failure already engraved in their faces."[49] Like punks, psychobillies often take a negativist perspective of beauty and manufacture their own ugliness. Some psychos actually don zombie makeup to look horrific; others stop at adopting eye-catching hairstyles and fashion that contrasts sharply with both rockabilly aesthetics and those of mainstream culture.

Unlike regular live human existence, zombie existence is worry-free. They have no money, no bills, no jobs, no responsibilities.[50] Zombies cannot help being zombies, just as psychobillies (and most subculture members) feel that they cannot help being psychobillies—they just happen to be that way. The zombie, as the undead, represents the formerly human; a psychobilly is the formerly "normal." Zombies stay up all night, eat brains, and terrorize the town; psychobillies want to stay up all night listening to psychobilly, participate in some sort of mind-rotting hedonistic activity (sex, drugs, and/or rock and roll, of course), and possibly get into trouble for it. Zombies are carnal, and they sustain themselves by eating flesh, an image that ties nicely to sexual activity. Like philosophical zombies, who look like everyone else but have no consciousness and are not aware of it, the psychobilly zombies want no consciousness, free will, or control over their own actions. They just want to be zombies, focused single-mindedly on psychobilly. The psychobilly ideal is to live fast, die young, leave a (not so) beautiful corpse, and then keep on going.[51] Once one is already dead—or of the mindset that they are—there are no worries about the fact that drugs, alcohol, and the general pleasure-seeking often associated with psychobilly (and other music-based subcultures) kill brain cells or that staying up all night leads to exhaustion; zombies eat brains, rather than think with them, and zombies are slow and uncoordinated like drunks even before imbibing, senses already dulled to all pain.

The Psychobilly Zombie Is a Joke!

At the risk of seeming to pull a 180-degree turn, it must be noted that, while serious analysis of zombie imagery offers key insights into the psychobilly choice of zombie as mascot, it does not fully account for one major element of the psychobilly mindset: humor. The psychobilly zombie is a caricature of negationist violence and monstrosity. "At one level the Psychobillies exhibited an alarming fixation with violence and wanton destruction, but this was always tempered by a wonderful, surreal sense of humour, which made you smile, even as you crossed hurriedly to the other side of the street," Polhemus summarizes.[52]

Whereas both rockabilly and punk subcultures take their nostalgia very seriously, striving for authenticity even when it does not exist, psychobilly actively embraces the aesthetics of kitsch, camp, and cheese. Kitsch, of course, refers to mass-produced popular or "low" art such as tchotchkes, knickknacks, souvenirs, or the classic Elvis on velvet. The artifacts of both classic rockabilly (dice, playing cards, cherries, pinup girls, bowling shirts, tiki bars, etc.) and horror movies (movie posters with shrieking starlets, monster action figures, the movies themselves, etc.) are kitschy and the accompanying retro-culture (for example, the space-age bachelor pad or the "cult" appeal of horror movies) often takes the form of camp.

Cheese takes camp one step further. Explains Annalee Newitz:

> Like *camp*, *cheese* describes both a parodic practice and a parodic form of textual consumption. It is the production of, and appreciation for, what is artificial, exaggerated, or wildly, explosively obscene. And like *camp*, *cheese* describes a way of remembering history, a kind of snide nostalgia for serious cultures of the past which now seems so alien and bizarre as to be funny.[53]

"Cheesy" is the best way to describe many old or classic horror films that, due to their bad acting, confusing plots, and cheap props, are amusing rather than frightening. Psychobilly straddles the line between camp and cheese, between trashy and outright ridiculous.

The psychobilly zombie is a parody of the Goth subculture's obsession with vampire imagery.[54] While Goth has moments of humor, as Polhemus notes is "evident in a fascination with the 1950s American cartoonists Charles Addams and Edward Gorey and with cult American TV shows of the 1960s such as *The Addams Family* and *The Munsters*," psychobillies are "creatures straight out of tacky comic books or ketchup-splattered horror movies brought to life(?)."[55] Psychobilly functions in the same space of self-conscious irony as horror comedy movies like the *Scream* trilogy that follow a traditional horror genre formula all the while parodying it.

Conclusion

Carolyn Joan Picart notes that "humour and horror have progressive and regressive political tendencies."[56] Thus, the humor of psychobilly culture should not be seen as negating the more serious symbolism of the psychobilly zombie. Zombies are retro, unattractive, and caricatures of death. The psychobilly zombie combines some aspects of the movie monster—all gory kitsch rather than the personification of sheer terror—even as it mirrors the behavior of the post–*Night of the Living Dead* zombie and punk ideal, destroying everything in its path. The zombie—an ugly, violent, brain-eating monster—epitomizes psychobilly—a trashy, sometimes violent, hedonistic subculture—in ways that no other monster can. A popular horror-genre monster, the zombie embodies both the kitschy Americana favored by rockabilly and the destructive attitude common to punk. The zombie is hideous yet fashionable, and mindless yet driven. Identification with the zombie represents a disassociation from mainstream society. Psychobilly zombies personify a frightful Other, but do so with humor, and they symbolize both death and a lust for live flesh. Quite simply, being a zombie means "You're human, I'm not like you, I'm the enemy, and now I'm going to destroy you and fortify my flesh by feeding off of your remains."

Notes

1. For brief published accounts of the history of psychobilly, see Ted Polhemus, *Streetstyle: From Sidewalk to Catwalk* (New York: Thames & Hudson, 1994), 102; and Martin Roach, *Dr. Martens: The Story of a British Icon* (London: Chrysalis Impact, 2003), 199–205.

2. Polhemus, *Streetstyle*, 102.

3. This is most likely due to a phenomenon Polhemus terms the "supermarket of style" whereby individuals—for whom he claims the history of previous subcultures

is "all part of their pop culture education"—pick and choose the elements of their look, musical selections, and entire subculture from among every choice that all earlier subcultures offer. The effect, Polhemus explains, is that "while five decades of rebellious teenagers explicitly set out to create new styletribes which (at least in their mythology) kicked aside their parents' past, since at least the mid-eighties we have been witness to a seemingly never-ending proliferation of Neo-Mods, Neo-Teds, Neo-Hippies, Neo-Psychedelics, Neo-Punks and now even New-New-Romantics" (Streetstyle, 130–31).

4. This is, perhaps, an allusion to the Dead Kennedys' (surprising) 1981 hit "Too Drunk to Fuck."

5. No doubt an intertextual reference to the famed book by Maurice Sendak.

6. Reprinted in Roach, Dr. Martens, 204–5.

7. Polhemus, Streetstyle, 7, 15.

8. Such as "Hippy beads, Skinhead/Punk DMs, Mod target motifs, Rocker leather, Perv rubber, Glam sequins"; Polhemus, Streetstyle, 134.

9. Polhemus, Streetstyle, 134.

10. Polhemus, Streetstyle, 131.

11. Paul Grainge, "Nostalgia and Style in Retro America: Moods, Modes, and Media Recycling," Journal of American and Comparative Cultures 23, no. 1 (2000): 28.

12. Grainge, "Nostalgia," 31.

13. Grainge, "Nostalgia," 33.

14. Scott W. Renshaw, "Postmodern Swing Dance and the Presentation of the Unique Self," in Postmodern Existential Sociology, ed. Joseph A. Kotarba and John M. Johnson (Walnut Creek, CA: Altamira Press, 2002), 72.

15. Robin Wood, "The American Nightmare: Horror in the 1970s," in Horror: The Film Reader, ed. Mark Jancovich (London: Routledge, 2002), 30.

16. Polhemus, Streetstyle, 98.

17. Andrew Tudor, "Why Horror? The Peculiar Pleasures of a Popular Genre," in Jancovich, Horror, 53.

18. Tudor, "Why Horror?" 53.

19. Tudor, "Why Horror?" 50.

20. Wood, "American Nightmare," 31.

21. Wood, "American Nightmare," 31.

22. Steven Jay Schneider, "Monsters as (Uncanny) Metaphors: Freud, Lakoff, and the Representation of Monstrosity in Cinematic Horror," in Horror Film Reader, ed. Alain Silver and James Ursini (New York: Limelight Editions, 2000), 167.

23. Schneider, "Monsters," 169–70.

24. Noël Carroll, "Why Horror?" in Jancovich, Horror, 34.

25. Schneider, "Monsters," 173–74 (emphasis in original).

26. Carroll, "Why Horror?" 35.

27. Neal Gabler, Life the Movie: How Entertainment Conquered Reality (New York: Knopf, 1998), 196, 205–6.

28. Gabler, 230–31.

29. Barry Keith Grant, "Taking Back the *Night of the Living Dead*: George Romero, Feminism, and the Horror Film," in *The Dread of Difference: Gender and the Horror Film*, ed. Barry Keith Grant (Austin: University of Texas Press, 1996), 210.

30. The abject, or the contemptible, refers to the human reaction (emotional or physical) to a potential breakdown of meaning caused when the differentiation between subject and object (or self and "Other") is blurred. For a detailed explanation, see Julia Kristeva, *Powers of Horror: An Essay on Abjection*, trans. Leon S. Roudiez (New York: Columbia University Press, 1982).

31. Barbara Creed, "Horror and the Monstrous-Feminine: An Imaginary Abjection," in Grant, *Dread of Difference*, 38.

32. Carroll, "Why Horror?" 39.

33. Wood, "American Nightmares," 31.

34. Paul O'Flinn, "Production and Reproduction: The Case of *Frankenstein*," in Jancovich, *Horror*, 105.

35. Robin Wood, "Neglected Nightmares," in Silver and Ursini, *Horror Film Reader*, 126.

36. Grant, "Taking Back the *Night*," 202.

37. Grant, "Taking Back the *Night*," 210–11.

38. Wood, "American Nightmare," 27.

39. There is a fair amount of gender-based difference in subcultural performance. While early punk was supposedly beyond sexism, many later subgenres (for example, hardcore) have been decidedly masculine. Even in politically correct subgenres, the key players—mainly musicians—are typically male. Even in riot grrrl, a feminist punk offshoot, many band members were men. Women are present in punk and psychobilly, however. Although relatively few are musicians, many women produce fanzines, blogs, and other written communiqués. They are fans and music collectors, in the audience at concerts, and vocal participants in online communities. Women are there, but their presence is often more subtle.

40. Whereas punk was inherently political, psychobilly has always been intentionally apolitical in order to prevent further divisiveness. This is in direct contrast to the skinhead scene, which is split between white supremacist factions and antiracist (or nonracist) factions. Punk, which, again, usually takes a staunch politically antiracist stance, is also primarily a white subculture.

41. Greil Marcus, *Lipstick Traces: A Secret History of the Twentieth Century* (Cambridge, MA: Harvard University Press, 1989), 9.

42. Marcus, *Lipstick Traces*, 67.

43. Marcus, *Lipstick Traces*, 69.

44. Joan Hawkins, "The Anxiety of Influence: George Franju and the Medical Horror Shows of Jess Franco," in Silver and Ursini, *Horror Film Reader*, 214–15.

45. Polhemus, *Streetstyle*, 15.

46. Peter Dendle, *The Zombie Movie Encyclopedia* (Jefferson, NC: McFarland, 2001), 10.

47. Dendle, *Zombie Movie Encyclopedia*, 11.

48. Marcus, *Lipstick Traces*, 73.

49. Dendle, *Zombie Movie Encyclopedia*, 74.

50. The zombie has even fewer responsibilities than other monsters. After all, someone has to pay for the upkeep on a vampire's castle and werewolves spend every night other than the full moon living a normal human existence.

51. The corpse's beauty depends on the eye of the beholder, of course. Psychobilly aesthetics find (faux) rotting flesh appealing. Mainstream notions of beauty do not.

52. Polhemus, *Streetstyle*, 102.

53. Annalee Newitz, "What Makes Things Cheesy? Satire, Multinationalism, and B-Movies," *Social Text* 18, no. 2 (2000): 59.

54. For examples of the ways in which Goths use vampire imagery, see Nancy Kilpatrick, *Goth Bible: A Compendium for the Darkly Inclined* (New York: St. Martin's Griffin, 2004).

55. Polhemus, *Streetstyle*, 98–99, 102.

56. Carolyn Joan Picart, "Humour and Horror in Science Fiction and Comedic Frankensteinian Films," *Scope*, May 2004, http://www.nottingham.ac.uk/film/journal/articles/humour-and-horror.htm.

CHAPTER TEN

Zombies in Gamespace:
Form, Context, and Meaning
in Zombie-Based Video Games

Tanya Krzywinska

Loading . . .

Pick up any recent horror-based video game and it is pretty likely that at least some of its monsters are zombies. They even appear in games that don't make direct claims on the horror genre. Whether zombies are encountered in the mainly third-person context of the *Resident Evil* (1996–) or *Silent Hill* (1999–) cycles, the first-person-shooter format of the *House of the Dead* cycle (1998–) or *Painkiller* (2004), or just as incidental enemies in action-shooter *Tomb Raider: The Last Revelation* (1999), it is clear that zombies are well suited to the medium of the video game.

The popularity of zombies in video games may in part be informed by the way that they articulate, in a mediated fantasy context, contemporary cultural fears about the loss of autonomy or the capacity of science to create apocalyptic devastation. Such meanings are certainly available to be read into zombie games, but the market value of zombies as a subgenre of horror, technological developments, and the limitations of animation in games have a lot do with the ubiquity of zombies in video games. Game zombies provide the ideal enemy: they are strong, relentless, and already dead; they look spectacularly horrific; and they invite the player to blow them away without guilt or a second thought.

If zombies are the only "modern myth," as Gilles Deleuze and Félix Guattari claim, then this is bound into the cultural and formal value placed on agency—something that might be seen as being heavily channeled in a work-based consumer culture.[1] Agency has a very special status within video games. By first addressing their market, aesthetic, and gameplay values, and then moving in to examine more closely the impact of player participation on the function and meaning of game-based zombies, I seek to consider the factors that shape the remediation of zombies into video game format and why they have proved such popular foes.

Market/Genre Values

It is important to consider the market context of games to understand why zombies feature so frequently in them. The industrial/market context has a strong bearing on the way video games remediate zombies, in terms of aesthetic and gameplay values. Within the last twenty years, the video game industry has moved from cottage industry to big business, with Sony and Microsoft now competing for market share in both hardware and software. With millions of dollars invested in the development of individual game titles, publishers are keen to ensure that they have a predefined market for any given game. Risk is carefully managed, and there is a tendency to stick with tried-and-tested formulas to minimize commercial failure. As with mainstream cinema, branding is instrumental to ensuring that products reach their intended markets.

As Rick Altman says, genre provides certain formal frameworks and patterns that enable audiences to predict to some extent what a product offers, as well as offering an interpretational framework that shapes the consumer's position in relation to the product.[2] Genre is a modal signifying system that communicates various messages designed to appeal to receptive audiences. The particular textual characteristics of the horror genre attracts aficionados across the age range who are committed to the genre, most lucratively, the general teen and twenty-something audience in search of thrills and forbidden fruit. To some extent, these map onto the specific market demographics of gaming: horror-based games attract "hardcore" gamers, particularly those that carry some form of gameplay or graphics innovation, as well as the more "casual" gamer, who may buy a game because of a franchise tie-in or because of a liking for a particular game type or cycle.[3]

Both video games and the gorier forms of horror have for various reasons tended to appeal to a male audience. Market-based surveys have shown that young males constitute the main market for violence-based games.[4] As with games in general, most zombie-based games are developed and created by men and tend to centralize activities likely to appeal to a male audience. Virtual violence is at the core of the majority of zombie-based games; rarely is the focus on character-based, interpersonal relationships of the type that might appeal to the majority of women. With games such as the *House of the Dead* cycle, *Doom3* (2004), and *Painkiller*, the player-character is gendered male and military-style weapons are used.

Games such as *Resident Evil* and the *Silent Hill* cycles, on the other hand, utilize mainly a third-person format and, while they demand some shooter action to kill zombies, they also introduce more "adventure"-style activities such as exploration of the gameworld, resource management, and puzzle solving. With a less frenetic pace, as wandering zombies are slower and more widely dispersed, more time and freedom to explore their atmospheric gameworlds, greater complexity of story lines, more emphasis on character development, and the option of playing as a man or a woman, these games are perhaps more interesting to a cross-gender market. This follows a general trend in the industry toward making games that appeal more widely, but in an effort to retain the more stable and predictable teenage-male market, aspects of the shooter-style action are nonetheless present.

In order to accommodate a range of players with different abilities, most games structure gameplay to create a learning curve. This usually means that the strength and number of zombie enemies increases as the player progresses through a game. In addition, games such as *Doom3* and *Painkiller* have different difficulty settings, so that less-able players will not give up playing a game because they fail to defeat foes. Other games enable players to control the difficulty of a game by providing toggle switches to turn on or off auto-aim (as in *Silent Hill*). These features are designed to help maximize potential markets.

The most commercially successful zombie films of the 1980s, such as *Evil Dead II* and *Return of the Living Dead*, attracted mainstream audiences to the zombie subgenre by using tension-relieving comedy. Laughing in the face of gory and disturbing horror enables some sense of control over its more unconscionable aspects. Zombie-based video games offer their own particular and more direct way for players to feel in control of on-screen events. The tag-lines of zombie games—"Can you Survive the Horror?" "Discover the Root of All Evil," "Stop the Unholy War"—challenge players to master the psychological and virtual-physical threat posed by zombies. What the player accrues by becoming skilled at a game is a sense of control of the gameworld and its horrors. Few games depart from the well-worn, familiar, flesh-eating zombie cliché, however.

The promise of mastery is intrinsic to games and important to their entertainment value. This tends to make them, in most cases, less ideologically or aesthetically challenging than, for example, art-horror films such as George Romero's low-budget independently produced films. Zombie-based games nonetheless raise issues of autonomy, identity, power/powerlessness, and control. Because the main target market for horror-based video games is roughly the same as for mainstream horror films, they tend to share similar generic, narrative, and thematic patternings, as indicated by the film versions of *House of the Dead*, *Resident Evil*, and *Resident Evil: Apocalypse*.

Technological/Graphical Values

As well as offering the potentially lucrative intertextual recognition factor that is important to establishing a market for a game, the use of conventionalized patterns give video game designers a ready-made formula through which to explore the capabilities and peculiarities of interactive entertainment. It took a range of developments in game technologies for the remediation of cinematic zombies to occur, however. The textual features of games cannot be considered without addressing the technological basis on which games are based.

One of the ways that the video game industry ensures continued interest in its products is through the added facilities and increasing graphical fidelity provided by new developments in game technologies. The capacity for greater graphical realism has proved important to the growth of the games industry generally as well as to the introduction of zombies into digital games. Early games offered limited movement and graphics that appeared in two dimensions, giving a flat effect to the gameworld and its objects. Blocky abstract graphics did not support well the textual particularities of body-horror. Games such as *Space Invaders* or *Defender*, for example, utilized the blank void of space as an easily rendered backdrop for shooting blocks of pixels that represented aliens or spacecraft. The subsequent development of 3-D video cards, giving rise to three-dimensionally rendered worlds, gave players a greater sense that they could move through a gameworld. This orientation enabled more effective shock tactics to be used.

In conjunction with greater capacity to produce graphical detail, these advances set the scene for the entry of zombies into the digital gaming arena. *Quake* (1996), for example, presented an array of demonic entities, including putrefying zombies, that the player was invited to shoot. A bare-bones narrative did little more than locate the player in a neo-medieval world infested with monsters that must be rapidly dispatched. Shambling across the screen, the gaunt zombies of *Quake* seek not to eat the player but merely to throw handfuls of their gloopy flesh at the player, causing health points to diminish. No explanation is provided for their presence in the game, and they are simply part of the army of demonic beings that lend the game its threatening atmosphere and challenge. Their lean visual appearance is unlike the more robust and muscular zombies of games such as *Resident Evil* and *Painkiller*. This is partly due to a decision about the use of resources; the first *Resident Evil* game was contemporary with *Quake*, but the latter utilized available resources to create a faster game, with more monsters to kill and larger playing arenas. Unlike *Resident Evil*, the game made little reference to zombie cinema.

Consonant with the availability of greater graphical resources, the fact that game zombies are digital creations affords artists greater freedom to construct more fantastical entities than is possible with the use of real people made up to look like zombies, and their digital origin accounts for the many diverse shapes and forms of zombies found in games.

With the first installment of the *Resident Evil* cycle in 1996, zombies became the main enemy. Its story arc drew on the mixture of science fiction and survival horror found in Romero's *Night of the Living Dead*, adding an extra X-Files-style conspiracy dimension to the mix that grew with additions to the cycle. The *Resident Evil* zombies are the product of a virus, manufactured by the powerful Umbrella Corporation, that reanimates the dead and causes them to aggressively pursue human flesh for sustenance. The game also adopts the neo-expressionist camera angles that appeared in Romero's first film. These serve a very specific purpose in the game.

While in many first- and third-person games the player's view of the gameworld is anchored to the player-character's perspective throughout gameplay, in the *Resident Evil* games the viewpoint often shifts radically away from the player's perspective to show events happening in other locations. This aspect of the game design is derived from cinema. It creates visual diversity and provides Hitchcock-style suspense by showing the viewer events happening beyond the player-character's view. This cross-cutting technique operates to jar the player's sense of visual control over the gameworld. A heightened sense of anticipation is created; the player knows that what they have been shown will soon impact on their activities. The use of canted angles throughout the game also adds to the sense that world has gone awry. These cinematic-style features add to the impression of threat and highlight the sense that the game is acting sometimes against the player's sense of agency and control.

The *Resident Evil* cycle also redeploys the more schlocky, B-movie elements of Romero's films, translated into the formal particulars of a game context. Illustrative of this is the use of the "splat" death screen. When the player dies, a cut scene ensues: the player-character is seen being eaten by zombies, blood drips down the screen, and the player-character writhes. The cartoonish qualities of the game are partly related to the technological resources available to the game's designers, and even though the game is set—like *Night of the Living Dead*—in an American small town, the fictional-fantasy status of the game is made apparent in overt terms.

Many other zombie-based games also adopt the schlock approach found in some horror/sci-fi cinema. Various games use cartoonish qualities to attract younger audiences, such as the one that was available on the BBC website in which members of a typical suburban family have become zombies through watching too much TV (the image of a zombie Mom doing the ironing is one to be savored). Also deploying schlocky zombie imagery designed for a more general audience is the innovative *Typing of the Dead* (2001), a game intended to increase the player's typing skills in an entertaining way (players must type the words that appear above each zombie enemy as quickly as possible to destroy it).

Perhaps the most atmospherically spooky and enigmatic of all zombie games is the *Silent Hill* cycle. With a muted color palette, a nonmusical sound track designed to disturb, a less linear and "zoned" structure to gameplay than many of its generic competitors, and a complex psychological-horror story line and visual style, the game has an aura of neo-Gothic foreboding gloom where nothing is what it seems. The townscape in which play takes place looks at first to be relatively normal (fog means it is hard to see beyond the player's immediate locale in some of the games). In each game in the cycle, the terrain has two dimensions: relative normality and gore-strewn nightmare. The naturalistically rendered buildings and the spaces of the former dimension become, in the latter, visceral, livid with spilled blood and entrails, harboring more dangerous, plentiful, and fantastical zombie foes. This two-tiered topology creates visual diversity and heightens the horror of the nightmare dimension through its relative difference, but it is also a resource-efficient device, as the same fundamental "map" is used for both modes. With each iteration of the cycle, the fidelity of the graphics has increased, with zombies becoming more detailed and bizarre, and the story line more convoluted—to the point where the status of the world and the source of the incursion of the horror itself becomes ever more obscure and enigmatic. And, rather than using a science-gone-awry virus-based premise, here the zombies are generated by supernatural means.

The *Resident Evil* and *Silent Hill* cycles were both designed for consoles. Two more-recent games, *Painkiller* and *Doom3*, were designed for higher-end PCs and therefore have even greater graphical and processing resources than the current consoles such as the Xbox and PS2. With dynamic lighting, more detailed graphics, more objects that can be moved or that react to being shot at, and increased artificial intelligence routines for nonplayer characters, both are able to create highly realistically detailed fantasy worlds, complemented by multilayered and spatially complex soundscapes. Both games are first-person shooters that require speedy dexterity on the part of the player; the games move at a dizzying pace and hordes of zombies assault the player in a relentless manner.

Painkiller and *Doom3* are predominantly shooters, but unlike earlier first-person shooters, they have a slightly richer contextualizing story line. The player-character of *Painkiller* has died and is charged by an angel to redeem himself by killing the massed denizens of Hell. *Painkiller*'s zombies are armed warriors and take various very detailed forms. Able to wield weapons and wear impressive armor, and looking like they stepped off the cover of a black-metal music CD, they are far from being the pitiable worker-zombies found in films such as *White Zombie* or the role-playing game *Planescape: Torment*. In contrast to the shuffling Romero-style zombies of *Resident Evil* and *Silent Hill*, from whom players can elect to run, and like the zombies of more recent films such as the 2004 remake of Romero's *Dawn of the Dead* and *28 Days Later*, the zombies of *Painkiller* and *Doom3* are capable of swift and decisive movement. Alert, smart, and heavily armed, these are no emblems of abjection or allegories of alienation. This development is pretty much due to the availability of greater resources for graphics and animation. If Romero's shuffling flesh-eating zombies are second generation to the worker-zombies of 1930s horror (as illustrated by the passive worker-zombies of *White Zombie*), then these are third-generation zombies, born of the digital era.

Gameplay Values

Games are not simply representational products. While the story arcs and aesthetics might borrow from other media, playing a zombie-based video game of whatever type places the player in the thick of the action as an active participant. All games are player-centric, designed precisely around player activity. This core feature is very different from other media, and it is essential to address the impact of player activity on the meanings and consumption of game zombies.

Any game is structured by a set of parameters implemented by designers to shape to some extent the player's experience.[5] The gameplay features of most zombie-based games are much the same as in other games: it is the *type* of game (first-person shooter, third-person action-adventure, role-paying game) that determines the set of activities available to the player, rather than the presence of either zombie foes or the use of an established zombie invasion story arc. (In the context of games, "horror" becomes a milieu that can accommodate different game types.) Within the preset parameters of the different game types, players are to varying degrees offered a certain freedom to move at will within and act upon the gameworld to accomplish set and sometimes self-directed tasks. This combination constitutes *gameplay*.[6] Gameplay might be tightly restricted to a set of limited activities, or it might be more "open," giving greater freedom to explore or to play in more diverse ways. The extent and forms of player freedom often depend on the type of game, which has an impact on the pace, rhythm, and style of gameplay.

At the most restricted end of the zombie-game spectrum is the first-person "rail" shooter format of *House of the Dead III* (2002). Player-character movement is limited, moving as if they are on a fixed rail. Players can look where they wish but only from a preset position—a factor that enables more effective play with the use of the limited facilities provided by an arcade-style light-gun controller. Play is geared around shooting zombies that pop up as the game moves forward, with no other activities. The players' set task is to shoot as many zombies as they can: reaction speed builds as the player gets to know the parameters set by the game and its capabilities. At the end of a level, points are awarded on the basis of how many zombies have been dispatched. Other than gaining as many points as possible and rescuing people to get extra lives, the actions of the player impact very little on the story line, which is delivered linearly through dialogue and interlevel cut scenes. As such, the game lends itself to being played in a fragmented rather than protracted way. There are no "adventure"-style components to the game: no scope for exploration, no puzzles to solve or objects to be found.

Although broadly in the same adrenalinized first-person vein as *House of the Dead III*, *Painkiller* offers greater capacity for player-directed movement and exploration than *House of the Dead III*. Arenas in which play takes place are, however, restricted through the use of "soft" boundaries: doors, gates, and other panels that open only after a set of zombies has been dispatched by the player. Keeping the player in close proximity to zombie enemies ensures that the pace of the game does not flag.

Both the *Resident Evil* and *Silent Hill* cycles offer a more open and exploratory style of gaming, combining shooter-style action with an adventure-style format. The third-person perspective used in these games (the player-character is seen on screen) enables the player to see more ably where zombies are positioned in a fight situation, including behind the player-character. Third-person mode is often found in action-adventure games, because it affords a wider perspective on the gamespace, better suited to exploration and tricky maneuvers, than does a first-person point of view. As with most adventure-style games, various objects need to be retrieved to help the player-character stay alive and progress: these might be weapons, various forms of power-ups, or save points. Investigating gamespace closely is required to find many of these items, as some are quite small and others are carefully hidden. Exploration may well be undertaken for its own sake but is more often based on finding objects that will increase the player's agency and competency in the gameworld.

The increased emphasis on exploration in the *Resident Evil* and *Silent Hill* games has an impact on the way they create suspense. While sound effects, music, and the general aura of danger go some way to build suspense, it is very often the act of exploring, in combination with a sense of anticipation about what might be found, that generates tension in the specific context of these games. By contrast, in *House of the Dead III*, *Doom3*, and *Painkiller*, there is little time available to build anticipatory suspense because of the relentless waves of zombie assaults on the player.

In the more exploratory, adventure-style context of the *Resident Evil* and *Silent Hill* games, the terrain is often far more expansive, with the enemies widely dispersed, yet because the player is unlikely to know where these are located, exploratory play becomes guarded and wary, exacerbated by the scarcity of firepower provided. In addition, zombies rarely roam beyond a small, predefined location, making it possible to run around them in some cases, thereby forcing players to make decisions about their actions (rather than simply shooting their way through as in first-person-shooter games). While players might learn over time and replayings where the zombies are located and what their scope for movement is—thus thereby the suspense of not knowing what to expect with the suspense of "Will I get through to the next save point this time?"—the player-character's first entry into a new space is nonetheless often filled with anxious trepidation. In staying alert to danger, which if it arises must be swiftly acted upon in a range of possible ways, the player is kept in a state of wary preparedness that is extremely suspenseful.

Many players have spoken of the creepiness induced by the *Silent Hill* games, and there are two devices built into the games' mise-en-scène that lend suspense and have a significant impact on gameplay. The first appears in the earlier games of the cycle. Outside spaces are veiled in thick fog, restricting what the player can see. While the zombies move fairly slowly, they are often not seen until they are close to the player-character and are therefore less easy to run from. As well as invoking a strong sense of claustrophobia, restricted vision means that players are likely to proceed with wary caution. The sense of danger created by the game is also compounded aurally. Player-characters are equipped with a radio that fizzes static when a zombie is close by. "Hearing" the zombies without being able to see them instills a palpable sense of panic, the player often swinging the viewpoint wildly around by virtue of the keypad to ascertain the direction of the zombies (including zombified flying entities that strike from above). In combination, these devices make gameplay agitated and edgy, mediating effectively the frisson of horror into a game context.

The story structures of the *Resident Evil* and *Silent Hill* games are also stitched into player activity and (limited) choice. While player actions do not affect the stories of *House of the Dead III* and *Painkiller* (they remain the same whatever the player does), in the *Resident Evil* and *Silent Hill* cycles at various nodal junctures, the player must choose from a set of written options what they will do next (a device found in earlier text-based adventure games and role-playing games, as well as book-based interactive fictions). What is chosen at these points determines the trajectory of the game and its story line. This certainly encourages replayings of the games, but most important lends the players a greater sense that their actions and choices are more deeply intrinsic to events—that they have consequences rather than simply trying to shoot one's way to the next level. Despite the branched story lines, these games do restrict gameplay in a range of ways: various barriers to full exploration are still in evidence, be it the zoning devices that appear in *Resident Evil* or the closed roads in some areas in *Silent Hill*, but more generally in the way that the games plant power-ups in specific places, the fairly limited store of story options, the lack of interaction with nonplaying characters, and the inability to change the moral alignment or capabilities of the player-characters (you can't, for example, decide to join the Umbrella Corporation or become a zombie). These set parameters are important, however, in shaping the player's experience and interaction with the games.

At the other end of the "freedom" spectrum are role-playing games, which are more responsive to different styles of play and offer a greater range of possible game tasks, nested story deviations, and larger, more complex worlds to roam in. In *Planescape: Torment*, for example, the player-character is himself a zombie, offering an innovative break from the usual Romero-inspired zombie-as-Other scenario. The overarching game task is for the player-character to recover memories that were lost when he was first turned into a zombie. Being a zombie amnesic affords enigmatic, other-to-oneself status, as well as attributes that directly relate to the ambience and trajectory of the game: for example, "dying" can be advantageous, as it releases the lost memories. Unlike *Resident Evil* and *Silent Hill*, where dialogue choices that affect the game trajectory are relatively limited, here they are plentiful and cumulative.

While the role-playing format of *Planescape: Torment* is perhaps less immediate in its cause-and-effect feedback to the player than shooter-style games and is less cinematic in style, the trajectory of gameplay is far more convoluted and multibranched. A multitude of quests and diversions are offered to the player, and the level structure is embedded rather than overt. The game can be played in various ways: for example, you can choose to fight your way through a situation, but this choice has significant consequences on the player-character, immediately as well as in the longer term. Less aggressive gameplay affords a far richer, if slower experience. As Diane Carr notes, the player-character "mutates in response to a player's prerogative, and continues to alter during play."[7]

Still, most zombie games are based on the survival-horror principles set out by Romero's *Night of the Living Dead*. The generic advantage of having zombies as the main enemy is that they are already dead, marked by their characteristic rotting flesh and unwholesome appearance. As well as being easier to animate than "real" people, killing the already dead is a neat strategy for getting around the morally loaded act of slaying nonplaying-characters. In the fast-paced context of a first-person shooter, being hesitant ends in the player-character's demise (whereas more careful consideration of options is necessary in *Planescape: Torment*).

Slow zombies are also easy targets, giving the player a reasonable amount of time to either aim and shoot or run away. The zombies of the more macho first-person shooters *Doom3* and *Painkiller* move like lightning: running away is never an option. In these games, in contrast to the explore-collect-conserve format of *Resident Evil* and *Silent Hill*, massive amounts of firepower are readily available to the player. In the main, what unites the gameplay features of shooter and action-adventure zombie-based games is that zombies are deployed as fleshly, killable obstacles that must be overcome for game mastery to be achieved.

Control

Most horror films work hard to manipulate the emotions of the viewer, who is unable to affect in any direct way the events that come to pass on-screen. On the other hand, while video games make use of some of the devices used to structure the experience of horror in films, they are predicated on the player having some control over events. If games are to generate the type of structured experiences that are expected of the horror genre, then they must create a balance between freedom to act and roam in the gameworld with certain features that manipulate the player's actions and emotional state. The spectacle of a half-rotted zombie toting a large weapon provides visual pleasure in its own right. But the reason most people play games is the sense of power and agency that they are afforded in relation to the game text. In games, the fate of the player-character, with whom we are invited to identify as well as act through, is very much in the hands of the player. And while, in a film or novel, viewers/readers can do nothing to help beleaguered characters, in games deft responses to set situations can enable becoming-hero players to rescue nonplaying characters from the clutches of zombies, a scenario that occurs in *House of the Dead III* and *Buffy the Vampire Slayer: Chaos Bleeds* (2003).

Games operate on the principle of cause and effect. The consequences of player-generated actions are felt directly in a range of ways, some of which may be progressive or regressive, while others are based on spectacle or story variation. Players are regularly placed as morally righteous in their zombie slaying, but it is only in *Planescape: Torment* that the consequences of moral choices impact fully on gameplay.

The leading pleasure (and frustration) of playing most zombie-based games is built around the challenge of overcoming zombie threats. Smaller, more immediate pleasures are produced by the use of visual and gameplay feedback for player's actions. Mowing down zombies in first-person shooters, for example, is made more exciting and satisfying because of the way they are animated when they die. In *Painkiller*, zombies don't simply drop to the floor on their death. When hit by a high-powered shotgun, they fly back with the force of the impact, and when the player continues to shoot them after they fall, the bodies jump limply about, using the "rag-doll" animation routine that has been adopted by a host of recently produced games. This (special) effect provides a neat visual reminder of the player's power.

I would argue that the primary theme of horror is the relationship between power and powerlessness. Autonomy and agency are regularly put to the test, undermined, or threatened in the genre. The particular combination between player autonomy and the shaping qualities of the game design that controls and limits player power to create a structured experience, story, or suspense is one that resonates well with the thematic concerns of the genre. I have argued elsewhere that players of horror-based games get a more direct experience of the autonomy and its loss in video games than in other media, because the two operate in a dynamic relation that heightens the experience of both.[8]

The fact that most zombie-based games enable the player to defeat the threat posed by zombies to the player-character and the order of things is one that requires some consideration. I would claim that most games present zombies simply as expendable and defeatable "cannon fodder," at least on the surface. When compared to Steven Shaviro's claim that the zombies of Romero's films have a compelling, ambiguous quality that "refigure[s] the very processes that produce and enforce the social order," game zombies can seem devoid of much deep psychological, aesthetic, or political meaning. But we have to remember that games have different properties than films.

Shaviro writes in affective prose about the ambiguous pleasures of waiting for the zombies to reach their targets in Romero's films, which he suggests is intrinsic to the passive pleasures he obtains from the films. Anticipation is also a significant experience in the playing of games, as I have already suggested. It is intensified because game events affect directly the player's progress and status as agent in the game. When the crackle of the radio indicates the as-yet unseen presence of a zombie in *Silent Hill*, I experience a palpable fear, my body stiffens, and I prepare for action. Where will it come from? What type of zombie is it? Do I have the firepower and dexterity to match it? Have I saved the game recently so that if it kills me, I will not have to retread much old ground? Such fear makes the blood pound and the head spin, often causing key-press sequences to be fumbled. If death ensues, I worry and mentally rehearse what I need to do to dispense with the threat the next time around. I am compelled less by the representational attributes of my zombie foe than by the desire to defeat the enemy, to try again. While Shaviro argues that the allegorical and mimetic qualities of Romero's zombies make them more than representation, I would argue that games are intrinsically more than representation precisely because player agency is at stake and games are about *doing* things in response to a given situation, which clearly goes beyond representation.

Academic analyses of horror, such as that provided by Shaviro, often refer to Kristeva's psychoanalytically informed concept of *abjection* in relation to the representation of zombies in an effort to uncover why they are so potentially disturbing. Zombies are abject because of their in-between status: as the animated dead, they disrupt and blur the categories of *dead* and *alive*. As Shaviro puts it of Romero's zombies, "The sheer exorbitance of zombies defies causal explanation or even simple categorization."[9] He suggests that these zombies are like us but not us—in other words, not entirely radically other from us.

However, the exaggerated style and fantastical form of zombies in video games means that they rarely achieve this disturbing ambiguous status: they are more conventionally monstrous, more radically other, more bestial-look-ing often than human. The zombie nurses of *Silent Hill*, for example, have certain mimetic qualities, but they do not have human faces; while they have human bodies and are clothed in their professional garb, their faces are more like that of insects. These are creepy when first encountered, but once the player gets into the swing of things, they are simply to be dispensed with so that new areas can be investigated and the game enigmas solved. Game zom-bies are easily shot, cut up with a chainsaw, or blasted by nail guns, requiring little hesitation or care. There is therefore little opportunity for players en-gaged in action to dwell on their possible meanings.

Only in *Planescape: Torment* do players inhabit the place of the zombie Other, although this is found in diluted form in the game version of *The Thing* (2002), where nonplaying characters with whom the player-character has fought as a team are often transformed into zombified creatures. Both these games create a deepened sense of the "us" and "not us" ambiguity (the former more so than latter). In all zombie-based games of whatever type, however, it is the direct experience of agency and its frequent loss that pre-vails, and it is this that excites, frustrates, disturbs, and compels and is di-rectly related to the particular attributes of the medium of video games.

The mediated presence of the abject in an aesthetic context might be con-sidered to be symptomatic of the drive to master such experiences. The frame of representation affords the abject with a different, attenuated status through the fictional/screen frame. Zombies can be said to invoke the ver-tiginous sense of the abject and yet, the smelly, gloopy, suffocating visceral-ity of the walking dead in its sensuous totality is signified only through sound and image, and is not therefore fully present except in imagination. In games, the fact that zombies directly affect player activity does, however, lend them a renewed vigor and quality; yet because they can be dealt with swiftly and finally, their abject potential is still somewhat diminished and contained—so you're really dead now!

Even though Shaviro makes a remarkable attempt to disregard the repre-sentational qualities that frame Romero's zombies, acknowledging yet also disavowing the B-movie tactics of the films, it is nonetheless the case that, as with games, the viewer is always aware at some level of the status of what they are watching. It is a structured and constructed experience in both cases. But in games, players are given a performative place in the game die-gesis, and what they do affects directly what happens there.

I would suggest that in games an interesting and as yet neglected situation occurs. When the game is going well and the zombies are beaten, the fictional/mediated frame diminishes in the heat of the action, but when the player dies, the whole fictional, constructed nature of the game crashes in on the player and is made patently apparent. In this sense, zombie games provide a forum within which players experience the impact of the Other more directly on their efforts to act out agency than can occur in other media. The Other here is not the zombies but the game apparatus itself.

Games generally demand far more commitment and effort from players than films require of viewers. Is it an indictment of our digital, consumerist age that so much "labor" is directed into gaming? While some critics of video games claim that players are themselves reactive zombies, sitting at their computers or consoles for hours, relentlessly pushing keys in a behaviorist response to actions, players do not experience gameplay in this way. To some extent, games provide us with the type of clear goals and moral regimes that are not available in the real world. Watching a zombie flip-flop about after I have pumped it full of bullets in *Painkiller* is testimony to my playing power—the power to create spectacle through action—and to the technological virtuosity of contemporary game technology, as well as providing an outlet for suppressed aggression generated by the frustrations of the daily grind (I could go to the gym, but I'd rather play at being a weapon-toting zombie slayer for a few hours before bedtime). Rather than sitting watching wall-to-wall television in a distracted way during an evening, games potentially afford a sense of progression and solicit active—and often frenetic and full—involvement in a text. Skill, dexterity, and knowledge of the peculiarities of both the game and the horror genre are all required to play zombie-based games, as is the drive to overcome set challenges. Within the arena of the zombie game, I can potentially become a hero.

Coda

The majority of zombie-based video games are informed in some way by the model found in Romero's zombie trilogy, particularly the survival-horror format of these films. The zombies of *House of the Dead* and the *Resident Evil* cycle, as well as *Doom3*, are the product of bioscience. The zombies of more neo-medievalist games, such as *Painkiller* and *Planescape: Torment*, are by contrast the product of supernatural forces. The *Silent Hill* cycle sits somewhere between: the zombies are supernatural, but the setting is a contemporary American small town, similar to those that appear in Romero's films. Supernatural zombies are to some extent informed by the voodoo-based zombies found in films such as *White Zombie* and *The Serpent and the Rainbow*. It is only in *Planescape: Torment* that the pitiful, passive, worker-zombies of the type used in these films are found. Most game zombies are, however, flesh-eating, aggressive creatures of the type found in Romero's films. The fact that they will not plead for their lives, run away, or cower when attacked plays to the characteristics of control and progression intrinsic to games.

Game zombies symbolize the perversion of the normative order, contagion, or science or power gone awry, and these meanings are perhaps easier to invoke by using models already established in cinema. The use of these by now well-worn clichés, however, means that the abject and deeper allegorical meanings are drained somewhat from game zombies. Nonetheless, zombies serve a very particular purpose in video games: in most zombie-based games, they are perfect enemies that can be killed without incurring guilt in the name of survival.

Notes

1. Cited in Steven Shaviro, *The Cinematic Body* (Minneapolis: University of Minnesota Press, 1993), 83.

2. Rick Altman, *Film/Genre* (London: BFI, 1999), 14.

3. For an extended analysis of the games market, see Stephen Kline, Nick Dyer-Witheford, and Greig De Peuter, *Digital Play: Interaction of Technology, Culture and Marketing* (Montreal: McGill-Queen's University Press, 2003).

4. For a summary of findings, see Aphra Kerr, "~~Girls~~ Women Just Want to Have Fun: A Study of Adult Female Players of Digital Games," in *Level Up*, ed. Marinka Copier and Joost Raessens (Utrecht, The Netherlands: DiGRA/Universiteit, 2003).

5. Various game theorists have focused on the relationship between game rules and play. For more, see Geoff King and Tanya Krzywinska, *Tomb Raiders and Space Invaders: Videogame Forms and Contexts* (London: IB Tauris, 2005); and Katie Salen and Eric Zimmerman, *Rules of Play* (Cambridge, MA: MIT Press, 2004).

6. See King and Krzywinska, *Tomb Raiders*, chapter 1, for more definitions and characteristics of gameplay.

7. Diane Carr, "Play Dead: Genre and Affect in *Silent Hill* and *Planescape Torment*," *Game Studies* 3, no. 1 (2003), http://www.gamestudies.org/0301/carr.

8. See Tanya Krzywinska, "Hands-on Horror," in *ScreenPlay: Cinema/Videogames/Interfaces*, ed. Geoff King and Tanya Krzywinska (London: Wallflower, 2002), 206–23.

9. Shaviro, *Cinematic Body*, 83.

CHAPTER ELEVEN

~

"Now I'm Feeling Zombified": Playing the Zombie Online

Ron Scott

The creation of a community of zombies might be a scary proposition, but it is one that Scott Heim uses to portray the loneliness of difference in a small town in the United States.[1] The protagonist in Heim's novel *In Awe* is a teenage orphan who lives in a Kansas farm town, and as a gay man Boris is an outsider, suffering from an alienation exacerbated by having to watch his best friend die of AIDS. The two of them, along with their small group of friends, endure a barrage of homophobic abuse from the community in which they live, and in order to soothe his pain, Boris has started writing a script for a movie in which he and his friends die and return as members of the undead. The act of scriptwriting allows him temporarily to escape the pain of being an outsider; reimagining himself as a member of the undead enables Boris to claim a power that he has never before possessed, one denied him by his sexual preference. The power of becoming "zombified" helps to lessen his suffering.[2]

Heim symbolizes Boris's outsider status with the culturally loaded image of the zombie, one that resonates as a representative of power in Boris's mind because of the horror movies he has grown up watching. What makes Heim's use of the zombie different from previous incarnations is the fact that Boris chooses a community to accompany his transformation, a choice not usually made by zombies in either film or literature. He creates a community that uses the image of the zombie to establish bonds among people of outsider status in the larger community around them, borrowing what Julia Kristeva identifies as the "abject power" of the horror genre in general to band together.[3] The power that this group lacks in real life comes to them in a form that both exemplifies their outsider status and amplifies the strength they find in the community they create for themselves.

In *Keywords: A Vocabulary of Culture and Society*, Raymond Williams traces the historical roots of the word *community*, noting that the term has grown from one that simply referred to a group of commoners—those who held no rank—to an increasingly "complex concept that on one hand relates to direct common concerns and on the other hand the materialization of forms of common organization."[4] In this definition, Williams implies that tension arises between the commonality of human needs and the "materialization" of the organization necessary to satisfy these needs. This tension may have arisen from the increasing commodification of human relations brought about by capitalism in the nineteenth and twentieth centuries, but even now Boris's community of zombies feels something similar, as they share the "common concern" of being outsiders while their relationship is codified in material as well as abstract ways. His community values specific standards for clothing and music as much as they do the more abstract relationships created from sexual preference and social status. These "common concerns" result in their adoption of the zombie as a symbol of their community, one that addresses what they have in common while encoding the material expressions of their relationships. As Heim's novel suggests, the idealized abstractions of communities represented in media portrayals of the small town underscore both American fears and dreams.

Online Zombies: A Test Case for Community

Williams locates the discussion of community in terms of the complexities the term itself engenders, and the possibilities presented by discussions of both zombiehood and new media demonstrate the viability of the question. However, to paraphrase Roland Barthes, in this chapter I want to try to "define things, not words," and thus I will examine the current state of an actual community rather than a fictional community of zombies in order to attempt to understand the effects of incorporating difference.[5] As a brief and extremely limited beginning, I will look at a community that combines the use of the zombie image with a community immersed in new media: online gamers who play games featuring the undead.

Since the new forms of media are the places where these changes are happening most rapidly, a particularly appropriate place to look at community is on the World Wide Web. Including usenet groups, online communities have been in existence since 1979, and their numbers continue to grow due to increased access to the Web.[6] The rapidity of the growth is one factor in understanding the future of American communities, as traditional communities are affected by the impact of the Web, and new ones form. In creating their own groups, gamers in particular figure out how to represent themselves online, initiate and instruct members on their expected roles, develop and become integrated into economic systems, and manipulate power relationships both among their peers and among the larger corporate entities that control the environment in which the gamers play. My analysis of the ways in which these communities work will describe ways in which community formation in the age of new media offers a location through which we can foresee and negate the potentially devastating long-term impacts some scholars such as Neil Postman say new media will have on our abilities to form vibrant communities.[7]

Gamers and the Games They Play

Computer games first became widespread in early 1970, but multiplayer online games began with the release of *Doom* by Id Software in 1993.[8] Since the advent of the four-player-at-a-time networking capability of *Doom*, online games have grown enormously, now involving hundreds of thousands of players and millions of dollars' worth of computer hardware, networking capability, and software development. Although Id released *Doom* as shareware, asking customers to send payment after they had received a copy, the contemporary game development scene is a billion-dollar industry. It features large corporations such as Sony and EA Sports and its own conventions. In fact, the games themselves have been grown into genres that have earned acronyms such as massively multiplayer online role-playing games (MMORPG) and real-time strategy (RTS) games. The community of players now numbers in the millions, many of whom play several games at a time.

Currently, the most popular online games include the fantasy-based *Everquest II*, *World of Warcraft*, *Diablo II*, and *The Dark Age of Camelot* and the science-fiction-based *Star Wars: Galaxies*, *Starcraft*, and *Final Fantasy*, but the horror and western genres have games as well. In fact, one game that has recently gone online—*The Sims*—can best be described as a version of MTV's *The Real World*, making it a genre all to itself. Gaining the attention of online gamers has become the subject of fierce competition among game developers, with enormous revenues in a dramatically increasing market at stake.[9] The online gaming community has come a long way from its early reliance on shareware for distribution, as it now possesses a financial impact that rivals that of the film industry.

The gaming community that I will focus on is Battle.net, administered by Blizzard Entertainment. Claiming to have as many as 400,000 gamers logged on to its servers at any one time, this community centers on the games *Warcraft* and *Diablo*, fantasy-based games that are among the best-sellers in game history.[10] Once consumers buy a copy of any Blizzard game, they get access to Battle.net at no extra charge, which means that they can instantly chat, download new maps and modules, challenge other players to online matches, or join clans. The games themselves—*Warcraft III* and *Diablo II* were the latest iterations of each series at the time of this writing—feature story lines and heroes derived from J. R. R. Tolkien and an amalgam of Greek, Roman, Norse, Middle Eastern, and Asian mythologies. *Warcraft*, for instance, recreates Tolkien's battles for Middle Earth, featuring orcs, humans, elves, and dwarves. *Diablo*, on the other hand, allows players to choose a lone hero to explore the depths of several labyrinths and wildernesses in pursuit of evil. The two games have even merged to a degree, as Blizzard has moved development of each to the same engine in order to save on development costs, and the two games now share some features. Battle.net houses both online gamer communities, and gamers routinely move between the two games in order to maximize their playing experience.

Creating Zombie Nation:
Battle.net and Developer Expectations

The history of both *Warcraft* and *Diablo* highlights the way control works in defining communities. *Warcraft II* was a huge success financially, but Blizzard discovered that its assumptions about its playing community were wrong. Assuming that few players would actually want to be orcs, the villain race in Tolkien's realm, Blizzard made the story line one in which "brutish" orcs threaten genocide against "noble" humans and their dwarven and elven allies.[11] Contrary to Blizzard's expectations, however, many players did choose to play as orcs, going against the game's story line.

In response to this adoption of the orc by a significant component of the *Warcraft II* community, Blizzard added a new race—the undead—to *Warcraft III*, again with the assumption that the vast majority of players would choose one of the other major races.[12] Blizzard even tried to stack the deck by making the undead difficult to play, as the undead require the use of unusual spells and strategies entirely different from those used by the other races.

Again, players confounded Blizzard's expectations, as many chose to play the undead instead of one of the other, more heroic races.

In Blizzard's latest release, *World of Warcraft*, the developer has stopped trying to decide the moral standing of the various races and has instead simply aligned one group of races into a team known as the Alliance (humans, dwarves, elves, and night elves) and another into one called the Horde (orcs, undead, tauren, and trolls). This latest development acknowledges the difficulties of corporate control within new media communities.

Blizzard faced a similar situation with *Diablo*. In the first version of the game, players had only three avatar options, all of which were "good" characters. In *Diablo II*, the attraction of playing evil characters led Blizzard to add a necromancer as a possible avatar. The Necromancer has similar powers to those of the devils he chases, and his description sounds much like the type of hero who can provide Heim's zombies with the fulfillment of their revenge:

> Though his goals are often aligned with those of the forces of Light, some do not think that these ends can justify his foul means. Long hours of study in dank mausolea have made his skin pale and corpselike, his figure, skeletal. Most people shun him for his peculiar looks and ways, but none doubt the power of the Necromancer, for it is the stuff of nightmares.[13]

The Necromancer is not a zombie, but he creates and controls zombies and other undead warriors, including golems, to penetrate the labyrinth and kill Diablo. Because of the fascination with zombies that each represents, those who play the role of either the Necromancer or Warcraft's undead form the basis of the group that in this chapter I will call Zombie Nation—those who choose to use zombies in their online battles. As a prime character for Zombie Nation, the Necromancer raises the dead to fight evil. In creating such a character, Blizzard has catered to what the developer thinks its fan base wants, in effect relinquishing some corporate control over the story line of their product.

While Blizzard's strategizing over "good" and "bad" heroes suggests the problems of all game manufacturers in determining what their customers want, the unique qualities of the online community increased the options available to Blizzard. Because *Diablo* was online before *Warcraft*, Blizzard was able to respond to its fan base's desire to play zombies quickly, transferring this knowledge to its development of *Warcraft III*. In earlier media, Blizzard would have had difficulty determining customer preferences, since their only avenue for receiving feedback would have been through more traditional marketing means. However, through Battle.net, Blizzard has a ready-made format for gathering both direct statistical information and user feedback on customer preferences. This sort of setup shows why online games are so enticing for developers: they can streamline their creative content while simultaneously marketing new products and receiving constant customer feedback. Blizzard does not even take full advantage of the revenue possibilities of creating online gaming environments, as the developer does not charge for Battle.net.[14] Constant customer feedback is what led Blizzard to include "evil" characters and races as options that players could choose to play, and because of Battle.net, Blizzard can back up anecdotal feedback about customer preferences with statistics gathered directly from its own servers in order to determine its best options.

Once a Ghoul, Always a Ghoul: Representation in Zombie Nation

As in most online communities that use avatars, members of Zombie Nation devote much time and energy to their visual representations in the digital world. Most zombies are known by their avatars, a word coined by Neil Stephenson in his 1992 novel *Snow Crash*, where he defined avatars as "the audiovisual bodies that people use to communicate with each other in Metaverse."[15] In *Snow Crash*, Stephenson assembled avatars into a hierarchy of access, describing people who connected to the Web through public phones as having weak, ghost-like avatars, while those who connected through high-speed lines used incredibly glamorized versions of their real selves. As Stephenson predicted, the personal avatar has since come to serve as a means of determining status in online communities. While gamers use improved software to imbue their avatar with visual images that match their self-perceptions, they also utilize avatars to show how players rank according to game skill and to show off their digital manipulation skills. In effect, avatars function metaphorically much like automobiles and other material symbols of status, enabling gamers to show visually how they fit into their specific online community.

For the Zombie Nation on Battle.net, representation happens in at least two different ways. Avatars serve as the player's game face for the purposes of the forum, and Blizzard assigns them avatars in Battle.net based on their skill level; once players attain a certain level, they are given a virtual image that corresponds to that level among characters in *Warcraft III*. The Blizzard avatar thus functions as a handy marker: a player knows instantly what rank their opponent has attained, and they can decide whom to play accordingly.

However, players also develop other avatars for non-refereed forums, and these avatars are often far more daring and digitally involved. These outside avatars, used for representation on clan forums and in chat rooms, allow players to showcase their digital manipulation skills, using images from around the Web and Photoshopping them in much the way that Heim has Boris wear black trench coats and eyeliner. Creating a scary or disturbing image enables the zombie gamer to engage in virtual intimidation, an intimidation whose effectiveness is impossible to measure but which still fits the gamer's need for self-expression in a strictly hierarchical system.

Players also represent themselves online with their choice of player name, in much the same way as chat room participants identify themselves. Trying to get names past the Blizzard name censor—which has a detailed set of words it will not allow—is a favorite game of players, but most choose some combination of words that shows their status and favorite character. This combination of avatar and player name marks the player: players of lower rank are given the picture of a low-level character as their avatar, denoting that they are either inexperienced or not very good, and these same players often choose names that either wittingly or unwittingly describe their experience in the community. Since players have to earn a certain number of wins to get a new, higher-level avatar, other players know immediately the capabilities of the player they have asked to join their game. Conversely, player names allow gamers to distinguish between high-level players in ways that the Blizzard-assigned avatars cannot. Online identity on Battle.net works to rigidly enforce the hierarchy of players, limiting the power of the avatar and demonstrating the ability of new media communities to enforce roles.

Diablo II offers one more possible avenue of representation: the weaponry and armor chosen by gamers for their characters. Individual character classes start out with the same basic armor and weaponry—for example, necromancers come equipped with a bone wand and black-and-white armor that makes them appear skeletal—but throughout the game players pick up items that enable them to develop their character's appearance. Players alter this template by choosing specific weapons and armor, occasionally creating their own implements and "hacking" them into the game in order to express their individuality. Some members of Zombie Nation even try to defeat the developer's intentions by creating a necromancer who does not use his necromantic skills, as several forum discussions focus on creating a melee-oriented or bow-using necromancer despite the character limitations built in by Blizzard. Online representation again becomes a matter of balancing the choices offered to players by the developer with the personal desires of the gamers—and for zombies, this balancing act often involves interfering with developer intentions while maintaining earned status among fellow players.

Planning the Learning Curve:
How to Become a (Successful) Zombie

For the members of Zombie Nation, initiating new players and instructing current ones in their roles within the community is an important activity for maintaining the health of the community as a whole. Since gamers invest literally thousands of hours in a game, their connection to it becomes intensely personal. Developers take advantage of this intensity by serializing their games, but revenue growth requires attracting new customers. In order to attain such growth, developers create new products that are close enough to accepted genre formulas to be familiar but different enough to evoke desire in the consumer. The risks for developers are apparent: if the game is too derivative, no one will buy it, but if it involves too steep a learning curve, gamers will not want to invest the time necessary to understand it. Gamers might complain if a new game is too similar to other, already existing ones, but they also do not subscribe to online games that fail to offer a set of the sort of easily recognizable hooks that make a game compelling.

Originally, gaming communities formed online as a response to the difficulties of learning to play various games, and Zombie Nation has a particular need for this sort of learning environment. In the early days of computer gaming, players frustrated by the difficulty of games formed their own communities through usenets and e-mail, but the development of company-run servers has resulted in strategy guides and Web forums that offer new players advice. In these forums, players learn about advanced game strategy and also socialize with other players. The forums have developed beyond mere basic gaming needs, as long-time players (distinguished, as we have seen, by their avatars and player names) use them to set standards for online conduct and to train new members while keeping these new players in their place. For Zombie Nation, these standards involve learning strategies that do not work for the other races and character classes, but the gamers who develop such standards also use them to initiate newcomers into both the uses of the forums and the gamers' relationship with the developer.

Newcomers initially might be attracted to *Warcraft III* or *Diablo II* because of their similarities to games they already know, but once they enter Battle.net they become aware that they have an entirely new language to learn. Part of this learning process occurs in the formation of clans. Clans are Blizzard-sanctioned groups of players who band together to practice and play online. While all gamers, regardless of clan, trade tips about games, review other games that participants like, and verbally chastise each other, clans form mainly to match like-minded players in order to teach each other new skills. Developers often make the creation of online teams necessary by including quests that players cannot solve on their own. These quests are designed to foster the sort of online community that game developers view as a key part of the addictive quality of the game. Thus, learning takes several forms: advanced game knowledge, game socialization, and community formation. All of these forms of learning are critical to the success of the community.

Working Together to Build a Better Zombie Nation

Zombie Nation is a prime example of the mutual dependency of game developers and players, a dependency that demonstrates the new media-styled relationship between consumers and producers. As the changes in *Warcraft III* and *Diablo II* make evident, gaming environments such as Battle.net have become collaborations between user groups and developers. As I have already discussed, from the developer's standpoint these communities offer unique marketing opportunities as well as places to monitor user feedback. More important, however, the addictive nature of the games and the intensity with which gamers pursue their online gaming means that players become committed to the environment in a way that perhaps only companies such as Harley-Davidson can match. The relationship is far more one of mutual dependence than communities developed under market-based economic systems usually allow, as developers build in interactive features that require gamers to bring change, and thus investment, to their games. Total control over the creative content of a game is impossible in the gaming community, due mainly to the ways that gamers hack the actual product itself.

As Ralph Koster, creative director of Sony Online Entertainment, argued in an interview: "You're making a mold but the players fill it. They'll shape their community to fit the rule sets you have, but you never really get to control it. And odds are pretty good they'll leak out of the mold and do something you never expected."[16] In this community, developers depend upon gamers building a relationship with the game that necessitates their active modification to its content, a relationship that would be impossible, for example, with manufacturers of refrigerators or books. Developers create story lines for games that encourage collaborative groups to solve problems within the game, and the intensity of the relationships formed within these quests contributes to the addiction. Even the language gamers use to plan these solutions is an invention of its own, and developers keep up only by having resources devoted solely to monitoring the games and their forums. Developers end up devoting extensive resources to the monitoring of the game and its community, tracking down cheaters, adding new content in the form of competitions and quests, and in general understanding the changes that have been wrought to a game they designed.[17] Essentially, the gaming community becomes a discursively active entity, as long as the servers remain functional.

The Economics of Zombie Nation

This mutual dependence between gamers and developers parallels the development of the backbone of new media, the Internet. In its original incarnation, the World Wide Web was developed to take advantage of the connectivity of the Internet in order to facilitate the exchange of scientific information. Tim Berners-Lee established the Web as a place where the purity of scientific research could take precedence over profit, a place where the needs of scientific users could be balanced with the wants of the programmers who were responsible for the Web's development. The utopian impetus behind this vision continues in the open source movement, a project begun by Richard Stallman, Linus Torvalds, and others who seek to provide open source code for the software applications that computer users rely on. The goal of the open source movement is to have both users and programmers take ownership of the applications they use in a way that is impossible with software developed by companies like Microsoft. The interdependence of programmers and users corresponds to the relationship in the online gaming community between developers and gamers. The Web is a place like many others in American culture, where commerce and democracy intermingle in ways that reveal both the frustrations and the promise of developing egalitarian, self-sustaining communities.

Zombie Nation exemplifies this relationship between commerce and democracy. All Blizzard games have a money-based economy in which players either find objects and sell them in towns (*Diablo*) or mine gold or harvest lumber to earn enough money to keep standing armies (*Warcraft*).[18] The developer/gamer's symbiotic relationship is built on this monetary exchange and thus is fraught with the complications found in all corporate–consumer relations, despite the utopian possibilities envisioned by the original designers of the Web. This exchange system presages a novel type of possibility for new media communities, as the promise of Internet open systems clashes with the reality of dollar-based exchanges of goods and services.

Earning money helps players level up their characters in *Diablo* and win battles in *Warcraft*, and at some level the relationship between Blizzard and its customers remains defined by the fact that Blizzard products cost consumers money. Blizzard maintains its Battle.net servers in order to earn profits and develop market share for Vivendi, its parent corporation, even if the resulting product is one over which they cannot maintain full content control. The Zombie Nation can influence the product, but ultimately Blizzard runs the show, and new media communities inevitably face this economic reality.

However, the new style of community found in this outlet makes defining this community as one strictly based on commerce difficult. Certainly, the relationship between Blizzard and its consumers is defined by money, but the community also takes advantage of the open-source possibilities of the Web, as Blizzard provides fans with the Worldcraft editor that gamers can use to develop their own maps. In fact, many online games provide this sort of custom creative input into their games as a way of helping players customize their own environments, and these editors enable fans to design their own maps, create their own weapons and armor, and even write story lines. Designing this type of custom content provides fans with input that comes at a far more detailed level than that ordinarily attained by consumers. However, this editor was not created by Blizzard without thorough cost-benefit analysis: because of the intensity with which gamers participate on Battle.net, Blizzard can devote far fewer personnel to maintaining and updating its games. In effect, these types of editors keep players interested in the game without adding developer costs. Still, the implications of providing this sort of access to what is in effect a portion of a game's source code are that online communities might well be based on far different interactions between developers and consumers than exist in more traditional notions of the consumer–producer relationship.[19]

Staying Pure Should Be Easy in an Algorithmic World

Members of Zombie Nation make difficult choices when they enter Battle.net. While the Necromancer may be just as powerful as any of the *Diablo II* heroes, the character is also the least satisfying, as he cannot kill his enemies himself but must rely instead on his necromantic skills. Zombie Nation members who play *Warcraft III* face the additional burden of learning a completely different set of game strategies, as the undead spells work in what is in effect reverse, sapping energy and hit points away from other players rather than blasting them with spells or swords, making them more difficult to win with. Additionally, players who play the undead or the Necromancer form clans that are often abused by other clans of "good" characters. The outcast status of Zombie Nation is one that its members have to actively embrace.

The fan fiction found on the Web forums located in Battle.net provides evidence of both the difficulties inherent and the desire evident for making this embrace. As John Cawelti argues in his seminal guide to generic fiction, *Adventure, Mystery, and Romance: Formula Stories as Art and Popular Culture*, cultural anxieties are often located in generic fiction, and the anxieties located in playing the undead online speak to the problems of redefining communities as well as any other more traditional type of genre storytelling.[20] Playing the undead invokes these cultural anxieties, appearing as both Kristevan fears about being drawn to the "place where meaning collapses" and anxieties about self-worth in a postmodern world.[21] Because playing the undead is more difficult than playing other races, and because being a Necromancer affects social status in the Battle.net community, the cultural anxieties awakened both within the subculture of the game itself and the culture at large help identify the problems of redefining community in the age of new media.

A major theme of the fan fiction that gamers publish on Battle.net forums is an anxiety that speaks directly to fears about conducting oneself in a situation with new rules: the extremes of purity and corruption. Stories in this forum often focus on concerns about the proper place of irony and the individual need to express joy at playing these games versus the fear that gamers are wasting their time. The story lines of the games themselves are not designed to be ironic, since the goal in both games is to rid the world of an evil that threatens the known world. But expressing too much belief in the purity of a consumer product originally developed to appeal to fans of Tolkien and *Dungeons & Dragons* becomes too much for some gamers. This irony expresses itself in their fiction in the form of fears of being too pure, as the paradox inherent in desiring to adopt the chivalrous nature of medieval knights in a postmodern world becomes hard to reconcile with material reality.

A story by a player named Magical Cow demonstrates these anxieties. In it, she uses a paladin—one of the pure knights who fight for virtue and are driven by their belief in a higher power to sacrifice themselves for the good of humanity—to investigate reasons why players choose to become part of Zombie Nation. The paladin in the story, John Archer, is chosen by a magical weapon to be the next leader of the undead, and he uses the weapon to kill the lead paladin, who seemingly did not fully appreciate Archer. In a flashback, the author tells us of Archer's frustration:

Things were becoming boring for me . . . much too boring. Slaying orcs had its kicks, but I grew weary of the monotonous fighting that seemed to always take place. And that pompous bastard Uther never acknowledged my brave deeds . . . no one ever did. So, it would appear that Paladins are used to protect, and then you can easily ignore them once they get their job done. . . . This angered me greatly, and for the first time I wished I had never become a Paladin. In fact, I started disobeying direct orders, and always did things halfway to protest my unjust treatment. . . . They took it as an act of treason. . . . I was convicted of flagrantly stopping and not saving a small family from demon worshiping orcs. Those bastards kicked me out like an unwanted mutt! I knew their time would come, and I'd be there dancing on their graves.[22]

The dissatisfaction with playing a "good" character is evident in the prose, as is a gamer's fear of betraying some sort of code about the need for irony. The simplicity of this scenario is obviously a product of the same sort of genre narrative established in mass productions like *Star Wars*, but the writer also indicates her general concerns about developing the feeling that she has become personally corrupted. Her sensibilities could be based on her gaming career, which she began as someone who played the human race but who eventually migrated to Zombie Nation. In any case, her fiction indicates her desire to distance herself from the trope of purity that dominates much of the fiction in fantasy and is evident in the fan forums as well. She is without a doubt aware of the irony in adopting a medieval sense of purity in a postmodern world, and the anxiety inherent in maintaining her sense of irony demonstrates the type of anxieties inherent in a new media community.[23]

"I'm OK, You're an Undead Demon from a Burning Legion of Doom"[24]

The definition of community in the new media world of the Zombie Nation is both a harbinger of new and unforeseeable relationships and a reminder that the new boss is often the same as the old boss. Even as symbols of alienation and outsider status, gamers who feel attracted to the idea of playing the undead can have a significant impact on a major game developer's prize product, in some ways even dictating its corporate direction. This sort of consumer power is countered by the fact that the community gets its direction from a major corporation, belying the democratic possibilities offered by the Web. That zombies, symbols of alienation and isolation and markers of teenage angst, serve as signifiers of this change makes sense: the redefining of the American community will most likely attain neither the utopic nor dystopic status envisioned by those who prophesy about the new media's effects on it, but it will certainly move in unexpected directions, encompassing both the anxieties and potential of its members.

The presence of online communities like Zombie Nation provides Americans a glimpse of the future of community in the world of new media, a future that offers the possibility of embracing the alienated self along with our democratic potential in a series of interconnected, self-sustaining communities. As members of Zombie Nation can perhaps best attest, the technological changes incorporated in new media need not destroy our cultural visions of community; instead, with luck, foresight, and planning, this sort of change can open up possibilities for community formation that may at this moment seem impossible to attain.

Notes

1. Scott Heim, *In Awe* (New York: HarperCollins, 1997).

2. The Goth band Alien Sex Fiend first popularized the turning of the noun *zombie* into a verb in a song from 1990 titled "Now I'm Feeling Zombified."

3. Julia Kristeva, *Powers of Horror: An Essay on Abjection*, trans. Leon S. Roudiez (New York: Columbia University Press, 1982), 1.

4. Raymond Williams, *Keywords: A Vocabulary of Culture and Society* (London: Croom Helm, 1976), 76.

5. In the final chapter of *Mythologies*, Barthes sets out to define exactly what he means by *myth*. After offering a definition, he uses a footnote to proclaim: "Innumerable other meanings of the word 'myth' can be cited against this. But I have tried to define things, not words." Roland Barthes, *Mythologies*, trans. Annette Lavers (New York: Noonday Press, 1957), 109.

6. According to the Pew Internet and American Life Project, 58 percent of Americans used the Internet on a regular basis in 2002; Susannah Fox, *Wired for Health: How Californians Compare to the Rest of the Nation* (Washington, DC: Pew Internet and American Life Project, 2003), 3 (available at http://www.pewinternet.org/pdfs/ pip_ca_health_report.pdf).

7. See, for example, Neil Postman's *Amusing Ourselves to Death* (New York: Penguin, 1985) and his speech "Five Things We Need to Know about Technological Change" at the "New Technologies and the Human Person: Communicating the Faith in the New Millennium" conference, Denver, March 27, 1998, http://itrs.scu .edu/tshanks/pages/Comm12/12Postman.htm.

8. "Online Gaming," *Game Research*, http://www.game-research.com/online -gaming.asp.

9. According to an article on the java.sun website, overall game revenues reached $23 billion worldwide in 2003 and were expected to jump to $30 billion by the end of 2006; Janice J. Heiss, "Java Technology Gets in the Game: A Conversa-

tion with Chief Gaming Officer, Chris Melissinos," March 2004, http://java
.sun.com/developer/technicalArticles/Interviews/games. The online gaming industry's share of that market, according to the Themis Group, a game consulting firm,
was $1.3 billion in 2003, with revenue expected to reach $2.9 billion by 2005; "The
Themis Report on Online Gaming 2004," January 6, 2004, http://www.themis-group
.com/view_news.phtml?id=24.

10. Blizzard Customer Support, e-mail to the author, May 14, 2004.

11. Blizzard Entertainment, "*Warcraft II*: Overview," http://www.blizzard.com/
war2bne.

12. The orcs suddenly became a "noble but savage" race; Blizzard Entertainment,
"*Warcraft III*: The Races," http://www.blizzard.com/war3/races.

13. Blizzard Entertainment, "*Diablo II*: The Necromancer," http://www.battle.net/
diablo2exp/classes/necromancer.shtml.

14. Several other companies, including Sony, run game servers that charge a sub-
scription fee of as much as $13 a month, taking advantage of a consistent revenue
stream to develop new products and expansions. For instance, *Everquest*, a Sony Online Entertainment Systems product, has more than 460,000 subscribers who pay
$9.95 a month, making it the largest MMORPG in the world in terms of both sub-
scribers and dollars. Curt Feldman, "Q & A: *Everquest II* Producer John Blakeley,"
Gamespot.com, http://www.gamespot.com/pc/rpg/everquest2/news_6094533.html.

15. Neil Stephenson, *Snow Crash* (New York: Bantam Books, 1992), 33.

16. Quoted in Tom Chick, "MMOs: Building Whole Societies," *Gamespy*, October 24, 2003, http://archive.gamespy.com/amdmmog/week5/index4.shtml.

17. Blizzard maintains one full-time employee to monitor the Battle.net forums,
while Everquest has employees act as "Games Masters" in order to "act as cops on the
beat within the game, trying to ensure that everyone plays nice."

18. *Warcraft* mimics a feudal economy in some ways, but its use of gold miners and
timber harvesters appropriates a capitalist hierarchy in which the lowest workers
spend all of their time ceaselessly, night and day, gathering resources to be used to
maintain social privilege.

19. The game *Neverwinter Nights* by Bioware has taken this move to open source
one step further. Bioware offers the toolset originally created by Aurora to any users
who want it, as long as they can download it from the Web. Builders can then create
modules based on their own interests and stories, providing content and art and mod-
ifying individual functions as necessary.

20. John Cawelti, *Adventure, Mystery, and Romance: Formula Stories as Art and
Popular Culture* (Chicago: University of Chicago Press, 1976).

21. Kristeva, *Powers of Horror*, 2.

22. Magical Cow, "A Death Knight's Betrayal!" Battle.net Fan Fiction Forum,
December 12, 2003, http://www.battle.net/forums/thread.aspx?FN=fanfiction&T=
20420&P=1.

23. Part of this dissatisfaction, though, seems to come from the idea of telling these
sorts of stories at all. The fan fiction forum is by far the smallest of all the Battle.net

forums, and it does not even feature much fan fiction. Instead, what fans tend to do is to create their own story line by having players submit characters and then have the characters walk through various quests, *Dungeons & Dragons* style. In effect, gamers create their own stories through a medium with which they are far more familiar. The collaborative nature of this style of writings marks the sort of storytelling that might well become the product of online collaborative communities.

24. ProjectXii, Battle.net Fan Fiction Forum, April 7, 2004, http://www.battle.net/forums/thread.aspx?FN=fanfiction&T=26533&P=1&ReplyCount=47#post26533.

~

CHAPTER TWELVE

The Funk of Forty Thousand Years; or, How the (Un)Dead Get Their Groove On

Marc Leverette

Turn and turn about; in these shadows from whence a new dawn will break, it is you who are the zombies.

—Jean-Paul Sartre

Thy dead men shall live, together with my dead body shall they arise. Awake and sing, ye that dwell in dust: for thy dew is as the dew of herbs, and the earth shall cast out the dead.

—Isaiah 26:19

And if you are undead—I'll find out about that too.

—J. Peterman on *Seinfeld*

Pleasures of the Flesh;
or, A (Brief) Propaedeutic on the Living Dead

I survived a zombie attack (perhaps it was a plague). No, seriously. I hold onto this moment in a highly apocryphal set of memories, and even though I can't recall what's real and what's not, I'll tell you anyway. Freud calls this "cryptonesia," an aberration of memory in writing.[1] I remember them stumbling their way down the main street, lumbering across the courtyard steps of my small town, shuffling their way through the strewn bodies. It was a very salient image.[2]

My father took me, as I recall. I even got a button proving it that I placed on the denim jacket I had covered with patches and pins of my favorite hair metal groups. What's funny about this to me is that I have no real recollection of the facts of that day—only glimpses, shock-cut flashes of the living dead wandering around downtown Fort Myers, Florida. Only when I recounted this story years later in preparation for this book did I realize that it was the filming of George Romero's third *Dead* movie and not an actual assault of the (un)dead. What this conflation does, however, is remind of the ambiguous dialectic that the zombie presents. In a constant flux between animation and reanimation, the walking, mumbling dead, full of the threat of something more terrifying than death, a contagion without seeming purpose, afford the opportunity to discuss what grips us, what enthralls us, what entertains us, and what terrifies us.[3]

While other traditional Hollywood monster types that scared us two generations ago are now spending their retirement on the cereal aisle with Frankenberry and company—able to watch the post-seventies, post-slasher horror generation try to outscare (or outgross) each other only from the sidelines—zombies, with that "plodding, 'never say die' quality," as Shawn McIntosh argued in chapter 1, are unique in that they have managed to endure as frightening monsters in an age of hyperrealistic splatter films and video games. This final chapter seeks to render problematic this conception of zombie fright and call into question their postmodern authenticity via an explicit "defanging," or rather a deconstructive "queering," of the zombie trope.

The more I became consumed with these living dead, these autoantonymic ontologies, the more I began to realize that the real question the (un)dead bring to the table is not what they say about schlock-horror or B-movie madness—rather, it is their Being that offers an unnerving commentary regarding the potential liminality of being human. For the zombie exists somewhere *between*. As Guy Debord says of the (really) dead in his *Comments on the Society of the Spectacle*, "They exist somewhere between the Acheron and the Lethe, these dead whom the spectacle has not properly buried, supposedly slumbering while awaiting the summons which will wake them all."[4] As such, I wish to here "wake" the living dead. I mean this in all its possible variants (i.e., from a funeral celebration wherein we watch the body and get drunk and celebrate, to literally waking up and causing a clatter). To examine the implications of the (un)dead, I will discuss the caesura separating living from dead, man from animal, the civil human from the cannibal corpse.

Our monsters must be considered from within the complex matrices that generate them, such as social, historical, and cultural relations. As a "mixed category," the monster inherently resists classification—and the zombie doubly so, for reasons discussed below.[5] According to Mark Jancovich, "Different groups will represent the monstrous in different ways and representations will develop historically."[6] And in her book *Skin Shows: Gothic Horror and the Technology of Monsters*, Judith Halberstam makes an almost identical claim: "The body that scares and appalls changes over time, as do the individual characteristics that add up to monstrosity, as do the preferred interpretations of monstrosity."[7]

While being a monster made up of more than one creature is not uncommon—that is, two physical states conflicting with one another as in lycanthropy, vampirism, the chimera, and so on—we find much of this discourse critiquing science in some way, the monsters often in some kind of procrustean internal and external struggle. They belong to neither species, inapposite to each, but maintaining the worst of both worlds.[8] As such, the monstrosity is to truly be found not in the Other that infects, but in the horror that some aspect of humanity remains, a corpse that is no longer an I. At the threshold of life and death, human and nonhuman, the zombie serves as an apparent deconstruction of our every ontology, with the binary of life and death now represented as illustrated in figure 12.1.

This is all, of course, to highlight the fact that the zombie, by its very nature, undergoes a kind of queering to serve its horror-ific function. As Sue Ellen Case noted almost two decades ago:

> The queer, unlike the rather polite categories of gay and lesbian, revels in the discourse of the loathsome, the outcast, the idiomatically proscribed position of same-sex desire. Unlike petitions for civil rights, queer revels constitute a kind of activism that attacks the dominant notion of the natural. The queer is the taboo-breaker, the *monstrous*, the uncanny.[9]

Queer thus offers a challenge to the "Platonic parameters of being—the *borders of life and death*."[10] Whereas Harry Benshoff has written a wonderful history of the relationship between homosexuality and the horror film, I am less

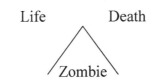

Figure 12.1.   The Binary of Life and Death

interested in sexuality here and more concerned with the possibilities of queering as a liminal Otherness.[11] According to Annamarie Jagose:

> It is not simply that queer has yet to solidify and take on a more consistent profile, but rather that its definitional *indeterminacy*, its elasticity, is one of its constituent characteristics.[12]

As such, I am interested in how audiences queer the zombie as a monster defined by indeterminacy, undecidability, liminality—in other words, an inbetweenness of difference. If, as Queer Nation activist Karl Knapper argues, "queerness is about acknowledging and celebrating difference, embracing what sets you apart,"[13] then the zombie as a trope in philosophy and art "rejects a minoritizing logic of toleration or simple political interest-representation in favor of a more thorough resistance to regimes of the normal."[14] While traditional critics of the horror film have focused on its tropes and genre in a great many ways, by queering what we fear, we can see a breakdown in what may actually be terrifying to us.

Noël Carroll, in his now-classic *The Philosophy of Horror*, pays close attention to horror's ooze, rot, slime, and blood—generic motifs reifying transition and transgression (hallmarks of "the queer"). Carroll ultimately argues that "what horrifies is that which lies outside cultural categories."[15] In short, Carroll is (perhaps unwittingly) arguing that what is most terrifying is the queer, or more specifically, a Derridean kind of cultural undecidability.

An(a)esthetic Undecidability; or, How I Learned to Start Worrying and Fear the Queer

A system's undecidability is . . . more powerful than the value of truth.

—Jacques Derrida

The zombie, as a philosophical monstrosity, thus resides at the edge of being, its status as neither alive nor dead undoing ontologies and dialectics. Here we must render problematic the dual purposes of the decidable center—that choice which renders something alive or dead: while on the one hand, that which is the dominant normative construct in a culture is centered, all else being marginalized and lowered to the status of subaltern, on the other, that which ontologically is in the middle of an either/or dialectic finds itself an undecidable. This is a most awkward place, a place where we often find Jacques Derrida looking about (using a variety of terms such as *pharmakon*, *supplement*, etc.), a place where indeterminacy, the cultural and physiological apprehensions about that which is not this or that, is the oft-horrific norm.

For a number of reasons, I avoid the term *ambiguity* here in favor of Derrida's term of choice: *undecidability*. In an analogy to mathematician Kurt Gödel's discovery of undecidable propositions, Derrida suggests that structures be described, provisionally at least, as undecidables.[16] Gödel, most famously in the essay *On Formally Undecidable Propositions of Principia Mathematica and Related Systems*, demonstrated that statements concerning the completeness of systems more complex than that of logical systems of the first order cannot be demonstrated within these systems.[17] Essentially, Gödel showed that no matter how perfect a language, it was always and already impossible to prove that some X could never be found to be not-X, forcing mathematics to join the physical sciences and philosophy in admitting that abstract reasoning could not be used to avoid ambiguities of decidability, deduction, paradox, and probability. In "The Double Session," Derrida appropriates the theorem as such:

> An undecidable proposition, as Gödel demonstrated in 1931, is a proposition which, given a system of axioms governing a multiplicity, is neither an analytical nor deductive consequence of those axioms, nor in contradiction with them, neither is true nor false with respect to these axioms.[18]

It is not coincidental, I think, that there is an idea similar in physics that was "discovered" within a few years of Gödel's formulation.

Erwin Schrödinger, in 1935, published a way of thinking about the circumstance of radioactive decay that is useful here. In a brief paragraph, he described (in more lucid, complex terms than I do below) what is now referred to as the paradox of Schrödinger's cat. We can imagine we have a living cat and we place that cat in a thick lead box. The cat, without question, is alive at this point. We then place a vial of cyanide in and seal the box. We do not know if the cat is alive or if it has broken the cyanide capsule and died, yet we may ask ourselves: Is the cat alive or dead? Must it not be one or the other? Since we do not know, the cat is both dead and alive, according to quantum law (given that zombified cats have yet to be recognized by the scientific community as a third choice). We find it is now an undecidable, in a superposition of states. It is only when we break open the box and learn the condition of the cat that the superposition is lost and the cat becomes one or the other (alive or dead) and its state of undecidability draws to close. We close the state, collapsing its decidability into an impossible possibility.[19]

Calling the system(s) by which life and death coexist undecidable is not what I am doing here. Rather, systematicity is undeniable; what is undecidable is its content. I am not merely attempting to stress the incompleteness and in-consistency with(in) a theory of the (un)dead, but rather I wish to remind the reader that we cannot deny the possibility of determining every element of the life/death dichotomy as both consequence and contradiction. Undecidability haunts the structure of life and death, while the structure of life and death haunts its undecidability.

In a 1971 *Tel Quel* interview with Jean-Louis Houdebine and Guy Scar-petta, reprinted in *Positions*, Derrida notes that to call structures *undecidables* is to argue that they are

> unities of simulacrum . . . "false" verbal properties . . . that can no longer be in-cluded within philosophical (binary) opposition, but which, however, inhabit philosophical opposition, resisting and disorganizing it, *without ever* constitut-ing a third term, without ever leaving room for a solution in the form of spec-ulative dialectics.[20]

Derrida, we must recall, emphasized that the notion of undecidability in its very negativity has such a sense only because of its irreducible reference to the ideal that is decidability, its revolutionary and disconcerting sense re-maining "essentially and intrinsically haunted in its sense of origin by the *te-los* of decidability—whose disruption it marks."[21]

Undecidability, then, must be considered a kind of incompleteness and inconsistency in which we find ourselves ensconced every time a fissure in the life/death binary occurs (whether in gamespace, on the silver screen—anywhere, for that matter). Undecidability constitutes a *medium*, the ele-ment between binary oppositions, a space between dyads, while at the same time reifying those structural distinctions. Structural undecidables are there-fore "the *medium* in which opposites are opposed, the movement and the play that links them among themselves, reverses them or makes one side cross over into the other."[22] This "floating indetermination" permits the substitu-tion and the play of conceptual binary oppositions, which, however *and* be-cause of this—the inescapable tendency of these denominations—are inca-pable of defining the medium from which they emerge, and their being is, thus, ontologically reliant on what they are not.[23]

This is why *ambiguity* is such a tricky term when discussing the con-tranymic ontological status of the "living dead": it does not offer any sense of distinction, whereas *undecidability* is not simply some ambivalent lack of clar-ity. In this way, binary opposition, as has been laid out by the history of West-ern thought and articulated in structuralism, is nothing more than the at-tempt to bring an end to the play of undecidability, to isolate and cut away the middle place. This kind of "restricted play" of philosophical coupling proceeds in its reconstituting of undecidables as dialectical contradictions that will ultimately succumb to eventual dissolution. But, notes Derrida, undecidability "is not contradiction in the Hegelian form of contradiction."[24] Undecidability is therefore what suspends decidability, particularly in dialectical forms involving the *mediation* of contraries and contradictions. In this middle space, we find decidability and dialecticism carving themselves out, along with definitiveness and structure. This undecidability, then, must remain irreducible, irresolvable.[25]

Undecidability, a zombie trope that is seemingly always coming to get us, floats indefinitely between the possibilities of mediation, between the structures of life and death, in a position of anteriority to the possibilities of that very systematicity. The state of being (un)dead—notice my marking both undead and dead at once—must as a result be considered structurally undecidable, a hymenal space that is (n)either one thing (alive) (n)or another (not alive).

Demonstrating how the structure of the "hymen" is undecidable because of this kind of syntactical (re)marking, Derrida writes:

> What holds for "hymen" also holds, *mutatis mutandis* for all other signs which, like *pharmakon, supplément, différance,* and others, have a double, contradictory, undecidable value that always derives from their syntax, whether the latter is in a sense "internal," articulating and combining under the same yoke, *huph'hen,* two incompatible meanings, or "external," dependent on the code in which the word is made to function. But the syntactical composition and decomposition of a sign renders this alternative between internal and external inoperative. One is simply dealing with greater or lesser syntactical units at work, and economic differences in condensation.[26]

Derrida himself occupies a hymenal space, in between (*entre*) literature and philosophy, deconstructing the binary oppositions between the two forms, *Glas* being the most obvious example, although another excellent example is the reading in "The Double Session" (*La double séance*) of Stéphane Mallarmé's *Mimique* inside of Plato's *Philebus*.[27] For Derrida, the hymen (in this most unusual sense) occupies the middlest of middle places: it is an either/or dichotomy in between another either/or dichotomy. Derrida uses this to dismantle Hegel's conception that there is any kind of synthesis that lies beyond the either/or of an argument. He also uses it to render problematic Lévi-Strauss's notion of the third space that mediates binary oppositions. This is to say that the concern is not "this/that," but simply "/."[28]

The hymen may then be considered a kind of "pharmacological supplement," one that can represent (n)either being unbroken (virginity) (n)or penetration (consummation). It is (n)either inside (n)or outside. It is, as I will now illustrate through a few extended examples, specifically, the folds and ambiguities of language and zombies, neither of which has meaning or ontology that can simply be *decided*.[29]

In this way, language is constantly presenting itself to us as a Janus figure. Janus, the Roman god whose name gives us January (*Januarius*), was the god of thresholds, gates, doors, doorways, beginnings, and endings and so, appropriately, was often portrayed as Janus Geminus (twin Janus) or Bifrons, with two heads looking in opposite directions (one to the past and one to the future).[30] Linguistically, the contranym is the differential equivalent of Janus's cleaved sight ("cleaved" itself being a contranym), polysemically presenting themselves as their own opposites.[31] Like the zombie with life and death, contranyms turn language itself into the aporetic object. We can say, "The sun is out." And by that we mean the sun can clearly be seen. But we could then go indoors, flick a switch, and proclaim, "The lights are out," which is to say they cannot be seen. This aporetic play leaves us with words meaning their own opposites—homonymic antonyms spelled the same and pronounced the same. But who would want to say such things?

As Derrida reminded us frequently, these occur somewhat often in English, making the translation of his Joycean puns indeed an albatross around the neck of his translators. Since English is such a confusing language to begin with, it is probably a good thing our vocabulary tends to suppress these antiological urges.[32]

Undecidability thus resembles syncategoremata, the secondary parts of discourse which, contra to that which is categorematic, are open expressions, unclosed in that they have no determined meaning, no fixity; they must predicate jointly, in a middle place.[33] *And, but, every, if, in between, only, or, not, some,* and so on—these expressions cannot be used categorematically, only in conjunction with other words, terms, expressions, *decidables*. These linguistic undecidables must be used with predicates with respect to their specific organizational function.[34] Furthermore, as decidability is ontologically reliant on undecidability, so goes the reverse. Undecidables can never semantically be their own signification; this void is part of the ontic-ethical orientation of grammar, the "priority" of "categoremata."[35] However, what we find in the work of someone like James Joyce or the Symbolist poet Mallarmé is a revealing of syncategoremata (such as *or* or *in between*) as a re-marking.

Speaking of Mallarmé's use of *entre*, Derrida strains to illustrate it "can be nominalized, turn into a quasi-categorem, receive a definite article, or even be made plural."[36] In "The Double Session," he illustrates that the writing of Mallarmé is an attempt to explore the possibilities of syntactical excess, where the medium becomes the message. Mallarmé plays with the undecidability of communication form in order to deconstruct the impossible possibility of the mediated center. His writing is, therefore, a kind of literature in which "the suspense is due only to the placement and not to the content of words."[37]

But I would like to move now from the destabilization of language to the destabilization of the life/death binary itself.

The idea of the "zombie" is a late arrival in the horror canon of Western culture. And without the clear binary distinctions between life and death, the idea of the undead or, contranymically, "living death," is rather meaningless. A better way to write it may be ~~life/death~~, as we are essentially left with an aesthetics under erasure. The dichotomy of life and death thus establishes a space, a site, of horrific violence against difference, where the pleasures of the flesh give over to the sins of transgression.

From the opening frames of the film version of *The Serpent and the Rainbow*, we read:

> In the legends of voodoo
> the Serpent is a symbol of Earth.
> The Rainbow is a symbol of Heaven.
> Between the two,
> all creatures must live and die.
> But because he has a soul
> Man can be trapped in a terrible place
> Where death is only the beginning.

This considering of the zombie as a liminal entity between life and death is clearly played for terror in most horror encounters. Perhaps this is what gives the living dead their dangerous touch. Perhaps there is nothing so frightening or monstrous as becoming something that is neither this nor that.

Even popular commentaries are quick to observe the deconstructive notes played by the living dead's liminality. For example, as Manohla Dargis notes in a *New York Times* review of *Land of the Dead*: "Neither fully alive or dead, zombies exist between the margins, in a twilight state that makes them among the most unsettling of all man-made creatures. That's the essential paradox of all zombie movies."[38] Additionally, as A. Loudermilk observes in his autoethnographic piece about *Dawn of the Dead*:

> Romero's postmodern zombie rises from a variety of tombs, a hybrid of corporeal and ideological monsters. Voodoo zombie, mummy and pod person, all

play into Romero's conception of the postmodern zombie in bodies that tread the liminal position between human and inhuman (or life and death).[39]

And according to Steven Shaviro, from his now-classic essay on Romero:

> Zombies always come in between: they insinuate themselves with the uncanny, interstitial space that separates (but thereby also connects) inside and outside, the private and the public, life and death. In this liminal position, they are obscene objects of voyeuristic fascination.[40]

This extended discussion of the undecidable has been to place the living dead within the context of their in-betweenness. Additionally, it is clear that Western culture does not like this third space, the space of the slash, the space of the slice, the space in the middle. This space is a space of horror (werewolves, etc.), but the zombie held a unique place in film and popular culture throughout most of the twentieth century. It responded to the terrors of race, colonization, capitalism, and so much more, all from a non-Gothic tradition. As such, the zombie has almost entirely entered the popular imagination as (or by way of) an Other—a monstrous Other. From its place in Haitian lore and the American misinterpretation of that culture to its addressing of issues of contagion in a post-AIDS era, the portrayals of the (un)dead have changed and evolved to fit contemporary fears, anxieties, and social issues. A main reason is, of course, their undecidable status, *between* life and death. Other reasons may be a (re)addressing of the question of liminality in relation to horror and their symbolic emptiness.

Priapism without Attention; or, "Get Off My Property, You Brain-Eatin' Zombie Bastards!"

> Eyewitness accounts described the assassins as ordinary-looking people, misshapen monsters, people who look like they're in a trance, and creatures that look like people but behave like animals.
>
> —Radio announcement in *Night of the Living Dead*

In the first scene of Romero's *Night of the Living Dead*, we encounter the first zombie of the contemporary era. Outside of the menacing effect he has on poor, dimwitted Barbara, I've always found this to be an incredibly sad creature, one that looks more in pain and suffering than filled with malice. As Gregory Waller observes in his book *The Living and the Undead*:

The first of the living dead that we see in the film is a man before he is a thing; he is one of us before we realize that he is one of them. He and all the rest of the living dead retain the physical appearance of human beings. They do not suddenly bare oversized canine teeth or stare with blood-red eyes. Even when they are eating the remains of the two teenagers, the living dead never cease to look like—and therefore in some fashion to be?—human beings. . . . The living dead, as Romero told an interviewer, are "the neighbors."[41]

Thus life, for Romero, is intensely entwined with death, just as death is with life. As such, death is always and already with(in) us, constantly, every day present. For this reason, we must take very seriously the living dead—they are us and we them under these terms. If this be the case, when we consider horror fiction and the us/them breakdown that usually ensues, what kind of ethical imperative are we faced with as we stare down the (un)dead? Are we killing ourselves?

Again, I wish to turn to Derrida's notion of the undecidable to help us navigate around the slippery bedrock that is morality in this case.

There is no responsibility, no ethico-political decision, that must not pass through the proofs of the incalculable or the undecidable. Otherwise everything would be reducible to calculation, program, causality, and at best "hypothetical imperative."[42]

So this imperative, then, is an ethico-political one, and for the zombies who, for many, function as the death-drive made flesh, we find this very wish perverted. There is no "true" death for the living dead. Even though their flesh is alive, it is a priapismic flesh beyond their control.[43] In other words, the living dead are basically just Thanatos in drag.

While modern culture is often haunted by the Freudian death wish, the zombie presents that simple psychoanalytic theory as a paradox. In a kind of Žižekian perversion, the zombie-Thanatos has nothing to do with death at all. Its horror lies in its embodiment as death and life not being the only choices. The horror of (an)other (non)life can be quelled only by living or dying. The death-drive as the unattainable *objet petit* that makes us alive is something lacked by the (un)dead (and here I would include other punished monsters such as vampires, ghosts [talk about a return of the repressed!], etc.). Thus the faux Thanatos that the zombie often represents is an affront to our Being (in both biological and existential senses). Zombies are transgression at its finest, since the living dead act as an affront to *both* the living and the dead.

Michel Foucault argues that the act of transgression is no doubt enthralling to witness because "the limit opens violently on to the limitless, find[ing] itself suddenly carried away by the content it had rejected and fulfilled by this alien plentitude which invades it to the core of its being."[44] The limit of which Foucault speaks is, of course, subjectivity. And those moments of transgression are when we strive to overstep the boundaries of our individual subjectivity. As a result, the *jouissance* we find in watching zombie cinema or experiencing the (un)dead in a video game is a kind of "mode of 'expenditure' or *dépense* that, pushed to the limit of all reason, utility, morality, sense of meaning, takes experience beyond experience itself, opening what was once oneself on to an apprehension of an impossible totality."[45]

The zombie crosses the boundary of what is taboo. It is at once corporeal and ephemeral. Yet we find intense pleasure in these transgressive moments—terrifying as they may be. Perhaps we consume zombie media in order to "hoodwink ourselves. . . . We want to get across without taking the final step."[46] Death is something we can never experience subjectively, and (un)death is something perhaps even more uncertain, undecidable, and horrific, yet these moments subvert and pervert the taboos of death. Georges Bataille explains it as such:

> As we are about to take the final step, we are beside ourselves with desire, impotent, in the clutch of a force that demands our disintegration. . . . How sweet it is to remain in the grip of the desire to burst without going the whole way, without taking the final step![47]

This kind of mediated escapism is a kind of queering, in that it celebrates a different and unknowable Other. The living dead are a celebration of the liminal space that we can only hope we never experience directly. As Victor Turner explains, "Liminal entities are neither here nor there; they are betwixt and between the positions assigned and arrayed by law, custom, convention, and ceremonial."[48] Thus the (un)dead can be considered a kind of liminal personae (or "threshold people").

Let us speak momentarily, then, of a liminal persona—one that might not immediately come to mind. I allude to *South Park*'s zombie send-up "Pinkeye," which featured a Chef-ified version of "Thriller." However, it's not Chef I want to examine here, but rather poor Kenny McCormick (the first zombie of that particular episode's Worcestershire sauce–induced plague). According to Brian Ott, Kenny is a televisual representation of liminality *par excellence*. Kenny "exists on the margin or limen between life and death," which is perhaps why his friends aren't shocked by his countless deaths and infinite returns (Kenny ultimately dies, "for real," in the episode "Kenny Dies"—yet he somehow returns a season later).[49] The fact that Kenny's deaths and resurrections are never explained cuts to the heart of why Kenny and other zombies are so interesting. While they at once breach and transgress social configurations, it is their liminality that "dissolves the norms that govern structured and institutionalized relationships and is accompanied by experiences of unprecedented potency."[50]

There is a pleasure "that accompanies liminality," as Ott argues, "a material one experienced on an extra- or pre-symbolic level." Thus, the liminal images of this "between" offer us *khōra* becomings, transgressive precisely because they cut to the core of the social and symbolic orders. How, then, does the liminal zombie unleash its monstrous capacity in relation to the living human? While there has been much recent critical attention given to the issues of contagion as found in the "cannibal cow," I wish here to hijack the name of an old death metal group and discuss the cannibal corpse.[51]

What we find in *Night of the Living Dead*'s move to distinguish its "ghouls" (the term *zombie*, we must remember, is never actually used) from humans is a reinforcement of the human as nonanimal. By engaging with the living dead on the level of the animal, we find the film in a profound disavowal of humanity's own animality, signaling what Derrida calls a "complicit, continued and organized involvement in a veritable war of the species."[52] For Derrida, the border that separates the human and the animal is not a clear, singular line; rather, it is heterogeneous, multiple. In late twentieth-century media culture, we find this history, this distinction, far from confident as we move through a phase where anthropocentric subjectivity is being called into radical uncertainty. The zombie is yet another example of what lies beyond the so-called human, unmaking our senses of self, hurling us into an uncertain ontology whereby human can be defined as beyond simply "not-zombie," "not-animal," but a multiplicity, a heterogeneous network of organizing relations. As Derrida says:

> No one can deny seriously, or for very long, that men do all they can in order to dissimulate this cruelty or to hide it from themselves, in order to organize on a global scale the forgetting or misunderstanding of this violence that some would compare to the worst cases of genocide.[53]

Let us now turn our attention to what could be seen as this Derridean zombie genocide to examine more closely the spaces of the (un)dead as this kind of cannibal corpse.

Living the Good Death;
or, The Ideological (Deconstructive) Work of Zombies

Edward Said, in *Culture and Imperialism*, argues against taking up any established, settled interpretive position, in favor of an outlook located "between domains, between forms . . . between languages."[54] For Said, this allows the critic to maintain a liminal (née undecidable) perspective whence one can read "contrapuntally."

Thus, in describing the flesh-devouring figure from Canadian lore, the Wendigo, acclaimed writer Margaret Atwood used language that skated dangerously close to recounting what it "means" to fear the living dead, a twofold fear: "fear of being eaten by one, and fear of becoming one." For Atwood, the real terror of the Wendigo is not in being consumed; rather, it is the becoming moment, explaining, "If you go Wendigo, you may end up losing your human mind and personality."[55]

As such, I propose that the zombie is a state of exception, enabled as the cultural construction of beings abandoned by law. According to Giorgio Agamben's theory, the sovereign holds the ability to define the state of exception. If we adjust Elspeth Probyn's discussion of the cannibal in *Carnal Appetites*, we can see that the zombie replicates the functions of Agamben's *homo sacer*. She writes: "The cannibal reminds us of that which cannot be in the polis, the social life of man."[56] This very exclusion defines humanity; to be human is to not be zombie. However, since *zombie* is a relatively new term for critical consumption, I wish to place this state of exception under a different critical lens and discuss how the West has conceptualized the "cannibal" as an Other (and not perhaps coincidentally a Caribbean Other) over the last two centuries.

In its purest form (I'm talking the *Oxford English Dictionary* here), the term *cannibal* primarily means "a man that eats human flesh; a man-eater, an anthropophagite." And while this definition says nothing of the living/dead status of the "man," it goes almost without saying that cannibalism has been the main modus operandi for zombies post-Romero ("Must . . . eat . . . brains," etc.). *28 Days Later* notwithstanding, the "goal" of the post-Romero cinematic zombie has been to consume the flesh of the living (the fact that it acts as a contagion is seemingly a by-product unbeknownst to the zombies themselves).

Etymologically *cannibal* was a neologism used to describe the acts of anthropophagy committed by Carib natives, yet the idea of the cannibal has long provided Western imaginations with an explosive cultural fantasy; the enduring power of cannibalism can be found, as Peter Hulme argues, in "its utility as a form of cultural criticism."[57] Thus, an ideological power behind the "cannibal" that can be transposed onto the "zombie" is a kind of motif underlying its symbolism. As Frank Lestringant points out, "The spectacular impact of the macabre feasts, which are so uninhibitedly played before the audience, is really intended to demonstrate the superabundance of meaning which they carry."[58] Considered in these terms, the cannibalistic, flesh- and brain-eating zombie acts as a multivalent sign, its polyvalence organized as a symbolic field around the spectacle of horrific consumption and corporeal violation. Perhaps this is why it makes the stuff of nightmares into horror fiction gold, or, in the words of Bataille, "The very prohibition attached to [it] is what arouses the desire."[59]

The zombie, then, like the cannibal, actually tells us a story about ourselves. As Priscilla Walton explains of the cannibal's relation to contemporary Western cultural practices (as well as those of the nineteenth and twentieth centuries), "Cannibalistic narratives can reveal more about Western discursive formulations than they do about actual cannibal practices."[60] As Walton notes, the narratives found within the imperialist writings of the eighteenth and nineteenth centuries found cannibals lurking in jungles, dangerous and dark figures, awaiting their chance to eat the "innocent" (and white) explorers. Much like the Haitian *zonbi* text, the images served as a kind of justification for missionary narratives that sought to civilize these "savage" Others, always from somewhere else (Haiti, Africa, etc.). The threat of this line of narrative, however, is that it is not untoward to the homeland; rather, it is an isolationist narrative that reminds us of the dangers of traveling elsewhere. This, of course, changed when Romero took "them" and made them "us." The displacement of the (un)dead from exotic Other to next-door neighbor rapidly changed the perception and possibilities of zombie horror.

By the late twentieth century, as Walton illustrates, the cannibal narrative became more focused on the discourses of disease, contagion, eating, and consumption. She notes, "Late 20th century consumer practices and commodity culture increasingly draw upon the rhetoric of the cannibal both to drive consumption and to shape conceptions of the body, suggesting a transformation from modern industrial culture to postmodern, postindustrial culture."[61] It is not a leap, then, to consider the zombie, after Walton's cannibal, as extending into the critique of the body and its relationship with the flows of contemporary global capital.

For example, in the 1980s and 1990s, cannibal narratives often took the form of articulating "new" diseases, such as SARS, Ebola, and, of course, AIDS, wherein we humans were eaten away from the inside out—cannibalizing ourselves, if you will. To Walton, this is a sign that cannibalism as a creation of Western colonialism has come home to haunt us. For her, these new infectious diseases are a reminder that globalization has taken us to a place where "we are all becoming increasingly savage in our civility, to the point where our civility is actually beginning to consume us"—which is to say that the postindustrial cannibal is essentially the "infected" of 28 *Days Later* and

28 Weeks Later, still deploying a rhetorical function yet responding not to colonial and imperialist fears or cold war isolationism, but rather to a world living under the looming specter of bird flu pandemic and bovine spongiform encephalopathy (BSE, or mad cow disease). Much as the cannibal was the nineteenth-century receptacle of the anxieties of savagery, industrialization, technology, and capitalism, the contemporary age offers us cannibalized images and (un)dead Others.[62]

Consider the dialectic of binaries laid out by Daniel Cottom, in *Cannibals and Philosophers: Bodies of Enlightenment*:

> The machine might press its image upon plants, animals, organs, humans, and everything else in the universe; the cannibal swallowed the distinctions among things. In place of the recursive modeling provided by the machine, we have the progressive destruction of identity imaged through the cannibal. The machine is the technological abstraction of the cannibal; the cannibal, the sensuous realization of the machine.[63]

Hence, the living dead aren't merely the rotting corpses of Romero's America or the slaves under Legendre's evil eye in Haiti—they are the post-Fordist somnambulist walking through *Fight Club*, the unsettled housewives of *Thelma and Louise*, the faux savior who can't tell if he's dreaming or not in *The Matrix* movies, and, perhaps most disturbing, the child psychiatrist so dis-tuned from the information economy that he doesn't even know he's dead in *The Sixth Sense*.[64] This technology/living dead articulation often forces the subject to blur the lines of (the) posthuman(ity) in the most corporeal of ways.[65] Yet the formation of this kind of Western subjectivity is crucial for theorizing the eternal present. The negative dialectic that occurs within the living dead function as a kind of Derridean speciesism that at once reifies yet undoes both the symbolic and political economies.

In "The Eighteenth Brumaire of Louis Bonaparte," Karl Marx summons the image of the living dead to distinguish a revolutionary evolution of the past and a reactionary one, the former found in the original French and English revolutions, the latter with the events of 1848:

> The awakening of the dead in those revolutions therefore served the purpose of glorifying the new struggles, not of parodying the old; of magnifying the given tasks in imagination, not taking flight from their solution in reality; of finding once more the spirit of revolution, not of making its ghost walk again.[66]

There is certainly something clearly Marxian in the treatment of the living dead in their representation (at least in their popular cinematic exorcisms), particularly the orthodox view of ideology often presented: "*Sie wissen das nicht, aber sie tun es*" ("They do not know it, but they are doing it").[67] Not all examples of undecidability, however, as it exists between the life/death binary are "horrific" in the entertainment sense: consider the 2005 media spectacle surrounding the "euthanasia" of Terri Schiavo.[68] I use these examples to show how the spaces between binaries are often where danger lurks behind every dark corner, how the controversies of modern life occupy third spaces of *neither* this *nor* that.

In *The New Rhetoric*, Chaïm Perelman and Lucie Obrechts-Tyteca provide a key insight worth noting here. They hold that arguments of social matters are not self-evident (unlike, for them, mathematics or other pure sciences). The answers to life's most difficult questions are never yes/no or true/false. Rather, they must be considered in degrees of *more or less*.[69] And it is how these answers materialize wherein we find the possibilities of imprinting one part of the dialectic.

χώρα (or *chora*)[70] is used in Plato in a sense close to *space* or *place*, describing the milieu in which forms materialize.[71] Elizabeth Grosz, after Derrida, insists that *khōra*

> must be understood without any definite article, has an acknowledged role at the very foundations of the concept of spatiality, place and placing: it signifies, at its most literal level, notions of "space," "location," "site," "region," "locale," "country," but it also contains an irreducible, yet often overlooked connection with the functions of femininity, being associated with a series of sexually-coded terms—"mother," "nurse," "receptacle," and "imprint-bearer."[72]

Both Julia Kristeva and Luce Irigaray have written widely adopted interpretations of Plato's reading of *khōra*—each, however, paying significantly more attention to its question of femininity (i.e., its placement as mother, receptacle, or nurse). Irigaray in particular criticizes Plato's connecting of the ideas of *khōra* and femininity in a way she sees as too unproblematical.[73]

As the nonspace from which everything arises, *khōra* is the slash of im/possibility. A Derridean economy of undecidability undermines not only the possibilities of life and death as dichotomous distinctions but also its very impossibility.[74] Hence, if we return to the interview with Derrida discussed earlier, "Eating Well," as well as its follow-up "The Animal That Therefore I Am (More to Follow)," we find the question of subjectivity itself placed under erasure as Derrida deconstructs the essentialist center of "the human definition." For Derrida, this *khōral* space of discourse splinters what he calls the "carnophallogocentrism" of the (un)fixed boundary between human and its Other.

Even though he is discussing the "animal" and not the zombie, I would still argue that Derrida's updating of his own neologism *phallogocentrism* is worth considering for our deconstructive purposes. For Derrida, phallogocentrism is the privileging of *logos* in Western culture (signified over signifier, logic over emotion, etc.), linked to the masculine/patriarchal bias of discourses of subjectivity. These definitions are founded on a kind of binary dualism that is in constant need of interrogating (such as human/animal, masculine/feminine, etc.—in our case, life/death). As such, it is our eating of flesh that, for Derrida, calls into question the unacknowledged hierarchy of human over animal (the sovereignty that allows us to "sacrifice" one life for another). Because "men have given themselves the right to give," we are not the "animal" in question and, thus, allow ourselves the "right" to the above-mentioned "genocide."[75] Derrida's concept of carno-phallogocentrism points our attention in the direction of this very sovereign subjectivity—we have the power to kill or let live all other animals. Yet when we consider the place of postindustrial processes, post-Fordist labor, and postmodern subjectivities, aren't we left with a constant question of this sovereignty as we further cannibalize the "standing reserve" that is ourselves?[76]

This is to say that the system of orderings we find in everyday life are always already being undone from within; these essentialist frameworks are always already deconstructing themselves. When we enjoy zombie media, we are reifying our own state of exception through that which we can never fully realize, nor would we seemingly want to. When we, as audiences and consumers, so engage with a celebration of "living death," we are, to paraphrase Zygmunt Bauman, living "through the deaths of others."[77] As we voyeuristically slash and slay our way through video games, movies, and other mediated zombie experiences, we are killing our deaths, while living our lives. To kill nondeath, to conquer the in-between, is, however, a melancholic drive from which there can be no victory. Our technology keeps getting better, but the zombies just keep coming back.[78]

The "gift" of nondeath that the zombies thus give is a kind of Derridean "quivering" where our mortal fear can become actualized, which is to say that it gives a gruesome, rotting face to those most dreadful of anxieties that haunt our world—a world in which our sovereignty is somehow governed by our capacity to live, die, and stave off the urge to eat ourselves. The zombie is, therefore, our Janus-faced Other, to invoke Bruno Latour's phrasing, in that its undecidable status falls as the slash between human/nonhuman, us/Other, living/dead, at once telling us explicitly about ourselves while often serving as a critical commentary on what we might become tomorrow.[79]

It is the zombie that reminds of the possibilities of what our tomorrows might make us.

As noted by Jamie Russell, the zombie (specifically that of Romero) has "a symbolic potential unmatched by any other horror movie monster."[80] But it may also be the symbolic emptiness that gives them their power; people can fill them with whatever fear they want.[81] From colonial capitalist nightmares and racist melodramas to parables of contagion and the post-human dilemma, the living dead seem to always and already serve some interpretive purpose.[82] The zombie as deconstruction, as has been shown, brings forth not simply apocalyptic chaos, as so many movies would imply, but a complete breakdown of the social and natural worlds: laws, dichotomies, food chains, and hierarchies all become meaningless (im)possibilities in a world where the limen is suspended as (ir)rational space. Even after the zombie plague is eradicated, the dead, as Michel de Certeau points out, will still "haunt the living."[83] There is, thus, no returning.

But what has happened to the zombie? Has it been "defanged"? I'd like to think not. Perhaps this is why they never entered the cereal aisle to room with old Count Chocula. Perhaps it's simply that a rotting corpse may not be the best way to market children's breakfast food. Perhaps the (un)dead are too complicated to pin down, too volatile to read, too open to interpret, too slow to be serious, but too numerous to stop. Perhaps we're trying too hard to domesticate that which is neither this nor that. Perhaps, as Derrida reminds us, "Monsters cannot be announced. One cannot simply say: 'Here are our monsters,' without immediately turning the monsters into pets."[84]

> Hail to your dark skin
> Hiding the fact you're dead again
>
> —The Shins, "Caring Is Creepy"

> Because of all we've seen, because of all we've said
> We are the dead
>
> —David Bowie, "We Are the Dead"

Notes

1. Sigmund Freud, "Analysis Terminable and Interminable," in *The Standard Edition of the Complete Psychological Works of Sigmund Freud* (London: Hogarth Press, 1964), 23:245.

2. Truth be told, I can now say I am one of the only people I know to have survived not one but two zombie attacks. As this book was being finished, I somehow

managed to get in the middle of a zombie onslaught in the streets of San Francisco. I am assuming this flash mob of the living dead was either protesting or supporting a critical mass of people on bicycles parading through Union Square. It was tough to tell the real purpose, as all I could discern was that these faux zombies just wanted my "braaaaiiiinnnsss."

3. For a brief but interesting take on the dialectic between animation and reanimation, see Ryan Bishop, "Animation/Re-animation," *Theory, Culture & Society* 23, nos. 2–3 (2006): 346.

4. Guy Debord, *Comments on the Society of the Spectacle*, trans. Malcolm Imrie (London: Verso, 1990), 55.

5. Jeffrey Jerome Cohen, "Monster Culture (Seven Theses)," in *Monster Theory: Reading Culture*, ed. Jeffrey Jerome Cohen (Minneapolis: University of Minnesota Press, 1996), 2–3.

6. Mark Jancovich, *American Horror from 1951 to the Present* (Staffordshire, England: Keele University Press, 1994), 9.

7. Judith Halberstam, *Skin Shows: Gothic Horror and the Technology of Monsters* (Durham, NC: Duke University Press, 1995), 8.

8. See, for example, the argument in the introduction to Kim Paffenroth, *Gospel of the Living Dead: George Romero's Visions of Hell on Earth* (Waco, TX: Baylor University Press, 2006).

9. Sue Ellen Case, "Tracking the Vampire," *Differences* 3, no. 2 (1991): 3, emphasis mine.

10. Case, "Tracking the Vampire," 3, emphasis mine.

11. Harry M. Benshoff, *Monsters in the Closet: Homosexuality and the Horror Film* (Manchester, England: Manchester University Press, 1997).

12. Annamarie Jagose, *Queer Theory: An Introduction* (New York: New York University Press, 1996), 1, emphasis mine.

13. Quoted in Lauren Berlant and Michael Warner, "What Does Queer Theory Teach Us about X?" *PMLA* 110, no. 3 (May 1995): 343.

14. Michael Warner, "Introduction," in *Fear of a Queer Planet: Queer Politics and Social Theory*, ed. Michael Warner (Minneapolis: University of Minnesota Press, 1993), xxvi.

15. Noël Carroll, *The Philosophy of Horror; or, Paradoxes of the Heart* (New York: Routledge, 1990), 35.

16. Jean-François Lyotard, in his classic treatise on the end of grand narratives (such as science or mathematics), claims that Gödel's theorem on logical uncertainty was a philosophical event that "necessitates a reformulation of the question of the legitimation of knowledge"; Jean-François Lyotard, *The Postmodern Condition: A Report on Knowledge*, trans. Geoff Bennington and Brian Massumi (Minneapolis: University of Minnesota Press, 1984), 43. Additionally, as Dale Cyphert notes, Gödel's proof necessitates a reformulation of the ancient relationship between logic and rhetoric, wherein Gödel "both justifies and illustrates the strategic role of paradox in a persuasive discourse of the unsayable"; Dale Cyphert, "Strategic Use of the Unsayable:

Paradox as Argument in Gödel's Theorem," *Quarterly Journal of Speech* 84, no. 1 (1998): 81.

17. Kurt Gödel, *On Undecidable Propositions in Formal Mathematical Systems*, Lecture Notes by S. C. Kleone and J. B. Rosser (Princeton, NJ: Institute for Advanced Study, 1934); and *On Formally Undecidable Propositions of Principia Mathematica and Related Systems*, trans. B. Meltzer (Edinburgh: Oliver & Boyd, 1962). For more on Gödel, see the recent work by Rebecca Goldstein, *Incompleteness: The Proof and Paradox of Kurt Gödel* (New York: W. W. Norton, 2005). The classic study is, of course, Douglas R. Hofstadter's Pulitzer Prize–winning *Gödel, Escher, Bach: An Eternal Golden Braid* (New York: Vintage, 1979). It is rather amazing when one considers that the proof was presented as an unassuming report on dissertation results at the Second Conference on Epistemology of the Exact Sciences in 1930 by a twenty-five-year-old newcomer. Some four decades later, in a 1970 letter to a graduate student, Gödel reminisced that "it was precisely his recognition of the contrast between the formal definability of demonstratability and the formal *un*definability of truth that led to his discovery of incompleteness"; John W. Dawson Jr., "The Reception of Gödel's Incompleteness Theorems," in *Gödel's Theorem in Focus*, ed. S. G. Shankar (London: Croom Helm, 1988), 92. Also see Cyphert, "Strategic Use," 84.

18. Jacques Derrida, "The Double Session," in *Dissemination*, trans. Barbara Johnson (Chicago: University of Chicago Press, 1981), 219. A very good explication of the theorem in relation to "testing" can be found in Avital Ronell, *The Test Drive* (Urbana: University of Illinois Press, 2005).

19. I need to thank Shawn McIntosh for introducing me to this poor unfortunate cat (who, of course, never actually existed). While I am not a physicist, nor will I pretend to even begin to comprehend the paradox's implications, what is interesting about this is what it implies about the nature of reality on the observable level (cats, for example, as opposed to electrons in Schrödinger's case). Because of this theorem, this is one of the stickiest areas of quantum mechanics (as well as deconstruction!). We must remember that the cat remains alive/dead until we interact and become the audience and open the box. In that way, the terror may not lie so much in the middle per se, but in that this middle reminds us that we have to make a choice at some point and may not like our decision. Supposedly, Schrödinger himself said, later in life, that he wished he had never met that cat. For the original proposition see Erwin Schrödinger, "Die gegenwartige Situation in der Quantenmechanik," *Naturwissenschaftern* 23 (1935): 807–49; and "The Present Situation in Quantum Mechanics: A Translation of Schrödinger's 'Cat Paradox Paper,'" trans. John D. Trimmer, *Proceedings of the American Philosophical Society* 124 (1980): 323–38 (available at http://www.qedcorp.com/pcr/pcr/qcat.html).

20. Jacques Derrida, *Positions*, trans. Alan Bass (Chicago: University of Chicago Press, 1981), 43.

21. Jacques Derrida, *Edmund Husserl's "Origin of Geometry": An Introduction*, trans. John P. Leavey (Stony Brook, NY: Nicolas-Hays, 1978), 53.

22. Jacques Derrida, "Plato's Pharmacy," in *Dissemination*, 127, emphasis mine.

23. Derrida, "Plato's Pharmacy," 93.

24. Rodolphe Gasché, "Infrastructures and Systematicity," in *Deconstruction and Philosophy: The Texts of Jacques Derrida*, ed. John Sallis (Chicago: University of Chicago, 1987), 11; Derrida, *Positions*, 101.

25. These "moments" of liminality, to use Victor Turner's phrase, find themselves always already victims of attempted rectification in culture. Considering my examples below and elsewhere, we modify and control our weather to maintain a climatic stasis, we render intersexed children one gender or another to protect them from an impossible life, and we usher away the dead to protect the living. These sutures, however, as Žižek (after Lacan) reminds, never hold, and the undecidable opening is always oozing. I wish to thank Cara Buckley for reminding me of these constant (failed) attempts to suture the wound of liminal undecidability and for our gruesome conversations in general.

26. Derrida, "Double Session," 221.

27. The first page of the essay, if we can even call it that, greets the reader with two columns of text, with the passage from *Philebus* on the left and the top, forming a kind of backward "7" or inverted "L," with the passage from *Mimique* literally being injected *inside* of Plato.

28. Derrida notes, "Lévi-Strauss will always remain faithful to this double intention: to preserve as an instrument something whose truth value he criticizes"; Jacques Derrida, "Structure, Sign, and Play in the Discourses of the Human Sciences," trans. Alan Bass, in *Critical Theory since 1965*, ed. Hazard Adams and Leroy Searle (Tallahassee: Florida State University Press, 1986), 88.

29. I elaborate on this further, with a discussion of humidity and human intersexuality, in Marc Leverette, "The Middle Place: Mediation and the (Im)possibility of Center" (Ph.D. diss., Rutgers University, 2006), 40–49.

30. This would make him, at times, like Hermes, a (Greek) god of the middle places. In some places he was Janus Quadrifrons (the four-faced), looking in every direction, yet always in the center.

31. Contranyms are also known as antilogies, antiphrasis, autoantonyms, enantiodromes, mirror words, oysterisms, polarities, self-antonymy, turncoat words, and, of course, Janus words. In Arabic, they are *addad* and *didh*; in German, *gegensinn*; in Greek, *enantiodromia*, *enantiosemy*, and *enantiosis*; and in Hebrew, *l'shon hefech*. See Richard Lederer, *Crazy English* (New York: Pocket Books, 1989). I think a compelling case could be made for their being called "zombie words."

32. In the interest of thoroughness (or is it playfulness?), here is a brief list of some of our lexicon's awkward middle places:

- bolt—to make secure and to leave precipitously
- bound—to move quickly and to be unable to move
- buckle—to make solid and to become weak
- certain—definite and vague
- cite—to award and to penalize
- cleave—to separate and to join

- clip—to fasten together and to cut apart
- commencement—a start and a finish
- critical—opposed to and essential to
- cut—to get into (a line) and to get out of (a class)
- dispense—to provide and to get rid of
- dust—to spread over and to remove from
- excrescence—abnormal growth or normal outgrowth
- fast—moving rapidly and fixed in a position
- feedback—interfering noise and reflective information
- garnish—to deduct from and to add to
- handicap—an advantage and a disadvantage
- inertia—the tendency to stand still and the tendency to stay in motion
- left—remaining and having gone
- let—to allow and to hinder
- limit—to include and to exclude
- literally—literally and figuratively
- lurid—bright, glowing and pale, deathly
- mind—to control and to be controlled
- off—having started and having finished
- out—seeable and not visible
- overlook—to ignore and to look over
- oversight—to look after and to not see
- patronize—to behave beneficently toward and to behave offensively toward
- qualified—competent and limited
- root—to plant and to pull out
- sanction—to approve and to punish
- scan—to examine thoroughly and to examine cursorily
- screen—to show and to hide
- seed—to plant seeds and to remove seeds
- simon-pure—genuinely pure and genuinely pretentious
- stem—to originate from and to stop
- stress—to reinforce and to increase pressure
- strike—to hit into place and to remove from place
- syzygy—two related things that are alike and two related things that are opposite to one another
- take—to get and to have removed
- temper—to soften and to harden
- trim—to add onto and to cut from
- trip—to stumble and to move with agility
- wear—to last and to disintegrate
- weather—to endure and to wear away

There are, of course, the possibilities for contranymic phrases, but I thought single words would suffice here in illustrating a point.

33. Gasché, "Infrastructures," 13.

34. Gasché, "Infrastructures," 13.

35. Gasché, "Infrastructures," 13.

36. Derrida, "Double Session," 222.

37. Derrida, "Double Session," 220.

38. Manohla Dargis, "Not Just Roaming, Zombies Rise Up; Review of *Land of the Dead*," *New York Times*, June 24, 2005.

39. A. Loudermilk, "Eating 'Dawn' in the Dark: Zombie Desire and Commodifed Identity in George A. Romero's *Dawn of the Dead*," *Journal of Consumer Culture* 3, no. 1 (2003): 85–86.

40. Steven Shaviro, *The Cinematic Body* (Minneapolis: University of Minnesota Press, 1998), 104.

41. Gregory A. Waller, *The Living and the Undead: From Bram Stoker's "Dracula" to Romero's "Dawn of the Dead"* (Urbana: University of Illinois Press, 1986), 267–77.

42. Jacques Derrida, "'Eating Well,' or the Calculation of the Subject," trans. Peter Connor and Avital Ronell, in *Who Comes after the Subject?*, ed. Eduardo Cadava, Peter Connor, and Jean-Luc Nancy (New York: Routledge, 1991), 273.

43. Priapism is, of course, a painful medical condition where the penis maintains an erection for more than four hours. I want to thank Michael Cole on this point, which he stuck in my head, perhaps unwittingly, with his phrasing of the (un)dead as a kind of consciousness without attention. Perhaps this isn't what he meant, or perhaps I misunderstood, as we had probably had way too many at Ginger Man at that point, but it got me thinking anyhow. So, thanks, Mike—and apologies for the perhaps crude and double-entendre-laden acknowledgment.

44. Michel Foucault, "A Preface to Transgression," in *Bataille: A Critical Reader*, ed. Fred Botting and Scott Wilson (Oxford, England: Blackwell, 1998), 28.

45. Fred Botting and Scott Wilson, "Introduction," in Botting and Wilson, *Bataille*, 1.

46. Georges Bataille, *Erotism: Death and Sensuality*, trans. Mary Dalwood (San Francisco: City Lights Books, 1986), 141.

47. Bataille, *Erotism*, 142.

48. Victor Turner, *The Ritual Process: Structure and Anti-Structure* (Chicago: Aldine, 1969), 95.

49. Brian L. Ott, "The Pleasures of *South Park* (An Experiment in Media Erotics)," in *"South Park" and Popular Culture*, ed. Jeffrey Weinstock (Albany: State University of New York Press, forthcoming).

50. Turner, *Ritual Process*, 128.

51. For more on the biopolitics of this kind of production and consumption, one where "mad cow" and the like become reflective or symptomatic of the times, see the overview presented in Gwendolyn G. Blue, "Consuming Flesh: The Biopolitics of Beef Consumption" (Ph.D. diss., University of North Carolina at Chapel Hill, 2006).

52. Jacques Derrida, "The Animal That Therefore I Am (More to Follow)," trans. David Wills, *Critical Inquiry* 28 (2002): 124. For the full version of the essay, see

Jacques Derrida, "L'animal que donc je suis (à suivre)," in *L'animal autobiographique: Autour de Jacques Derrida*, ed. Marie-Louise Mallet (Paris: Galilée, 1999), 251–301.

53. Derrida, "Animal," 120.

54. Edward Said, *Culture and Imperialism* (New York: Vintage, 1994), 332.

55. Margaret Atwood, *Strange Things: The Malevolent North in Canadian Literature* (Oxford: Oxford University Press, 1995), 67. For another interesting take from her, see Margaret Atwood, "Cannibal Lecture," *Saturday Night*, November 1995, 81–90.

56. Elspeth Probyn, *Carnal Appetites: FoodSexIdentities* (London: Routledge, 2000), 88. On the state of exception, see Giorgio Agamben, *The Open: Man and Animal*, trans. Kevin Attell (Stanford, CA: Stanford University Press, 2004); *State of Exception*, trans. Kevin Attell (Chicago: University of Chicago Press, 2005); and *Homo Sacer: Sovereign Power and Bare Life*, trans. Daniel Heller-Roazen (Stanford, CA: Stanford University Press, 1998). Also see Andrew Norris, ed., *Politics, Metaphysics, and Death: Essays on Giorgio Agamben's "Homo Sacer"* (Durham, NC: Duke University Press, 2005).

57. Peter Hulme, "Introduction: The Cannibal Scene," in *Cannibalism and the Colonial World*, ed. Francis Barker, Peter Hulme, and Margaret Iversen (Cambridge: Cambridge University Press, 1998), 37. Hulme makes the argument that the cannibal is a key figure in the process of colonization and colonial discourse operating to separate the indigenous "savages" from the "civilized" Europeans. This is extremely similar to the construction of Haiti in the mind of the United States during and after its 1915–1934 occupation (the book *The Magic Island* and the film *White Zombie*, for example, are all about this kind of colonial propagandizing). For an extremely brief introduction to Hulme's take, see Peter Hulme, "Columbus and the Cannibals," in *The Post-Colonial Studies Reader*, ed. Bill Ashcroft, Gareth Griffiths, and Helen Tiffin (London: Routledge, 1995), 365–69. See also W. B. Seabrook, *The Magic Island* (New York: Harcourt Brace, 1929).

58. Frank Lestringant, *Cannibals: The Discovery and Representation of the Cannibal from Columbus to Jules Verne* (Berkeley: University of California Press, 1997), 116. For a good general collection, see also Kristen Guest, ed., *Eating Their Words: Cannibalism and the Boundaries of Cultural Identity* (Albany: State University Press of New York, 2001).

59. Bataille, *Erotism*, 72.

60. Priscilla L. Walton, *Our Cannibals, Ourselves: The Body Politic* (Urbana: University of Illinois Press, 2004), 33.

61. Walton, *Our Cannibals*, 6. On the relationship between the cannibal narrative of exoticism and cultural imperialism/orientalism, see Deborah Root, *Cannibal Culture: Art, Appropriation, and the Commodification of Cultural Difference* (New York: Westview Press, 1996), 30; despite its rather seductive title, there is surprisingly little flesh eating in what is otherwise a good book.

62. Daniel Cottom, *Cannibals and Philosophers: Bodies of Enlightenment* (Baltimore: Johns Hopkins University Press, 2001).

63. Cottom, *Cannibals and Philosophers*, 173.

64. An excellent argument in this vein regarding the last film can be found in Christina R. Foust and Charles Soukup, "Do I Exist? Transcendent Subjects and Secrets in *The Sixth Sense*," *Western Journal of Communication* 70, no. 2 (2006): 115–33.

65. For example, the sanguinary, often oral, "money shots" of *28 Days Later* or the scene in *Fight Club* when Tyler allows himself to get beaten to a pulp by Lou, only to proceed to cough up blood on him, clearly aiming to spit down his throat, all while screaming: "You don't know where I've been!"

66. Karl Marx, "The Eighteenth Brumaire of Louis Bonaparte," in *The Marx-Engels Reader*, ed. Robert C. Tucker (New York: Norton, 1972), 596.

67. Slavoj Žižek, *The Sublime Object of Ideology* (New York: Verso, 1989), 28; see also Karl Marx, *Capital: A Critique of the Political Economy*, trans. Ben Fowkes (New York: Penguin, 1992), 1:166–67. See also Joshua Gunn and Shaun Treat, "Zombie Trouble: A Propaedeutic on Ideological Subjectification," *Quarterly Journal of Speech* 91, no. 2 (2005): 144–74.

68. See Douglas Kellner, "The Media and Death: The Case of Terri Schiavo and the Pope," *Flow* 2, no. 2 (2005), http://flowtv.org/?p=567.

69. A great metaphor for this was explained to me by Martín Carcasson, whom I thank. The concept here is like comparing a light switch to a dimmer. From a rhetorical standpoint, through argumentation, people do not necessarily persuade their audiences to convert to the speaker's perspective. Instead, what happens is simply the movement to a point on a continuum closer to the speaker's point of view. Within this view, opposing viewpoints are thereby redefined as residing on various points along this continuum, rather than being antagonistic sides. This allows for a more productive, evolutionary kind of thinking, rather than requiring an absolutist conversion and/or revolution. See Chaïm Perelman and Lucie Obrechts-Tyteca, *The New Rhetoric: A Treatise on Argumentation*, trans. John Wilkinson and Purcell Weaver (Notre Dame, IN: University of Notre Dame Press, 1969); Martín Carcasson, "The Rhetorics of Contemporary Political Philosophy: Toward a Grammar of American Values," unpublished paper.

70. The spelling and diacritical marks of the term are highly inconsistent across authors and disciplines. For purposes of consistency, I am using Derrida's phrasing of the term; see his *Khōra* (Paris: Galilée, 1993) and " *Khōra*," trans. Ian McLeod, in *On the Name*, ed. Thomas Dutoit (Stanford, CA: Stanford University Press, 1995), 87–127.

71. For a good recent work that questions *khōra*, see Dana Miller, *The Third Kind in Plato's "Timaeus"* (Göttingen, Germany: Vandenhoeck & Ruprecht, 2003).

72. Elizabeth Grosz, "Women, *Chora*, Dwelling," in *Space, Time and Perversion: Essays on the Politics of Bodies* (New York: Routledge, 1995), 112. As Ruben Berezdivin points out, regarding the latter connections: "Between the ideal and the things which the ideals haunt, akin to that χώρα which in the *Timaeus* is said to nurse and generate everything that comes into being"; Ruben Berezdivin, "In Stalling Metaphysics: At the Threshold," in *Deconstruction and Philosophy: The Texts of Jacques Derrida*, ed. John Sallis (Chicago: University of Chicago, 1987), 55. For a good example of a kind

of intentional undecidability of *khōral* space from a popular-culture source, see the film *Blade Runner* (1982). When the character of Roy Batty (leader of the renegade replicants) confronts his creator, Dr. Tyrell, to make the demand, "I want more life," the line is followed by an odd melding of the words *father* and *fucker*. Actor Rutger Hauer was explicitly directed to say it in such a way where the audience could and would read both meanings into the line.

73. See Luce Irigaray, *Speculum of the Other Woman*, trans. Gillian C. Gill (Ithaca, NY: Cornell University Press, 1985), and Julia Kristeva, *Revolution in Poetic Language*, trans. Margaret Waller (New York: Columbia University Press, 1984). For Kristeva, in her psychoanalytic mode, *khōral* is the earliest stage in one's psychosexual development, which happens between the ages from zero to six months. It is in this prelingual stage of development that we are dominated by a blend of perceptions, feelings, and needs (all of which are quite chaotic). We do not distinguish ourselves from that of our mothers, or even from the world around us. Rather, we spend time taking in everything that is being experienced as pleasurable, without acknowledging any kind of boundary—thus there is no separation, no mediation, between ourselves and the world. This *khōral* stage, then, is when we are closest to a pure kind of materiality of existence, what Lacan refers to as the "Real." At this point, we are, according to Kristeva, dominated by our drives on a pure level (both life- and death-drives).

74. On the politics of impossibility, see Andrew Ross, "The Politics of Impossibility," in *Psychoanalysis and . . .* , ed. Richard Feldstein and Henry Sussman (New York: Routledge, 1990), 113–28. See also Jacques Derrida, "Not Utopia, the Im-Possible," in *Paper Machine*, trans. Rachel Bowlby (Stanford, CA: Stanford University Press, 2005), 121–35.

75. Derrida, "Animal," 120.

76. On the Heideggerian notion of "standing reserve," see Martin Heidegger, "The Question Concerning Technology," in *"The Question Concerning Technology" and Other Essays*, trans. William Lovitt (New York: Vintage Books, 1977), 3–35.

77. Zygmunt Bauman, *Mortality, Immortality and Other Life Strategies* (Stanford, CA: Stanford University Press, 1992), 34.

78. As Avital Ronell once remarked, "The death of God has left us with a lot of appliances"; Avital Ronell, "TraumaTV: Twelve Steps beyond the Pleasure Principle," in *Finitude's Score: Essays for the End of the Millennium* (Lincoln: University of Nebraska Press, 1994), 305–28.

79. Jacques Derrida, "Beyond: Giving for the Taking, Teaching and Learning to Give, Death," in *The Gift of Death*, trans. David Wills (Chicago: University of Chicago Press, 1995), esp. 31–40. I came to this citation by way of David Scott Diffrient, "*My So-Called Life* in the Balance: Metaphors of Morality and Uncertainty in a Short-Lived Television Series," in *Dear Angela: Remembering "My So-Called Life,"* ed. Michele Byers and David Lavery (Lanham, MD: Lexington, 2007). See also Bruno Latour, *We Have Never Been Modern*, trans. Catherine Porter (Cambridge, MA: Harvard University Press, 1993).

80. Jamie Russell, *Book of the Dead: The Complete History of Zombie Cinema* (Godalming, England: FAB Press, 2005), 190. Romero himself, for example, over four films, had the living dead seemingly represent Vietnam's dead, the silent majority of Nixon's America, vapid consumers, and an oppressed ethnic underclass.

81. As Shaviro notes, "These walking corpses are neither majestic and uncanny nor exactly sad and pitiable. . . . *They are blank*, terrifying, and ludicrous in equal measure, without any of these mitigating the others" (*Cinematic Body*, 85, emphasis mine).

82. See, for example, Annalee Newitz, *Pretend We're Dead: Capitalist Monsters in American Pop Culture* (Durham, NC: Duke University Press, 2006), esp. chap. 3, "The Undead: A Haunted Whiteness"; Harry Benshoff, "Blaxploitation Horror Films: Generic Reappropriation or Reinscription?" *Cinema Journal* 39, no. 2 (2000): 31–50; Kevin Heffernan, "Inner-City Exhibition and the Genre Film: Distributing *Night of the Living Dead* (1968)," *Cinema Journal* 41, no. 3 (2002): 59–77; Julian Cornell, "Toward a Cultural Theory of Zombie Cinema," paper presented at the annual meeting of the International Communication Association, New York, May 30, 2005; Marc Leverette, "The Living Dead World: The 'Multitude,' the 'Standing Army,' and the Zombie as Cannibalized Image of Global Capitalism," paper presented at the International Association for the Fantastic in the Arts, Fort Lauderdale, FL, March 15, 2006; and chapter 8 in this volume.

83. Michel de Certeau, "Psychoanalysis and Its History," in *Heterologies: Discourse on the Other*, trans. Brian Massumi (Minneapolis: University of Minnesota Press, 1986), 3.

84. Jacques Derrida, "Some Statements and Truisms about Neologisms, Newisms, Parasitisms, and Other Small Seismisms," in *The States of "Theory": History, Art, and Critical Discourse*, ed. David Caroll (New York: Columbia University Press, 1990), 80.

~

Filmography

28 Days Later . . . (Danny Boyle, 2002, United Kingdom/France)

28 Weeks Later . . . (Juan Carlos Fresnadillo, 2007, United Kingdom/Spain)

Alien (Ridley Scott, 1979, United Kingdom)

The American Nightmare (Adam Simon, 2000, United States/United Kingdom)

Anthropophagus also known as *Anthropophagous: The Beast*; *Antropofago*; *The Grim Reaper*; *Man Beast*; *The Savage Island*; *The Zombie's Rage* (Aristede Massaccesi [as Joe D'Amato], 1980, Italy)

Army of Darkness also known as *Army of Darkness: Evil Dead 3*; *Army of Darkness: The Medieval Dead*; *Army of Darkness: The Ultimate Experience in Medieval Horror*; *Bruce Campbell vs. Army of Darkness*; *Evil Dead 3*; *Evil Dead III: The Medieval Dead* (Sam Raimi, 1993, United States)

The Aztec Mummy also known as *Attack of the Aztec Mummy*; *La momia azteca* (Rafael Portillo, 1957, Mexico)

The Aztec Mummy vs. the Human Robot also known as *El roboto humano*; *La momia azteca contra el robot humano*; *The Robot vs. the Aztec Mummy* (Rafael Portillo and Manuel San Fernando, 1958, Mexico)

Bad Taste (Peter Jackson, 1987, New Zealand)

Baron Blood also known as *The Blood Baron*; *Chamber of Tortures*; *Gli orrori del castello di Norimberga*; *The Thirst of Baron Blood*; *The Torture Chamber of Baron Blood* (Mario Bava, 1972, West Germany/Italy)

The Beyond also known as *And You Will Live in Terror: The Afterlife*; *. . . E tu vivrai nel terrore! L'Aldilà*; *L'Aldilà*; *Seven Doors of Death* (Lucio Fulci, 1981, Italy)

Beyond the Darkness also known as *Blue Holocaust; Buio Omega; Buried Alive; The Final Darkness; In quella casa . . . buio omega* (Aristede Massaccesi [as Joe D'Amato], 1979, Italy)

The Bird with the Crystal Plumage also known as *Bird with the Glass Feathers; Das Geheimnis der schwarzen Handschuhe; The Gallery Murders; L'Uccello dalle piume di cristallo; Phantom of Terror; Point of Terror* (Dario Argento, 1970, Italy/West Germany)

Blade Runner (Ridley Scott, 1982, United States)

The Blair Witch Project (Daniel Myrick and Eduardo Sánchez, 1999, United States)

Bloodsuckers from Outer Space (Glen Coburn, 1984, United States)

Braindead also known as *Dead Alive* (Peter Jackson, 1992, New Zealand)

The Bride of Frankenstein (James Whale, 1935, United States)

The Brood (David Cronenberg, 1979, Canada)

Bud Abbott Lou Costello Meet Frankenstein also known as *Abbott and Costello Meet Frankenstein; Abbott and Costello Meet the Ghosts* (Charles Barton, 1948, United States)

Burial Ground also known as *Burial Ground: The Nights of Terror; La Notti del Terrore; Night of Terror; Nights of Terror; Zombie 3: Le Notti del Terrore; The Zombie Dead; Zombie Horror* (Andrea Bianchi, 1980, Italy)

Cannibal Apocalypse also known as *Apocalipse cannibal; Apocalipsis caníbal; Apocalisse domani; Apocalypse domani; Cannibal apocalipsis; Cannibal Apocalypse; Cannibal Massacre; The Cannibals Are in the Streets; Cannibals in the City; Cannibals in the Street; Invasion of the Fleshhunters; Savage Apocalypse; Savage Slaughterers; The Slaughterers; Virus* (Antonio Margheriti, 1980, Italy/Spain)

Chopper Chicks in Zombietown also known as *Cycle Sluts* (Dan Hoskins, 1989, United States)

The Curse of Frankenstein (Terence Fisher, 1957, United Kingdom)

The Curse of the Aztec Mummy also known as *La maldición de la momia azteca* (Rafael Portillo, 1957, Mexico)

Dawn of the Dead (George A. Romero, 1978, United States)

Dawn of the Dead (Zack Snyder, 2004, United States)

Day of the Dead (George A. Romero, 1985, United States)

Deep Red also known as *Deep Red Hatchet Murders; Dripping Deep Red; The Hatchet Murders; Profondo rosso; The Sabre Tooth Tiger* (Dario Argento, 1975, Italy)

Dellamorte Dellamore also known as *Cemetery Man* (Michele Soavi, 1994, Italy/France/Germany)

Dracula (Tod Browning, 1931, United States)

Dracula also known as *Dracula 1958; Horror of Dracula* (Terence Fisher, 1958, United Kingdom)

The Earth Dies Screaming (Terence Fisher, 1965, United Kingdom/United States)

Eraserhead (David Lynch, 1977, United States)

The Evil Dead (Sam Raimi, 1981, United States)

The Evil Dead II (Sam Raimi, 1987, United States)
eXistenZ (David Cronenberg, 1999, Canada/United Kingdom/France)
The Exorcist (William Friedkin, 1973, United States)
Fight Club (David Fincher, 1999, Germany/United States)
A Fistful of Dollars also known as *Per un pugno di dollari* (Sergio Leone, 1964, West Germany/Spain/Italy)
Flesh for Frankenstein also known as *Andy Warhol's Frankenstein; Andy Warhol's Young Frankenstein; Carne per Frankenstein; De la chair pour Frankenstein; The Devil and Dr. Frankenstein; Flesh for Frankenstein; Frankenstein; The Frankenstein Experiment; Il mostro è in tavola; Il mostro è in tavola barone Frankenstein; Up Frankenstein* (Antonio Margheriti and Paul Morrissey, 1973, United States/Italy/France)
The Fly (David Cronenberg, 1986, United States)
Frank Capra's It's a Wonderful Life (Frank Capra, 1946, United States)
Frankenstein (James Whale, 1931, United States)
From Dusk till Dawn (Robert Rodriguez, 1996, United States)
The Gates of Hell also known as *City of the Living Dead; The Fear; Fear in the City of the Living Dead; Pater Thomas; Paura nel città dei morti viventi; Twilight of the Dead* (Lucio Fulci, 1981, Italy)
The Ghost Breakers (George Marshall, 1940, United States)
Ginger Snaps (John Fawcett, 2000, Canada/United States)
Gods and Monsters (Bill Condon, 1998, United Kingdom/United States)
Hard Rock Zombies (Krishna Shah, 1985, United States)
Hellraiser (Clive Barker, 1987, United Kingdom)
Hercules in the Haunted World also known as *Ercole al centro della terra; Hercules at the Center of the Earth; Hercules in the Center of the Earth; Hercules vs. the Vampires; The Vampires vs. Hercules; With Hercules to the Center of the Earth* (Mario Bava and Franco Prosperi, 1961, Italy)
The Horror at Party Beach (Del Tenney, 1964, United States)
House of 1,000 Corpses (Rob Zombie, 2003, United States)
House of the Dead (Uwe Boll, 2003, Canada/United States/Germany)
The Incredibly Strange Creatures Who Stopped Living and Became Mixed-Up Zombies!!? also known as *Diabolical Dr. Voodoo; The Incredibly Mixed Up Zombie; The Incredibly Strange Creature; or, Why I Stopped Living and Became a Mixed-Up Zombie; The Teenage Psycho Meets Bloody Mary* (Ray Dennis Steckler, 1964, United States)
Invasion of the Body Snatchers (Don Siegel, 1956, United States)
Invisible Invaders (Edward L. Cahn, 1959, United States)
The Invisible Man (James Whale, 1933, United States)
It's Alive (Larry Cohen, 1974, United States)
I Walked with a Zombie (Jacques Tourneur, 1943, United States)
I Was a Teenage Zombie (John Elias Michalakis, 1987, United States)
John Carpenter's The Thing (John Carpenter, 1982, United States)
King of the Zombies (Jean Yarbrough, 1941, United States)

Land of the Dead (George A. Romero, 2005, United States)

Lara Croft: Tomb Raider (Simon West, 2001, United Kingdom/Germany/United States/Japan)

Lara Croft Tomb Raider: The Cradle of Life (Jan de Bont, 2004, United States/Germany/Japan/United Kingdom/Netherlands)

The Last Man on Earth also known as *L'ultimo uomo della terra*; *Naked Terror*; *The Night Creatures*; *Night People*; *Vento di morte*; *Wind of Death* (Ubaldo Ragona/Sydney Salko, 1964, United States/Italy)

Let Sleeping Corpses Lie also known as *Breakfast at the Manchester Morgue*; *Don't Open the Window*; *The Living Dead at Manchester Morgue*; *Non si deve profanare il sonno dei morti*; *No profanar el sueño de los muertos*; *Sleeping Corpses Lie*; *Zombi 3 (Da dovè vieni?)* (Jorge Grau, 1974, Spain/Italy)

The Lord of the Rings: The Fellowship of the Ring (Peter Jackson, 2001, New Zealand/United States)

The Lord of the Rings: The Return of the King (Peter Jackson, 2003, New Zealand/United States)

The Lord of the Rings: The Two Towers (Peter Jackson, 2002, New Zealand/United States/Germany)

May (Lucy McKee, 2002, United States)

Meet the Feebles (Peter Jackson, 1989, New Zealand)

Michael Jackson's "Thriller" (John Landis, 1983, United States)

Monty Python and the Holy Grail (Terry Gilliam and Terry Jones, 1975, United Kingdom)

Monty Python's Meaning of Life (Terry Jones and Terry Gilliam, 1983, United Kingdom)

The Mummy (Karl Freund, 1932, United States)

My Boyfriend's Back (Bob Balaban, 1993, United States)

National Lampoon's Animal House (John Landis, 1978, United States)

Nightmare City also known as *City of the Walking Dead*; *Incubo sulla città contaminate*; *Invasion by the Atomic Zombies*; *La Invasión de los zombies atómicos* (Umberto Lenzi, 1980, Italy/Mexico/Spain)

Night of the Living Dead (George A. Romero, 1968, United States)

The Omega Man (Boris Sagal, 1971, United States)

Ouanga also known as *Crime of Voodoo*; *Drums in the Night*; *Drums of the Jungle*; *Love Wanga* (George Terwilliger, 1936, United States)

Peeping Tom (Michael Powell, 1960, United Kingdom)

The Plague of the Zombies also known as *The Zombies* (John Gilling, 1966, United Kingdom)

Plan 9 from Outer Space (Edward D. Wood Jr., 1959, United States)

Porky's (Bob Clark, 1982, United States)

Psycho (Alfred Hitchcock, 1960, United States)

Rabid also known as *Rage* (David Cronenberg, 1977, Canada)

Re-Animator (Stuart Gordon, 1985, United States)

Repulsion (Roman Polanksi, 1965, United Kingdom)

Resident Evil (Paul W. S. Anderson, 2002, United Kingdom/Germany/France/United States)

Resident Evil: Apocalypse (Alexander Witt, 2004, Germany/France/United Kingdom/Canada)

The Return of the Living Dead (Dan O'Bannon, 1985, United States)

Revenge of the Nerds (Jeff Kanew, 1984, United States)

Revenge of the Zombies also known as *The Corpse Vanished* (Steve Sekely, 1943, United States)

Revolt of the Zombies (Victor Halperin, 1936, United States)

Rock 'n Roll Wrestling Women vs. the Aztec Mummy also known as *Las luchadoras contra la momia*; *Wrestling Women vs. the Aztec Mummy* (René Cardona, 1964, Mexico)

Scared Stiff (George Marshall, 1953, United States)

Scream (Wes Craven, 1996, United States)

Scream 2 (Wes Craven, 1997, United States)

Scream 3 (Wes Craven, 2000, United States)

The Serpent and the Rainbow (Wes Craven, 1988, United States)

Shaun of the Dead (Edgar Wright, 2004, United Kingdom/France)

Shivers also known as *The Parasite Murders*; *They Came from Within* (David Cronenberg, 1975, Canada)

Shock Waves also known as *Almost Human*; *Death Corps* (Ken Weiderhorn, 1977, United States)

Species (Roger Donaldson, 1995, United States)

Super Mario Bros. (Annabell Jankel, Rocky Morton, Roland Joffe [uncredited], and Dean Semler [uncredited], 1993, United Kingdom/United States)

Suspiria (Dario Argento, 1977, Italy)

Terminator 2: Judgment Day (James Cameron, 1991, France/United States)

The Texas Chain Saw Massacre (Tobe Hooper, 1974, United States)

Tombs of the Blind Dead also known as *A noite do terror cego*; *The Blind Dead*; *Crypt of the Blind Dead*; *La noche de la muerta ciega*; *La noche del terror ciego*; *Mark of the Devil, Part 4: Tombs of the Blind Dead*; *Night of the Blind Dead* (Amando de Ossorio, 1971, Spain/Portugal)

Torso also known as *Bodies Bear Traces of Carnal Violence*; *Carnal Violence*; *I corpi presentano tracce di violenza carnale* (Sergio Martino, 1973, Italy)

The Vampires also known as *The Devil's Commandment*; *Evil's Commandment*; *I vampiri*; *Lust of the Vampire* (Riccardo Freda with Mario Bava [uncredited], 1956, Italy)

Videodrome (David Cronenberg, 1983, Canada/United States)

Voodoo Man also known as *The Tiger Man* (William Beaudine, 1944, United States)

War of the Zombies also known as *Night Star: Goddess of Electra*; *Roma contra Roma* (Giuseppe Vari, 1964, Italy)

Westworld (Michael Crichton, 1973, United States)

White Zombie (Victor Halperin, 1932, United States)

X-tro (Harry Bromley Davenport, 1983, United Kingdom)

Young Frankenstein (Mel Brooks, 1974, United States)

Zombi 2 also known as *Gli Ultimi Zombi; Island of the Flesh-Eaters; Island of the Living Dead; Zombie; Zombie 2: The Dead Are among Us; Zombie Flesheaters* (Lucio Fulci, 1979, Italy)

Zombi 3 also known as *Zombie Flesh Eaters 2* (Lucio Fulci, Claudio Fragasso [uncredited], and Bruno Mattei [uncredited], 1988, Italy)

Zombie Holocaust also known as *Doctor Butcher M.D.; Dr. Butcher M.D.; Dr. Butcher, Medical Deviate; Island of the Last Zombies; La regina dei cannibali; Medical Deviate; Queen of the Cannibals; Zombi Holocaust; Zombie 3* (Marino Girolami, 1980, Italy)

Zombies of the Stratosphere (Fred C. Bannon, 1952, United States)

Zombies on Broadway (Gordon Douglas, 1945, United States)

~

Bibliography

Aarne, Antti. *The Types of the Folktale: A Classification and Bibliography*. 2nd rev. ed. Trans. and enl. by Stith Thompson. Helsinki: Suomalainen Tiedeakatemia/Akademia Scientiarum Fennica, 1981.

Agamben, Giorgio. *Homo Sacer: Sovereign Power and Bare Life*. Trans. Daniel Heller-Roazen. Stanford, CA: Stanford University Press, 1998.

———. *The Open: Man and Animal*. Trans. Kevin Attell. Stanford, CA: Stanford University Press, 2004.

———. *State of Exception*. Trans. Kevin Attell. Chicago: University of Chicago Press, 2005.

Altman, Rick. *Film/Genre*. London: BFI, 1999.

Arnzen, Michael. "Who's Laughing Now? The Postmodern Splatter Film." *Journal of Popular Film and Television* 21, no. 4 (1994): 176–85.

Atwood, Margaret. "Cannibal Lecture." *Saturday Night*, November 1995, 81–90.

———. *Strange Things: The Malevolent North in Canadian Literature*. Oxford: Oxford University Press, 1995.

Badley, Linda. *Film, Horror and the Body Fantastic*. Westport, CT: Greenwood Press, 1995.

Bakhtin, Mikhail. *Problems of Dostoevsky's Poetics*. Ed. and trans. Caryl Emerson. Minneapolis: University of Minnesota Press, 1984.

———. *Rabelais and His World*. Trans. Hélène Iswolsky. Bloomington: Indiana University Press, 1984.

Barber, Paul. *Vampires, Burial, and Death: Folklore and Reality*. New Haven, CT: Yale University Press, 1988.

Barthes, Roland. *Mythologies*. Trans. Annette Lavers. New York: Noonday Press, 1957.

Bataille, Georges. *Erotism: Death and Sensuality*. Trans. Mary Dalwood. San Francisco: City Lights Books, 1986.

Bauman, Zygmunt. *Mortality, Immortality and Other Life Strategies*. Stanford, CA: Stanford University Press, 1992.

Baxter, John. *Science Fiction in the Cinema*. New York: Paperback Library, 1970.

Beard, Steven. "No Particular Place to Go." *Sight and Sound* 3, no. 4 (1993): 30–31.

Beck, Ulrich. "Zombie Categories." In *The Art of Life: On Living, Love and Death*, edited by Jonathan Rutherford, 35–51. London: Lawrence & Wishart, 2000.

Becker-Leckrone, Megan. *Julia Kristeva and Literary Theory*. New York: Palgrave Macmillan, 2005.

Bellour, Raymond. "Alternation, Segmentation, Hypnosis: An Interview with Raymond Bellour." Interview by Janet Bergstrom. *Camera Obscura*, nos. 3/4 (1979): 58–103.

Benshoff, Harry M. "Blaxploitation Horror Films: Generic Reappropriation or Reinscription?" *Cinema Journal* 39, no. 2 (2000): 31–50.

———. *Monsters in the Closet: Homosexuality and the Horror Film*. Manchester, England: Manchester University Press, 1997.

Berezdivin, Ruben. "In Stalling Metaphysics: At the Threshold." In *Deconstruction and Philosophy: The Texts of Jacques Derrida*, edited by John Sallis, 47–59. Chicago: University of Chicago, 1987.

Berger, James. *After the End: Representations of Post-Apocalypse*. Minneapolis: University of Minnesota Press, 1999.

Bergson, Henri. *Laughter: An Essay on the Meaning of the Comic*. Trans. C. Breretson. New York: Macmillan, 1926.

Berlant, Lauren, and Michael Warner. "What Does Queer Theory Teach Us about X?" *PMLA* 110, no. 3 (May 1995): 343–49.

Bishop, Ryan. "Animation/Re-animation." *Theory, Culture & Society* 23, nos. 2–3 (2006): 346.

Blue, Gwendolyn G. "Consuming Flesh: The Biopolitics of Beef Consumption." Ph.D. diss., University of North Carolina at Chapel Hill, 2006.

Botting, Fred, and Scott Wilson. "Introduction." In *Bataille: A Critical Reader*, edited by Fred Botting and Scott Wilson, 1–23. Oxford, England: Blackwell, 1998.

Brophy, Philip. "Horrality—the Textuality of Contemporary Horror Films." In *The Horror Reader*, edited by Ken Gelder, 276–84. London: Routledge, 2000.

Brottman, Mikita. *Funny Peculiar: Gershon Legman and the Psychopathology of Humor*. London: Analytic Press, 2004.

Bryce, Allan, ed. *Zombie*. Liskeard, England: Stray Cat, 1999.

Carr, Diane. "Play Dead: Genre and Affect in *Silent Hill* and *Planetscape Torment*." *Game Studies* 3, no. 1 (2003).

Carroll, Noël. *The Philosophy of Horror; or, Paradoxes of the Heart*. New York: Routledge, 1990.

———. "Why Horror?" In *Horror, the Film Reader*, edited by Mark Jancovich, 33–46. London: Routledge, 2002.

Case, Sue Ellen. "Tracking the Vampire." *Differences* 3, no. 2 (1991): 1–20.

Cawelti, John. *Adventure, Mystery, and Romance: Formula Stories as Art and Popular Culture*. Chicago: University of Chicago Press, 1976.

Certeau, Michel de. "Psychoanalysis and Its History" In *Heterologies: Discourse on the Other*, 3–16. Trans. Brian Massumi. Minneapolis: University of Minnesota Press, 1986.

Cherry, Brigid. "Refusing to Refuse to Look: Female Viewers of the Horror Film." In *Identifying Hollywood's Audiences*, edited by Melvyn Stokes and Richard Maltby, 187–203. London: British Film Institute, 1999.

Chick, Tom. "MMOs: Building Whole Societies." *Gamespy*, October 24, 2003.

Christiansen, Reidar Th. *Folktales of Norway*. Trans. Pat Shaw Iversen. London: Routledge & Kegan Paul, 1964.

Clarens, Carlos. *An Illustrated History of the Horror Film*. New York: Capricorn Books, 1967.

Clark, Katerina, and Michael Holquist. *Mikhail Bakhtin*. Cambridge, MA: Belknap Press of Harvard University Press, 1984.

Clover, Carol J. "Her Body, Himself: Gender in the Slasher Film." In *The Dread of Difference: Gender and the Horror Film*, edited by Barry Keith Grant, 66–113. Austin: University of Texas Press, 1996.

———. *Men, Women and Chainsaws: Gender in the Modern Horror Film*. Princeton, NJ: Princeton University Press, 1992.

Cohen, Jeffrey Jerome. "Monster Culture (Seven Theses)." In *Monster Theory: Reading Culture*, edited by Jeffrey Jerome Cohen, 3–25. Minneapolis: University of Minnesota Press, 1996.

Collins, John J. "Introduction: Toward the Morphology of a Genre." *Semeia* 14 (1979): 1–19.

Cornell, Julian. "Toward a Cultural Theory of Zombie Cinema." Paper presented at the annual meeting of the International Communication Association, New York, May 30, 2005.

Cottom, Daniel. *Cannibals and Philosophers: Bodies of Enlightenment*. Baltimore: Johns Hopkins University Press, 2001.

Cozzi, Luigi. *Giallo Argento*. Rome: Profondo Rosso, 2001.

Craige, John Houston. *Black Baghdad*. New York: Minton, Balch, 1933.

———. *Cannibal Cousins*. New York: Minton, Balch, 1934.

Creed, Barbara. "Bad Taste and Antipodal Inversion: Peter Jackson's Colonial Suburbs." *Postcolonial Studies* 3, no. 1 (2000): 61–68.

———. "Horror and the Carnivalesque: The Body Monstrous." In *Fields of Vision: Essays in Film Studies, Visual Anthropology, and Photography*, edited by Leslie Devereaux and Roger Hillman, 127–59. Berkeley: University of California Press, 1995.

———. "Horror and the Monstrous-Feminine: An Imaginary Abjection." In *The Dread of Difference: Gender and the Horror Film*, edited by Barry Keith Grant,

35–65. Austin: University of Texas Press, 1996. Reprinted in *Horror: The Film Reader*, edited by Mark Jancovich, 67–76. London: Routledge, 2002.

———. *The Monstrous-Feminine: Film, Feminism, Psychoanalysis.* New York: Routledge, 1993.

Critchley, Simon. *Very Little . . . Almost Nothing: Death, Philosophy, Literature.* London: Routledge, 1997.

Cyphert, Dale. "Strategic Use of the Unsayable: Paradox as Argument in Gödel's Theorem." *Quarterly Journal of Speech* 84, no. 1 (1998): 80–93.

Davis, Wade. *Passage of Darkness: The Ethnobiology of the Haitian Zombie.* Chapel Hill: University of North Carolina Press, 1988.

———. *The Serpent and the Rainbow.* London: Time Warner, 1987.

Dawson, John W., Jr. "The Reception of Gödel's Incompleteness Theorems." In *Gödel's Theorem in Focus*, edited by S. G. Shankar, 74–95. London: Croom Helm, 1988.

Debord, Guy. *Comments on the Society of the Spectacle.* Trans. Malcolm Imrie. London: Verso, 1990.

Deleuze, Gilles. *Cinema 1: The Movement Image.* Trans. Hugh Tomlinson and Barbara Habberjam. Minneapolis: University of Minnesota Press, 1988.

———. *Cinema 2: The Time Image.* Trans. Hugh Tomlinson and Robert Galeta. London: Athlone Press, 1989.

———. *The Fold: Leibniz and the Baroque.* Trans. Tom Conley. London: Athlone Press, 2001.

Deleuze, Gilles, and Félix Guattari. *A Thousand Plateaus: Capitalism and Schizophrenia.* Trans. Brian Massumi. London: Athlone Press, 1987.

Del Guercio, Gino. "The Secrets of Haiti's Living Dead." In *Magic, Witchcraft and Religion: An Anthropological Study of the Supernatural*, 2nd ed., edited by Arthur C. Lehmann and James E. Myers, 327–31. Mountain View, CA: Mayfield, 1989.

Delius, Peter. "Witches and Missionaries in Nineteenth-Century Transvaal." *Journal of Southern African Studies* 27, no. 3 (2001): 429–43.

Dendle, Peter. *The Zombie Movie Encyclopedia.* Jefferson, NC: McFarland, 2001.

Derrida, Jacques. "The Animal That Therefore I Am (More to Follow)." Trans. David Wills. *Critical Inquiry* 28 (2002): 369–418.

———. "Beyond: Giving for the Taking, Teaching and Learning to Give, Death." In *The Gift of Death*, translated by David Wills, 35–52. Chicago: University of Chicago Press, 1995.

———. "The Double Session." In *Dissemination*, translated by Barbara Johnson, 173–286. Chicago: University of Chicago Press, 1981.

———. "'Eating Well,' or the Calculation of the Subject." Trans. Peter Connor and Avital Ronell. In *Who Comes after the Subject?*, edited by Eduardo Cadava, Peter Connor, and Jean-Luc Nancy, 96–116. New York: Routledge, 1991.

———. *Edmund Husserl's "Origin of Geometry": An Introduction.* Trans. John P. Leavey. Stony Brook, NY: Nicolas-Hays, 1978.

———. *Khōra.* Paris: Galilée, 1993.

———. "Khōra." Trans. Ian McLeod. In *On the Name*, edited by Thomas Dutoit, 87–127. Stanford, CA: Stanford University Press, 1995.

———. "L'animal que donc je suis (à suivre)." In *L'animal autobiographique: Autour de Jacques Derrida*, edited by Marie-Louise Mallet, 251–301. Paris: Galilée, 1999.

———. "Not Utopia, the Im-Possible." In *Paper Machine*, translated by Rachel Bowlby, 121–25. Stanford, CA: Stanford University Press, 2005.

———. "Plato's Pharmacy." In *Dissemination*, translated by Barbara Johnson, 67–171. Chicago: University of Chicago Press, 1981.

———. *Positions*. Trans. Alan Bass. Chicago: University of Chicago Press, 1981.

———. "Some Statements and Truisms about Neologisms, Newisms, Parasitisms, and Other Small Seismisms." In *The States of "Theory": History, Art, and Critical Discourse*, edited by David Carroll, 63–94. New York: Columbia University Press, 1990.

———. "Structure, Sign, and Play in the Discourses of the Human Sciences." Trans. Alan Bass. In *Critical Theory since 1965*, edited by Hazard Adams and Leroy Searle, 83–94. Tallahassee: Florida State University Press, 1986.

Diffrient, David Scott. "My *So-Called Life* in the Balance: Metaphors of Morality and Uncertainty in a Short-Lived Television Series." In *Dear Angela: Remembering "My So-Called Life"*, edited by Michele Byers and David Lavery. Lanham, MD: Lexington, 2007.

Duggan, Christopher. *A Concise History of Italy*. Cambridge: Cambridge University Press, 1994.

Firsching, Robert. "Italian Horror in the Seventies." *Images*, no. 5 (1997).

Foucault, Michel. "A Preface to Transgression." In *Bataille: A Critical Reader*, edited by Fred Botting and Scott Wilson, 24–40. Oxford, England: Blackwell, 1998.

Foust, Christina R., and Charles Soukup. "Do I Exist? Transcendent Subjects and Secrets in *The Sixth Sense*," *Western Journal of Communication* 70, no. 2 (2006): 115–33.

Freud, Sigmund. "Analysis Terminable and Interminable." In *The Standard Edition of the Complete Psychological Works of Sigmund Freud*, 23:209–53. London: Hogarth Press, 1964.

Fuery, Patrick. *New Developments in Film Theory*. New York: St. Martin's, 2000.

Gabler, Neal. *Life the Movie: How Entertainment Conquered Reality*. New York: Knopf, 1998.

Gasché, Rodolphe. "Infrastructures and Systematicity." In *Deconstruction and Philosophy: The Texts of Jacques Derrida*, edited by John Sallis, 3–20. Chicago: University of Chicago, 1987.

George, Julia. "The Horror Film: An Investigation of Traditional Narrative Elements." *Folklore Forum* 15 (1982): 159–79.

Gibson, William. *Neuromancer*. New York: Ace Books, 1984.

Ginsborg, Paul. *A History of Contemporary Italy: Society and Politics*. New York: Palgrave MacMillan, 2003.

Gödel, Kurt. *On Formally Undecidable Propositions of Principia Mathematica and Related Systems*. Trans. B. Meltzer. Edinburgh: Oliver & Boyd, 1962.

——. *On Undecidable Propositions in Formal Mathematical Systems.* Lecture notes by S. C. Kleone and J. B. Rosser. Princeton, NJ: Institute for Advanced Study, 1934.

Goldsmith, Stephen. *Unbuilding Jerusalem: Apocalypse and Romantic Representation.* Ithaca, NY: Cornell University Press, 1993.

Goldstein, Rebecca. *Incompleteness: The Proof and Paradox of Kurt Gödel.* New York: W. W. Norton, 2005.

Graham, Elaine L. *Representations of the Post/Human: Monsters, Aliens, and Others in Popular Culture.* New Brunswick, NJ: Rutgers University Press, 2002.

Grainge, Paul. "Nostalgia and Style in Retro America: Moods, Modes, and Media Recycling." *Journal of American & Comparative Cultures* 23, no. 1 (2000): 27–34.

Grant, Barry Keith. *A Cultural Assault: The New Zealand Films of Peter Jackson.* Studies in New Zealand Culture, no. 5. London: Kakapo Books, 1999.

——, ed. *The Dread of Difference: Gender and the Horror Film.* Austin: University of Texas Press, 1996.

——. "Taking Back the *Night of the Living Dead*: George Romero, Feminism, and the Horror Film." In *The Dread of Difference: Gender and the Horror Film*, edited by Barry Keith Grant, 200–212. Austin: University of Texas Press, 1996.

Grant, Michael. "Cinema, Horror and the Abominations of Hell: Carl-Theodor Dreyer's *Vampyr* (1931) and Lucio Fulci's *The Beyond* (1981)." In *The Couch and the Silver Screen: Psychoanalytic Reflections on European Cinema*, edited by Andrea Sabbadini, 145–55. London: Brunner-Routledge, 2003.

Grosz, Elizabeth. "Women, Chora, Dwelling." In *Space, Time and Perversion: Essays on the Politics of Bodies*, 111–24. New York: Routledge, 1995.

Guattari, Félix. "In Order to End the Massacre of the Body." In *Soft Subversions*, 29–36. Trans. Jarred Becker. New York: Semiotext(e), 1996.

Guest, Kristen, ed. *Eating Their Words: Cannibalism and the Boundaries of Cultural Identity.* Albany: State University of New York Press, 2001.

Gunn, Joshua, and Shaun Treat. "Zombie Trouble: A Propaedeutic on Ideological Subjectification," *Quarterly Journal of Speech* 91, no. 2 (2005): 144–74.

Halberstam, Judith. *Skin Shows: Gothic Horror and the Technology of Monsters.* Durham, NC: Duke University Press, 1995.

Halliwell, Leslie. *The Dead That Walk: Dracula, Frankenstein, the Mummy and Other Favorite Movie Monsters.* London: Continuum, 1988.

Haraway, Donna J. *Simians, Cyborgs, and Women: The Reinvention of Nature.* London: Free Association Books, 1991.

Hawkins, Joan. "The Anxiety of Influence: George Franju and the Medical Horror Shows of Jess Franco." In *Horror Film Reader*, edited by Alain Silver and James Ursini, 111–28. New York: Limelight Editions, 2000.

Hayles, N. Katherine. *How We Became Posthuman: Virtual Bodies in Cybernetics, Literature, and Informatics.* Chicago: University of Chicago Press, 1999.

Heffernan, Kevin. "Inner-City Exhibition and the Genre Film: Distributing *Night of the Living Dead* (1968)." *Cinema Journal* 41, no. 3 (2002): 59–77.

Heidegger, Martin. "The Question Concerning Technology." In *The Question Concerning Technology" and Other Essays*, 3–35. Trans. William Lovitt. New York: Vintage Books, 1977.

Heim, Scott. *In Awe*. New York: HarperCollins, 1997.

Hill, Annette. "'Looks Like It Hurts': Women's Responses to Shocking Entertainment." In *Ill Effects: The Media/Violence Debate*, 2nd ed., edited by Martin Barker and Julian Petley, 135–49. New York: Routledge, 2001.

Hofstadter, Douglas R. *Gödel, Escher, Bach: An Eternal Golden Braid*. New York: Vintage, 1979.

Hulme, Peter. "Columbus and the Cannibals." In *The Post-Colonial Studies Reader*, edited by Bill Ashcroft, Gareth Griffiths, and Helen Tiffin, 365–69. London: Routledge, 1995.

———. "Introduction: The Cannibal Scene." In *Cannibalism and the Colonial World*, edited by Francis Barker, Peter Hulme, and Margaret Iversen, 1–38. Cambridge: Cambridge University Press, 1998.

Hunt, Leon. "A (Sadistic) Night at the Opera: Notes on the Italian Horror Film." *Velvet Light Trap*, no. 30 (1992): 65–75.

Hurston, Zora Neale. *Tell My Horse: Voodoo and Life in Haiti and Jamaica*. London: Harper & Row, 1938.

Irigaray, Luce. *Speculum of the Other Woman*. Trans. Gillian C. Gill. Ithaca, NY: Cornell University Press, 1985.

Jagose, Annamarie. *Queer Theory: An Introduction*. New York: New York University Press, 1996.

Jancovich, Mark. *American Horror from 1951 to the Present*. Staffordshire, England: Keele University Press, 1994.

———. "'A Real Shocker': Authenticity, Genre and the Struggle for Distinction." In *The Film Cultures Reader*, edited by Graeme Turner, 469–80. New York: Routledge, 2002.

Johnson, Gary. "The Golden Age of Italian Horror." *Images*, no. 5 (1997), www.images journal.com/issue05/infocus/intro.htm.

Jones, Allen. "Morti Viventi." In *Zombie*, edited by Allan Bryce, 12–27. Liskeard, England: Stray Cat, 1999.

Jones, Leslie. "'Last Week We Had an Omen': The Mythological X-Files. " In *Deny All Knowledge: Reading the X-Files*, edited by David Lavery, Angela Hague, and Marla Cartwright, 77–98. London: Farber & Farber, 1996.

Kayser, Wolfgang. *The Grotesque in Art and Literature*. Trans. Ulrich Weisstein. New York: McGraw-Hill.

Kellner, Douglas. "The Media and Death: The Case of Terri Schiavo and the Pope." *Flow* 2, no. 2 (2005).

Kermode, Frank. *The Sense of an Ending: Studies in the Theory of Fiction*. Oxford: Oxford University Press, 1967.

Kerr, Aphra. "~~Girls~~ Women Just Want to Have Fun: A Study of Adult Female Players of Digital Games." In *Level Up*, edited by Marinka Copier and Joost Raessens. CD-ROM. Utrecht, The Netherlands: DiGRA/Universiteit, 2003.

Kilpatrick, Nancy. *Goth Bible: A Compendium for the Darkly Inclined.* New York: St. Martin's Griffin, 2004.

King, Geoff. *Film Comedy.* London: Wallflower, 2002.

King, Geoff, and Tanya Krzywinska. *Tomb Raiders and Space Invaders: Videogame Forms and Contexts.* London: I. B. Tauris, 2005.

Kline, Stephen, Nick Dyer-Witheford, and Greig De Peuter. *Digital Play: Interaction of Technology, Culture and Marketing.* Montreal: McGill-Queen's University Press, 2003.

Kohler, Chris. "Mmmmmmmm, Brains." *Wired Online,* October 28, 2005, http://www .wired.com/news/games/0,2101,69349,00.html.

Koven, Mikel J. "Folklore Studies and Popular Film and Television: A Necessary Critical Survey." *Journal of American Folklore* 116, no. 2 (2003): 176–95.

Kristeva, Julia. *Powers of Horror: An Essay on Abjection.* Trans. Leon S. Roudiez. New York: Columbia University Press, 1982.

———. *Revolution in Poetic Language.* Trans. Margaret Waller. New York: Columbia University Press, 1984.

Krzywinska, Tanya. "Hands-on Horror." In *ScreenPlay: Cinema/Videogames/Interfaces,* edited by Geoff King and Tanya Krzywinska, 206–23. London: Wallflower, 2002.

Kuhn, Annette. "The Body and Cinema: Some Problems for Feminism." In *Grafts: Feminist Cultural Criticism,* edited by Susan Sheridan, 11–23. London: Verso, 1988.

Laclos, Michel. *Le Fantastique au Cinema.* Paris: J. J. Pauvert, 1958.

Latour, Bruno. *We Have Never Been Modern.* Trans. Catherine Porter. Cambridge, MA: Harvard University Press, 1993.

Lederer, Richard. *Crazy English.* New York: Pocket Books, 1989.

Lestringant, Frank. *Cannibals: The Discovery and Representation of the Cannibal from Columbus to Jules Verne.* Berkeley: University of California Press, 1997.

Leverette, Marc. "The Living Dead World: The 'Multitude,' the 'Standing Army,' and the Zombie as Cannibalized Image of Global Capitalism." Paper presented at the International Association for the Fantastic in the Arts, Fort Lauderdale, FL, March 15, 2006.

———. "The Middle Place: Mediation and the (Im)possibility of Center." Ph.D. diss., Rutgers University, 2006.

Liehm, Mira. *Passion and Defiance: Film in Italy from 1942 to the Present.* Berkeley: University of California Press, 1984.

London, Rose. *Zombie: The Living Dead.* New York: Bounty Books, 1976.

Loudermilk, A. "Eating 'Dawn' in the Dark: Zombie Desire and Commodifed Identity in George A. Romero's *Dawn of the Dead.*" *Journal of Consumer Culture* 3, no. 1 (2003): 83–108.

Lowry, Edward, and Richard deCordova. "Enunciation and the Production of Horror in *White Zombie.*" In *Planks of Reason: Essays on the Horror Film,* edited by Barry Keith Grant, 346–89. Metuchen, NJ: Scarecrow Press, 1984.

Lyotard, Jean-François. *The Postmodern Condition: A Report on Knowledge.* Trans. Geoff Bennington and Brian Massumi. Minneapolis: University of Minnesota Press, 1984.

MacCormack, Patricia. "Masochistic Cinesexuality: The Many Deaths of Giovanni Lombardo Radice." In *Alternative Europe: Eurotrash and Exploitation Cinema since 1945*, edited by Xavier Mendik and Ernest Mathijs, 106–16. London: Wallflower, 2004.

Marcus, Greil. *Lipstick Traces: A Secret History of the Twentieth Century*. Cambridge, MA: Harvard University Press, 1989.

Marx, Karl. *Capital: A Critique of the Political Economy*, vol. 1. Trans. Ben Fowkes. New York: Penguin, 1992.

———. "The Eighteenth Brumaire of Louis Bonaparte." In *The Marx-Engels Reader*, edited by Robert C. Tucker, 436–525. New York: Norton, 1972.

Massumi, Brian. "Realer than Real: The Simulacrum According to Deleuze and Guattari." *Copyright* 1 (1999).

McCarthy Brown, Karen. "Voodoo." In *Magic, Witchcraft and Religion: An Anthropological Study of the Supernatural*, 2nd ed., edited by Arthur C. Lehmann and James E. Myers, 321–26. Mountain View, CA: Mayfield, 1989.

McCarty, John. *Splatter Movies*. New York: Fanta Co Enterprises, 1981.

McDonagh, Maitland. *Broken Mirrors/Broken Minds: The Dark Dreams of Dario Argento*. New York: Citadel Press, 1994.

Meers, Phillipe. "Is There an Audience in the House? New Research Perspectives on (European) Film Audiences." *Journal of Popular Film and Television* 29, no. 3 (2001): 138–44.

Metcalf, Peter A. "Death Be Not Strange." In *Magic, Witchcraft and Religion: An Anthropological Study of the Supernatural*, 2nd ed., edited by Arthur C. Lehmann and James E. Myers, 332–35. Mountain View, CA: Mayfield, 1989.

Metz, Christian. *The Imaginary Signifier: Psychoanalysis and the Cinema*. Trans. Celia Britton et al. Bloomington: Indiana University Press, 1983.

Miller, Dana. *The Third Kind in Plato's "Timaeus."* Göttingen, Germany: Vandenhoeck & Ruprecht, 2003.

Modleski, Tania. "The Terror of Pleasure: The Contemporary Horror Film and Postmodern Theory." In *The Film Cultures Reader*, edited by Graeme Turner, 268–75. New York: Routledge, 2002.

Morris, Gary. "Review of *Baron Blood*, dir. Mario Bava." *Images*, no. 8 (2004).

Mulvey, Laura. "Visual Pleasure and Narrative Cinema." *Screen* 16 (1975): 6–18.

Newitz, Annalee. *Pretend We're Dead: Capitalist Monsters in American Pop Culture*. Durham, NC: Duke University Press, 2006.

———. "What Makes Things Cheesy? Satire, Multinationalism, and B-Movies." *Social Text* 18, no. 2 (2000): 59–82.

Newman, Kim. *Nightmare Movies: A Critical History of the Horror Film, 1968–88*. London: Bloomsbury, 1988.

———. "Review of *The Last Man on Earth*, dir. Ubaldo Ragona." In *Eaten Alive! Italian Cannibal and Zombie Movies*, edited by Jay Slater, 31–34. London: Plexus, 2002.

———, ed. *Science Fiction/Horror: A Sight and Sound Reader*. London: BFI Press, 2002.

Norris, Andrew, ed. *Politics, Metaphysics, and Death: Essays on Giorgio Agamben's "Homo Sacer."* Durham, NC: Duke University Press, 2005.

Nowell-Smith, Geoffrey, with James Hay and Gianni Volpi. *The Companion to Italian Cinema.* London: Cassell, 1996.

O'Connor, Barbara, and Elisabeth Klaus. "Pleasure and Meaningful Discourse: An Overview of Research Issues." *International Journal of Cultural Studies* 3, no. 3 (2001): 369–88.

O'Flinn, Paul. "Production and Reproduction: The Case of *Frankenstein*." In *Horror: The Film Reader,* edited by Mark Jancovich, 105–14. London: Routledge, 2002.

Olkowski, Dorothea. "Flows of Desire and the Body-Becoming." In *Becomings: Explorations in Time, Memory, and Futures,* edited by Elizabeth Grosz, 98–116. Ithaca, NY: Cornell University Press, 1999.

Ott, Brian L. "The Pleasures of *South Park* (An Experiment in Media Erotics)." In *"South Park" and Popular Culture,* edited by Jeffrey Weinstock. Albany: State University of New York Press, forthcoming.

Paffenroth, Kim. *Gospel of the Living Dead: George Romero's Visions of Hell on Earth.* Waco, TX: Baylor University Press, 2006.

Palmerini, Luca M., and Gaetano Mistretta. *Spaghetti Nightmares: Italian Fantasy-Horrors as Seen through the Eyes of Their Protagonists.* Trans. Gilliam M. A. Kirkpatrick. Key West, FL: Fantasma, 1996.

Paul, William. *Laughing Screaming: Modern Hollywood Horror and Comedy.* New York: Columbia University Press, 1994.

Perelman, Chaïm, and Lucie Obrechts-Tyteca. *The New Rhetoric: A Treatise on Argumentation.* Trans. John Wilkinson and Purcell Weaver. Notre Dame, IN: University of Notre Dame Press, 1969.

Picart, Carolyn Joan. "Humour and Horror in Science Fiction and Comedic Frankensteinian Films." *Scope,* May 2004, http://www.nottingham.ac.uk/film/journal/articles/humour-and-horror.htm.

Pinedo, Isabel Cristina. *Recreational Terrors: Women and the Pleasures of Horror Film Viewing.* Albany: State University of New York Press, 1997.

Polhemus, Ted. *Streetstyle: From Sidewalk to Catwalk.* New York: Thames & Hudson, 1994.

Poole, Steven. *Trigger Happy: Videogames and the Entertainment Revolution.* New York: Arcade, 2000.

Postman, Neil. *Amusing Ourselves to Death.* New York: Penguin Books, 1985.

———. "Five Things We Need to Know about Technological Change." Paper presented at the "New Technologies and the Human Person: Communicating the Faith in the New Millennium" conference, Denver, March 27, 1998.

Probyn, Elspeth. *Carnal Appetites: FoodSexIdentities.* London: Routledge, 2000.

Pryor, Ian. *Peter Jackson: From Prince of Splatter to Lord of the Rings: An Unauthorized Biography.* New York: St. Martin's, 2003.

Radice, Giovanni Lombardo. "Male Masochism, Male Monsters: An Interview with Giovanni Lombardo Radice." In *Alternative Europe: Eurotrash and Exploitation Cin-*

ema since 1945, edited by Xavier Mendik and Ernest Mathijs, 117–23. London: Wallflower, 2004.

Renshaw, Scott W. "Postmodern Swing Dance and the Presentation of the Unique Self." In *Postmodern Existential Sociology*, edited by Joseph A. Kotarba and John M. Johnson, 63–85. Walnut Creek, CA: Altamira Press, 2002.

Rigaud, Milo. *Secrets of Voodoo*. San Francisco: City Lights, 1969.

Roach, Martin. *Dr. Martens: The Story of a British Icon*. London: Chrysalis Impact, 2003.

Ronell, Avital. *The Test Drive*. Urbana: University of Illinois Press, 2005.

———. "TraumaTV: Twelve Steps beyond the Pleasure Principle." In *Finitude's Score: Essays for the End of the Millennium*, 305–28. Lincoln: University of Nebraska Press, 1994.

Root, Deborah. *Cannibal Culture: Art, Appropriation, and the Commodification of Cultural Difference*. New York: Westview Press, 1996.

Ross, Andrew. "The Politics of Impossibility." In *Psychoanalysis and . . .* , edited by Richard Feldstein and Henry Sussman, 113–28. New York: Routledge, 1990.

Russell, Jamie. *Book of the Dead: The Complete History of Zombie Cinema*. Godalming, England: FAB Press, 2005.

Said, Edward. *Culture and Imperialism*. New York: Vintage, 1994.

Salen, Katie, and Eric Zimmerman. *Rules of Play*. Cambridge, MA: MIT Press, 2004.

Savini, Tom. "Fast Foreword." In *Still Dead: Book of the Dead 2*, xiii–xvi. New York: Bantam, 1992.

Schatz, Thomas. *Hollywood Genres*. New York: McGraw-Hill, 1981.

Schneider, Steven Jay. "Monsters as (Uncanny) Metaphors: Freud, Lakoff, and the Representation of Monstrosity in Cinematic Horror." In *Horror Film Reader*, edited by Alain Silver and James Ursini, 167–92. New York: Limelight Editions, 2000.

———. "Notes on the Relevance of Psychoanalytic Film Theory to Euro-Horror Film." In *The Couch and the Silver Screen: Psychoanalytic Reflections on European Cinema*, edited by Andrea Sabbadini, 119–27. London: Brunner-Routledge, 2003.

Schrödinger, Erwin. "Die gegenwartige Situation in der Quantenmechanik." *Naturwissenschaftern* 23 (1935): 807–49.

———. "The Present Situation in Quantum Mechanics: A Translation of Schrödinger's 'Cat Paradox Paper.'" Trans. John D. Trimmer. *Proceedings of the American Philosophical Society* 124 (1980): 323–38.

Sconce, Jeffrey. "Trashing the Academy: Taste, Excess, and the Emerging Politics of Cinematic Style." *Screen* 36, no. 4 (1995): 371–93.

Seabrook, W. B. *The Magic Island*. New York: Harcourt Brace, 1929.

Shaviro, Steven. *The Cinematic Body*. Minneapolis: University of Minnesota Press, 1993.

Simpson, Jacqueline. *Icelandic Folktales and Legends*. London: B. T. Batsford, 1972.

———. *Legends of Icelandic Magicians*. Cambridge, England: D. S. Brewer and Rowman & Littlefield for the Folklore Society, 1975.

Skal, David J. *The Monster Show: A Cultural History of Horror*. New York: Norton, 1993.

Slater, Jay, ed. *Eaten Alive! Italian Cannibal and Zombie Movies*. London: Plexus, 2002.

Smith, Gary A. *Uneasy Dreams: The Golden Age of British Horror Films, 1956–1976*. Jefferson, NC: McFarland, 2000.

Sobchack, Vivian. *The Address of the Eye: A Phenomenology of Film Experience*. Princeton, NJ: Princeton University Press. 1992.

———. *Screening Space: The American Science Fiction Film*. New York: Ungar, 1987.

Stallybrass, Peter, and Allon White. *The Politics and Poetics of Transgression*. Ithaca, NY: Cornell University Press, 1986.

Stephenson, Neil. *Snow Crash*. New York: Bantam Books, 1992.

Tasker, Yvonne. "Having It All: Feminism and the Pleasures of the Popular." In *Off-Centre: Feminism and Cultural Studies*, edited by Sarah Franklin, Celia Lury, and Jackie Stacey, 85–96. London: HarperCollins Academic, 1991.

Thompson, Stith. *The Folktale*. New York: Dryden Press, 1946. Reprint, Berkeley: University of California Press, 1977.

———. *Motif-Index of Folk-Literature: A Classification of Narrative Elements in Folk-tales, Ballads, Myths, Fables, Mediaeval Romances, Exempla, Fabliaux, Jest-Books, and Local Legends*. 6 vols. Bloomington: Indiana University Press, 1955–1958.

Thomson, Philip. *The Grotesque*. London: Methuen, 1972.

Thrower, Stephen. *Beyond Terror: The Films of Lucio Fulci*. Godalming, England: FAB Press, 2002.

Totaro, Donato. "Gilles Deleuze's Bergsonian Film Project." *Offscreen* 3, no. 3 (March 1999).

———. "The Italian Zombie Film: From Derivation to Reinvention." In *Fear without Frontiers: Horror Cinema across the Globe*, edited by Steven Jay Schneider, 161–73. Godalming, England: FAB Press, 2003.

———. "Review of *Dellamorte Dellamore*, dir. Michele Soavi." In *Eaten Alive! Italian Cannibal and Zombie Movies*, edited by Jay Slater, 231–35. London: Plexus, 2002.

———. "Review of *The Beyond*, dir. Lucio Fulci." In *Eaten Alive! Italian Cannibal and Zombie Movies*, edited by Jay Slater, 165–69. London: Plexus, 2002.

———. "Your Mother Ate My Dog! Peter Jackson and Gore-Gag Comedy." *Offscreen* 5, no. 4 (September 2001).

Trencansky, Sarah. "Final Girls and Terrible Youth: Transgression in 1980s Slasher Horror." *Journal of Popular Film and Television* 29, no. 2 (2001): 63–73.

Tudor, Andrew. "Why Horror? The Peculiar Pleasures of a Popular Genre." In *Horror: The Film Reader*, edited by Mark Jancovich, 47–56. London: Routledge, 2002.

Turner, Victor. *The Ritual Process: Structure and Anti-Structure*. Chicago: Aldine, 1969.

Virilio, Paul, and Sylvère Lotringer. *Crepuscular Dawn*. Los Angeles: Semiotext(e), 2002.

Waller, Gregory A. *The Living and the Undead: From Bram Stoker's "Dracula" to Romero's "Dawn of the Dead."* Urbana: University of Illinois Press, 1986.

Walton, Priscilla L. *Our Cannibals, Ourselves: The Body Politic.* Urbana: University of Illinois Press, 2004.

Warner, Marina. *Fantastic Metamorphoses, Other Worlds: Ways of Telling the Self.* Oxford: Oxford University Press, 2002.

Warner, Michael. "Introduction." In *Fear of a Queer Planet: Queer Politics and Social Theory,* edited by Michael Warner, vii–xxxi. Minneapolis: University of Minnesota Press, 1993.

Warren, Bill. *The Evil Dead Companion.* New York: St. Martin's, 2000.

Warwick, Kevin. "Cyborg 1.0." *Wired* 8, no. 2 (2000): 151.

William, Tony. *The Cinema of George Romero: Knight of the Living Dead.* London: Wallflower, 2003.

Williams, Linda. "Film Bodies: Gender, Genre and Excess." *Film Quarterly* 44, no. 4 (1991): 2–13. Reprinted in *Feminist Film Theory: A Reader,* edited by Sue Thornham, 267–81. New York: New York University Press, 1999.

———. "When the Woman Looks." In *Re-Vision: Essays in Feminist Film Criticism,* edited by Maryanne Doane, Patricia Mellencamp, and Linda Williams, 67–82. Los Angeles: University Publications of America, 1984.

Williams, Raymond. *Keywords: A Vocabulary of Culture and Society.* London: Croom Helm, 1976.

Wimberly, Lowry C. *Folklore in the English and Scottish Ballads.* New York: Frederick Unger, 1928.

Wood, Robin. "The American Nightmare: Horror in the 1970s." In *Horror: The Film Reader,* edited by Mark Jancovich, 25–32. London: Routledge, 2002.

———. *Hollywood from Vietnam to Reagan.* New York: Columbia University Press, 1986.

———. "Introduction." In *American Nightmare: Essays on the Horror Film,* edited by Andrew Britton, Richard Lippe, Tony Williams, and Robin Wood, 7–28. Toronto: Festival of Festivals, 1979.

———. "Neglected Nightmares." In *Horror Film Reader,* edited by Alain Silver and James Ursini, 111–28. New York: Limelight Editions, 2000.

Zillman, Dolf, and Peter Vorderer. *Media Entertainment: The Psychology of Its Appeal.* Mahwah, NJ: Erlbaum, 2000.

Žižek, Slavoj. *The Sublime Object of Ideology.* New York: Verso, 1989.

Index

~

About the Contributors

Linda Badley is professor of English at Middle Tennessee State University and general editor of the Traditions in World Cinema series at Edinburgh University Press. She has published widely on horror and related genres in literature, television, and film and is the author of *Film, Horror, and the Body Fantastic* (1995) and *Writing Horror and the Body: The Fiction of Stephen King, Clive Barker, and Anne Rice* (1996) and coeditor of *Traditions in World Cinema* (2006). Current projects include *Contemporary American Independent Cinema* (with Barton Palmer) and a study of intersections/interactions between horror film and auteur theory.

Mikel J. Koven is senior lecturer in film studies at the University of Worcester, England. His main research area is the interrelation between folklore and film, specifically urban legends and horror films. He is editing both a special issue of *Western Folklore* and a companion book collection on folklore and film. His articles have appeared in such journals as *Literature/Film Quarterly, Scope, The Journal of American Folklore, Midwestern Folklore, Ethnologies, Contemporary Legend,* and *Culture & Tradition.* He is working on a book-length study of the Italian *giallo* film.

Tanya Krzywinska is a reader in film and television studies at Brunel University. She is the author of *A Skin for Dancing In: Possession, Witchcraft and*

Voodoo in Film (2000), *Science Fiction Cinema: From Outerspace to Cyberspace* (2000, with Geoff King), *Sex and the Cinema* (forthcoming, with Geoff King), and *Tomb Raiders and Space Invaders: Videogame Forms and Contexts* (forthcoming) and coeditor, with Geoff King, of *ScreenPlay: Cinema/Videogames/Interfaces* (2002). She has written several articles on *Buffy the Vampire Slayer* and has recently begun work on *Imaginary Worlds: A Cross-Media Study of the Aesthetic, Formal, and Interpolative Strategies of Virtual Worlds in Popular Media.*

Marc Leverette is assistant professor of media studies in the Department of Speech Communication at Colorado State University, where he teaches courses in aesthetics, cultural studies, and critical theory. His books include *Professional Wrestling, the Myth, the Mat, and American Popular Culture* (2003) and the coedited collection *It's Not TV: Watching HBO in the Post-Television Era* (forthcoming). His articles have appeared in such journals as *Image & Narrative* and *Studies in Popular Culture.*

Patricia MacCormack is senior lecturer in the Department of Communication and Film at Anglia Ruskin University, Cambridge, England. Her most recent publications have been in perversion theory and feminist teratology in *Thirdspace*, masochism in Italian horror film in the anthology *Alternative Europe*, and continental philosophy, in particular the works of Deleuze, Guattari, and Lyotard, in *Theory, Culture, and Society*. She is a regular contributor to film and alternative music magazines including *Senses of Cinema*. Her Ph.D. was awarded the Mollie Holman Doctorate Medal for best thesis. She is currently writing on the areas of cinesexuality, necrophilia films, and ecstasy in the work of Blanchot, Foucault, and Bataille.

Shawn McIntosh is coauthor of *Converging Media: Introduction to Mass Communication* (2003), a textbook for undergraduate media courses, and is lecturer in the Strategic Communications Program at Columbia University's School of Continuing Education. He has been an editor and freelance writer for ten years for various newspapers and magazines in the United Kingdom, the United States, and Japan. He was an adjunct faculty member at Iona College in New Rochelle, New York, where he taught online journalism, website publishing, feature writing, and information visualization, and he has taught media ethics at Rutgers University. He taught online journalism at Vidzeme University College in Valmiera, Latvia, as a Fulbright scholar. His research interests include communication dynamics in media organizations, social media, and the relation of media, power, and democracy. He received a B.S. in microbiology from the University of Idaho and an M.S. in journalism with a concentration in new media from Columbia University, and is pursuing his Ph.D. in media studies from Rutgers University.

Brad O'Brien teaches English at Coastal Carolina University in Myrtle Beach, South Carolina. His essay "Fulcanelli as a Vampiric Frankenstein and Jesus as His Vampiric Monster: The Frankenstein and Dracula Myths in Guillermo del Toro's *Cronos*" appears in the collection *Monstrous Adaptations*. He has also written about horror films for a local newspaper in his hometown of Columbia, South Carolina.

David Pagano directs the English general-education program at Old Dominion University in Norfolk, Virginia, where he also teaches classes in film, American literature, and critical theory.

Natasha Patterson is pursuing her doctorate in the Department of Women's Studies at Simon Fraser University, British Columbia. Her research interests include horror cinema, audience research, gender and popular culture, and feminist cultural studies.

Martin Rogers, an instructor at the University of Georgia, has taught classes on composition, literature, and anime. His current research and criticism explores post-human narrative systems and genre hybridity.

Ron Scott is assistant professor of English at Walsh University in Ohio. He is interested in understanding the power of the immersive capabilities of much of the phenomenon called New Media, and he writes on the way that the usual suspects of race, gender, and class both impact and are impacted by emerging technologies. He focuses his teaching efforts on helping his students become professionally literate, assisting them in developing their abilities to think through problems. In his spare time, he guides whitewater rafts, climbs rocks, and enjoys the pursuit of nearly any activity that produces adrenaline.

Annelise Sklar holds an MSLS from the University of North Carolina and a B.A. in American studies from the University of New Mexico. She works in the Reference and Government Information departments of Zimmerman Library at the University of New Mexico. She spends a lot of time thinking about psychobilly and the imagery therein, even when she doesn't want to.